INDABA98
BOOKS
& *children*

Zimbabwe International Book Fair Trust

Note to the Reader

When compiling the papers from Indaba98, we were unable to include all the papers in full. We have used extracts from some of the longer papers and others have been shortened. Some papers were linked to visual aids and thus may have lost some of their original impact. Some of the presentations have only been included in the report-backs or discussions either because the papers were not available or because they were too long to include and not easily shortened without compromising the original.

However, the proceedings convey the essence of all the presentations and discussions and anyone who would like the full text of any of the papers, may contact the writer of the paper directly (all the addresses appear in the list of contributors) or contact the Zimbabwe International Book Fair.

Published by the Zimbabwe International Book Fair Trust
PO Box CY 1179, Causeway, Harare, Zimbabwe
© Zimbabwe International Book Fair Trust, 1998
ISBN: 0-7974-1925-X

Contents

List of Contributors

Dayo Alabi
Managing Director CSS Limited,
Nigeria PO Box 174 Lagos
Tel: (234) 266 33081
Virgilio Almario
Managing Director
Children's Communication Centre
PO Box 10011, Main Post Office
Quezon City Philippines
Tel 9274416/7 Fax: 9266636
E-mail: adama@mozcom.com
Meshack Asare
Author and illustrator, Ghana
18 Cintra Court Patterson Road
London SE 19 2LB Tel: (181) 653 9294
Miriam Bamhare
Director, ZBDC
PO Box CY 1179 Causeway Harare
Tel: (263-4) 749176/7
Fax (263-4) 749190
E-mail: zbdc@samara.co.zw
Babette Brown
Author, UK Flat One 51 Granville
Road, London N12 OJH
Tel: (181) 446 7056
Fax: (181) 446 7591
Mary Bugembe
Managing Publisher, Foundation for the
Promotion of Children's Science
Publications in Africa (CHISCI), Kenya
PO Box 61301, Nairobi
Tel: (254-2) 573029
Fax (254-2) 573029
Henry Chakava
EAEP, APNET, Kenya
PO Box 45314, Nairobi
Tel: (254-2) 534020/ 545903
Fax: (254-2) 532095/448753
Maria Chiswanda
Consultant, Zimbabwe
3353 Glen Norah A Harare
Tel: (263-4) 612116
E-mail: webbie@baobab.cszim.co.zw

Richard Crabbe
APNET Chairman, African Christian
Press, Ghana PO Box 30, Achimota
Tel: (233-21) 220271
Fax: (233-21) 220271/668115
Margaret Crampton
National Inquiry Services Centre
(NISC), South Africa
PO Box 377 Grahamstown 6140
Tel: (27-46) 622-9698
Fax: (27-46) 622-9550
E-mail: nisc@ru.ac.za
Eldorado Dabula
Dramatist Orpheus Theatre
Mozambique C.P. 34 Maputo
Tel: (258-1) 491748
Fax: (258-1) 492196
Niki Daly
Illustrator, South Africa
36 Strubens Road, Mowbray
Tel: (27-21) 685 1032
Fax (27-21) 685 4679
E-mail: inkman@iafrica.com
Woeli Dekutsey
Woeli Publishing Services, Ghana
PO Box K601, Accra New Town
Fax: (233-21) 229294/777098
Yohannes Gebregeorgis
San Francisco Public Library
PO Box 21365 Oakland CA 94620
Tel: (510) 658 0462
Fax: (510) 658 6685
E-mail: africansun@igc.apc.org
F. M. Genga-Idowu
IBBY, Kenya
PO Box 23730, Nairobi
Tel: (254-2) 533309
Fax: (254-2) 533309
Wangui wa Goro
Translator, Kenya 11B Waterloo Terrace
London N1 1TQ UK

7

Jay Heale
IBBY, South Africa
PO Box 541, Grabouw 7160
Tel (27-21) 859 3081
Fax: (27-21) 859 4000
Cynthia Hugo
National Director, READ Educational
Trust, South Africa
PO Box 30994, Braamfontein 2017
Tel: (27-11) 339 5941
Fax: (27-11) 339 5709
Teresa Ibrahim
Women Training and Promotion
Association, Sudan
PO Box 11227 Khartoum
Fax: 777785
Chukweumeka Ike
President, Nigerian Book Foundation
PO Box 1132 Awka
Tel: (406) 551403 Fax: (406) 552615
Charles Kalugula
Head, Book Management Unit,
Ministry of Education, Tanzania
PO Box 9121 Dar es Salaam
Tel: (255-51) 110146
Fax: (255-51) 113271
Pamela Kola
Author, Kenya's Children's Book
Project, Kenya PO Box 48611 Nairobi
Tel/Fax: (254-2) 569786
Charles Larson
Professor of Literature, American
University, Washington
3600 Underwood Street
Chevy Chase MD 20815
Tel: (301) 656 9370
Fax: (202) 885 2994
Marie Laurentin
Ministry of Culture and
Communication, France
361 Avenue du General de Gaulle
92140 Clamart France
Tel: (33-0-1) 40 83 1462
Fax: (33-0-1) 40 94 0404
E-mail: interculturel.ajpl@wanadoo.fr

O.M. Lawal-Solarin
Literamed Publications, APNET,
Nigeria P Bag 21068 Ikeja Lagos State
Tel: (234-1) 962512/ 960450
Fax: (234-1) 497 2217
Don Long
Learning Media Limited, New Zealand
PO Box 3293 Wellington
Tel: (644) 4725522 Fax: (644) 4726444
Myrna Machet
Children's Literature Research Unit,
UNISA, South Africa
PO Box 392 Pretoria 0001
E-mail: MACHEMP@alpha.unisa.ac.za
Gabriel Machinga
Minister of Education and Culture,
Zimbabwe PO Box CY 121 Causeway
Tel: (263-4) 734051
John Manyarara
Chairman, ZIBF Trust; retired High
Court judge, Zimbabwe 47B Fort Street/
Third Avenue, Bulawayo
Tel: (263-9) 540731
Fax: (263-9) 78053
E-mail: manyarara@telconet.co.zw
Ali Mazrui
Albert Schweitzer Professor in the
Humanities and Director of the Institute
of Global Cultural Studies,
Binghampton University, USA
PO Box 6000 Binghampton
New York 13902-6000
Tel: 607 777 4494
Fax: 607 777 2642
Lydia Mhango
Data Processing Limited
PO Box 20072 Kitwe Zambia
Tel:02-227723/225186
Fax:02-220412
E-mail: silwamba@mail1.zamnet.zm
Gcina Mhlophe
Author/storyteller, South Africa
63 Macdonald Street Kensington 2094
Tel/Fax: (27-11) 614 5221

Alois Mlambo
ZIBF Trustee; Zimbabwe Academic and
Non-Fiction Authors Association;
Department of Economic History,
University of Zimbabwe PO Box
MP167 Mt Pleasant Harare
Tel: (263-4) 303211 ext. 139

Tsletsi Mohapi
Deputy Director, State Language
Services, Department of Arts, Culture,
Science and Technology, South Africa
636 Makou Street Monument Park
Extension 0181
Tel. (27-12) 347 6967/ 16301

Elibariki Moshi
Executive Secretary, Tanzania
Children's Literature Project
PO Box 78245 Dar es Salaam
Tel: (255-51) 760750/ 666957
Fax: (255-51) 761562/150387

Tsidi Moshoeshoe-Chadzingwa
Lesotho Publishers Association, ADEA/
APNET trade study researcher, Lesotho
PO Box 180 Roma
Tel: (166) 340601 Fax (266) 34004

Godfrey Moyo
Children's Active Literature Project
P.O. Box FM 322 Famona Bulawayo

Egidio Mpanga
Book and Publishers Association of
Malawi, ADEA/APNET
P Bag 39 Blantyre
Tel: (265) 670880 Fax: (265) 670021

David Muita
Kenya Publishers Association
PO Box 18560 Nairobi
Tel: (254-2) 223262
Fax: (254-2) 336771

Ray Munamwimbu
Booksellers and Publishers Association
of Zambia, Managing Director
PO Box 32708 Lusaka
Tel: (260-1) 229240 Fax: (260-1) 225073

David Mungoshi
Zimbabwe Writers' Union
PO Box 6170 Gweru
Tel: (163-54) 3284 Fax: (263-54) 53147

James Ng'ombe
Jhango Publishing House, Malawi
PO Box 1259 Blantyre
Tel/Fax: (265) 652908

Janet Njoroge
Publisher, Longhorn, Kenya
PO Box 18033 Nairobi
Tel: (254-2) 532579/80/81
Fax: (254-2) 569786

Asenath Odaga
Author, Kenya PO Box 1743 Kisumu
Tel/Fax: (254-35) 22707/22291
E-mail: gadod@arcc.or.ke

Thomas Odhiambo
Chairman, Foundation for the
Promotion of Children's Science
Publications in Africa (CHISCI), Kenya
PO Box 61301 Nairobi
Tel: (254-2) 573027/8/9
Fax: (254-2) 573029/ 571944

Mervin Ogle
National Director, English Language
Educational Trust, South Africa 6th
Floor 74 Aliwal Street Durban 4001
Tel: (27-31) 332 0501
Fax: (27-31) 3370002
E-mail: elet@iafrica.com

Olalede Oladitan
REPRONIG, Nigeria, Department of
Foreign Languages Ile-Ife
Fax: (234-36) 230 214

Sandra Olen
Children's Literature Research Unit,
South Africa PO Box 392 Pretoria 0001
Tel: (27-12) 429 3316
Fax: (27-12) 429 3221

Roger Oze
Nouvelles Editions Ivoiriennes,
APNET, Côte d'Ivoire 1 Boulevard de
Marseille B.P. 1818 Abidjan 01
Tel: (225) 24 07 66
Fax (255) 24 24 56

Terence Ranger
Institute of Development Studies,
University of Zimbabwe, ZIBF Hon.
Trustee; Historian/Author, UK
PO Box MP 167 Mt Pleasant Harare
Tel (263-4) 333342

Abdullah Saiwaad
Publishers Association of Tanzania
PO Box 1408 Dar es Salaam
Tel: (255-51) 185432
Fax: (255-51) 181624
E-mail: pata@cctz.com

Helene Schar
Baobab Children's Book Fund,
Switzerland
Steinenring 49 CH 4051 Basel
Tel: (61) 281 3763
Fax: (61) 381 3767

Susan Scull-Carvalho
Managing Director, Jacaranda Designs,
Kenya PO Box 76691, Nairobi
Tel: (254-2) 47145/6
Fax: (254-2) 568353

Monica Seeber
Publishers Association of South Africa
PO Box 31134 Braamfontein 2017
Tel: (27-11) 622 6937
Fax: (27-11) 622 6899
E-mail: seeber@icon.co.za

Simon Sikwese
The Story Workshop, Malawi
PO Box 642 Zomba

Elinor Sisulu
Author, South Africa PO Box 2406
Glenwood Goodwood 7460 Cape Town
Tel: (27-21) 593 525
Fax: (27-21) 592 5325

Irene Staunton
Baobab Books PO Box 567 Harare
Tel: (263-4) 755034/5/6/7/8/
Fax: (263-4) 781913

Claudia Stein
Frankfurt Book Fair, Germany
Reineckstr. 3 D-60313 Frankfurt
Postfach 10 01 16 D 60001 Frankfurt
Tel: (69) 21 020 Fax: (69) 210 2227
E-mail: litprom@book-fair.com

Olav Stokkmo
Secretary General, International
Federation of Reproduction Rights
Organization (IFRRO), Norway
Rue du Prince Royal 87 B-1050
Brussels Belgium
Tel: (32-2) 551 08 99
Fax (32-2) 551 08 95
E-mail: ifrro@skynet.be

Sebenzile Thango
Umdladla Swazi Writers Association
PO Box 1153 Manzini

Brenda Townsend
Director of Professional Development,
International Reading Association, USA
PO Box 8139 Newark DE 19714-8139
Tel: (302) 731 1600 ext. 235
Fax: (302) 731 1057

James Tumusiime
Managing Director, Fountain Publishers,
APNET, Uganda PO Box 488 Kampala
Tel: (41) 259163 Fax (41) 251160

Emmie Wade
Kawi Project, African
Publishers Network, Zimbabwe
PO Box 3773 Harare
Tel: (263-4) 705105/726405
Fax: (263-4) 705106
E-mail: apnet@mango.zw

Gabriela Wenke
Eselshor Magazine, Germany
Layenhot/Ostfluegel Am Finther Building
5801 D-55126 Mainz
Tel: (49) 6131 40678
Fax: (49) 6131 40915

Welcome

It is a great honour to welcome all of you to ZIBF 1998. I welcome all from near and far. I hope that the SADC nationals among you did not require visas to enter Zimbabwe, particularly if your passport had the unfortunate entry 'journalist'. One of the aims expressed in the declaration treaty of SADC signed on 17 August 1992 in Namibia promised that it would facilitate the movement of SADC nationals in the region. This promise is yet to be fulfilled.

Also a special welcome to our Kenyan visitors. Kenya is the country focus for the Book Fair this year. We have with us the young Kenyan winners of the UNESCO competitions. The winner of the essay writing competition will be reading an extract from his award-winning essay and he will be accompanied by the winner of the poster part of the competition. They will then join the Chipawo children and have fun in Zimbabwe.

I take my cue from the words 'to have fun'. The theme of this year's Book Fair is 'Books and children'. Children should have a special place in the hearts of all people. The abuse of children is not limited to sexual abuse, abhorrent though this is or child labour although we all regret this. But this extends to little heralded abuses of children. One watches with dismay child soldiers carrying loads twice their weight in weapons for destruction. Again one is dismayed when children are taught hate speeches and made to sing hate songs by the greedy, the ambitious and other species of humanity of that ilk.

So one is delighted to hear that special provision has been made for these honoured young guests to be with us.

JUSTICE JOHN MANYARARA

Opening Remarks

GABRIEL M. MACHINGA

Once again, Zimbabwe is proud and privileged to provide environment of frank exchanges on different aspects of the book industry. Each year the ZIBF Indaba continues to improve in scope and content as a unique forum which brings together all the links in the book publishing chain. I am confident that the focus of Indaba 98, 'Books and Children', will effectively highlight the production of books for children and various aspects of the marketing of these books within Africa and the rest of the world.

As a nation we are delighted that over the years the ZIBF Indaba has become internationally renowned as a highly significant gathering of prominent professionals working in the African book industry in its widest possible sense. It is our sincere hope that once again authors, publishers, policy-makers, donors, academics and librarians will find this Indaba a most appropriate forum for very constructive debate on issues concerning book publishing.

I am happy to learn from the Executive Director of the Book Fair, that both the African Publishers Network and the ADEA Books Working Group have been instrumental in co-ordinating special sessions at this year's Indaba to look at structures and strategies in the promotion of children's books and reading development as well as an overview of the African publishing industry, past, present and future.

As you all know, one of the characteristics of this year's ZIBF is the special focus on Kenya — the home of the Pan-African Children's Book Fair. I would like to say a special *Karibu* — welcome — to the large delegation of distinguished Kenyans at this year's Indaba led by Professor Mazrui, David Muita, the chairperson of the Kenya Publishers Association, and Thomas Odhiambo, the Managing Trustee of the Foundation for the Promotion of Children's Science Publications in Africa. We hope that this special attention on Kenya will broaden our scope of publishing for children while providing particular examples of how to deal with problems that hinder the growth of a book industry.

The
Plenary
Sessions

1
Fewer Heroes and More Martyrs

Africa's Post-Colonial Experience:
Implications for the African Child

ALI A. MAZRUI

I am particularly indebted to Dr Ousseina Alidou for suggestions and stimulation in preparing this keynote address. In one of his immortal speeches Kwame Nkrumah, the founder President of Ghana, quoted from William Wordsworth's 'Ode on Intimations of Immortality' from *Recollections of Early Childhood*. Nkrumah lamented to fellow Ghanaians:

Whither is fled the visionary gleam?
Where is it now, the glory and the dream?

What was the visionary gleam which had fled? What was the glory and the dream which had been lost ?

To Wordsworth, it was the loss of imaginative power which occurs as a child grows into adulthood. Perhaps *grows* into adulthood is a misnomer. A child *shrinks* into adulthood in terms of imaginative power.

There was a time when meadows, grove, and stream,
The earth, and every common sight,
to me did seem
Apparelled in celestial light,
The glory and the freshness of a dream.
It is not now as it hath been of yore: —
Turn wheresoever I may,
By night or day,
The things which I have seen I now can see no more.
II
The Rainbow comes and goes,
And lovely is the Rose,
The Moon doth with delight
Look round her when the heavens are bare,
Waters on a starry night
Are beautiful and fair;

The sunshine is a glorious birth;
But yet I know, where'er I go,
That there hath past away a glory from the earth.

Whither is fled the visionary gleam?
Where is it now, the glory and the dream?

Between the Transnatural and the Supernatural

Depending upon their age, children have heroes who traverse more than one branch of nature. The imaginary hero can combine the characteristics of a cat with the attributes of a human being: A lion who speaks fluent Kikuyu language or a bull who is in command of Maasai proverbs.

When I was a child my mother told me a story about a child who not only survived when eaten by a big fish but could sing to call for his brother to save him. My mother had to repeat the story night after night. The kind of hero might be regarded as transnatural — traversing more than one branch of nature.

Disney's *The Lion King* successfully titillated the transnatural imagination of children — an anthropomorphic treatment of beasts of the jungle as a lively pseudo-human society. The owl and the rabbit recur in many transnatural children's tales in different countries.

A second category of heroes is that of the supernatural. In what sense is this different from the transnatural? Of course lions do not speak human languages, nor do human beings pounce like lions on their prey. But both lions and humans exist. What Disney and children's imaginations do is to criss-cross the attributes, like making humans fly and making birds attend book fairs. All this is transnatural.

The supernatural comes into play when we have heroes whom we have never witnessed on earth — like gods at war or angels at prayer. Supernatural heroes are products of either the imagination or faith. Grown-ups draw their supernatural mainly from religion; children mainly from the imagination.

The third category of heroes for children are natural heroes including regular human heroes who walk instead of flying, and who exist in the lives of their societies. The children may know them by name. They may be their own parents or Heads of State. African children who grew up during the struggle for independence lived in an age of super-heroes. As adversaries, European empires seemed huge and all-encompassing. African nationalists challenging those empires appeared like courageous Davids confronting imperial Goliaths.

In those days names like Kwame Nkrumah of Ghana, Eduardo Mondlane of Mozambique, Albert Luthuli of South Africa, Kenneth Kaunda of Northern Rhodesia, Joshua Nkomo and Robert Mugabe of Southern Rhodesia, and Jomo Kenyatta of Kenya captured many a youthful imagination in far away Senegal or Uganda. When I finally became an academic the role of heroes in that phase of African history still preoccupied me.

In 1967 I published one of my earliest books. It was entitled *On Heroes and Uhuru Worship* (London: Longman).

Kwame Nkrumah again quoted William Wordsworth very aptly:

Bliss was it in that dawn to be alive
But to be young was very heaven.

Wordsworth was talking about the youth during the era of the French revolution. Nkrumah was talking about the youth in the struggle to regain Africa's sovereignty. Those were the years of super-ideas and super-heroes.

From heroes to martyrs

Since independence, where have all the super-heroes gone? Great liberation fighters were not necessarily great nation-builders. The lustre has often faded from our super-heroes for two main reasons, first, most of the leaders were not as impressive in dealing with problems of independence as they had been in fighting for that independence. Secondly, we (their youthful fans) grew older and had lost that sense of wonderment and adoration as we had matured.

Heaven lies about us in our infancy!
Shades of the prison-house begin to close
Upon the growing boy . . .

. . . the radiance which was once so bright
Be now for ever taken from my sight,
. . . nothing can bring back the hour
Of splendour in the grass, of glory in the flower; . . .

Whither is fled the visionary gleam?
Where is it now, the glory and the dream?
(Wordsworth, Intimations of Immortality, Ibid).

After independence Africa produced a whole generation of young people deprived of super-heroes in the political domain. Africa has had heroes, but fewer and fewer super-heroes since the last years of colonial struggle. Figures much larger than life were more common then than now. The one single

17

towering political super-hero of the last years of the 20th century has been Nelson Mandela, who has been in a class almost by himself.

What Africa has produced instead of super-heroes in the last few decades of the 20th century has been super-martyrs. Heroes are symbols of achievement; martyrs are symbols of anguish. Heroes are ultimate victors; martyrs are ultimate victims.

Steve Biko was a victim; Nelson Mandela survived to be a victor. Biko was a symbol of anguish; Mandela became a symbol of achievement.

Eduardo Mondlane of Mozambique was, in our sense, more a martyr than a hero. Augustinho Neto of Angola was more a hero than a martyr. Samora Machel of Mozambique was definitely a hero. But was he also a martyr? Was his plane shot down by apartheid South Africa and then was he killed? Or did he survive the aircrash only to be murdered on the ground while awaiting medical attention?

Many of the recent martyrs elsewhere in Africa have suffered at the hands of African dictators. They have been made martyrs by fellow Africans. Ken Sarowiwa in Nigeria was a champion of the Ogoni people and a crusader for environmental protection. He and a number of others were brutally executed by the Abacha regime in Nigeria in 1995.

My friend and benefactor, Chief Moshood Abiola, died in 1998 on the eve of his being released from military detention. The military regime in Nigeria may not have poisoned him but it is virtually certain that the Abacha regime shortened his life by five to fifteen years through ruthless neglect.

Chief Abiola's last words to me were in 1974 when he called me at home, and then at Lincoln University in Pennsylvania, to tell me that he was going home to Nigeria to become President. When I asked for further explanation, he simply said confidently before hanging up, 'See you at the Inauguration'.

I did go to see the late General Abacha personally to plead for Chief Abiola's release. I even used the argument concerning Chief Abiola's health. But the General pooh-poohed the arguments as a mere ruse.

Two years later Chief Abiola died. Was it a case of heroism or martyrdom? Sometimes martyrdom can escalate to heroism if the impact of the martyrdom leads on to new achievements as was the case of Nelson Mandela's own martyrdom in prison.

But with Moshood Abiola we are still at a stage of a super-martyr rather than a super-hero though Abiola was heroic in non-political ways long before he was locked up. For example, he was a self-made millionaire who also became Nigeria's leading private philanthropist.

As a former President of the African Studies Association (ASA) of the US

I once wrote to Chief Abiola to help the association, the largest African studies body in the world which acts as a major institutional friend of Africa in the US. I asked Abiola for US$50,000. Within 24 hours, he phoned my home in Binghamton, New York, and asked for my bank account number. I got the money and gave it to the association at a time when another donor was prepared to raise the value of every dollar the African Studies Association raised.

The association decided to name its annual Distinguished Lecture after Chief Moshood Abiola. This tradition continues every time they hold the annual convention. The donation was one of Abiola's many contributions to the academic world. But he also helped the poorer sectors of Nigeria and often came to the rescue of the most vulnerable, especially the children.

Just as some martyrs become bigger and bigger heroes (as in the case of Nelson Mandela), some heroes later become bigger and bigger martyrs (as in the case of John F. Kennedy). Mandela's prison-martyrdom propelled him towards greater and greater heroism. Kennedy's assassination propelled his memory towards greater and greater martyrdom.

Sylvanus Olympio was Africa's first presidential martyr. He was assassinated in January 1963. Since then other great African leaders who have been assassinated include Patrice Lumumba of Congo, Emperor Haile Selassie of Ethiopia, Hendrik Verwoed of South Africa, Murtala Muhammad of Nigeria, Thomas Sankara of Burkina Faso, Eduardo Mondlane of Mozambique, Anwar Sadat of Egypt, and Muhammad Farrah -Aideed of Somalia.

Female succession to male martyrdom

The martyrdom of male heroes in Asia has sometimes led to a phenomenon which might be called female succession to male martyrdom.

It started in Ceylon (now Sri Lanka) when Solomon Bandaranaike was assassinated. His wife, Sirimavo Bandaranaike, succeeded as leader of the party and eventually as Prime Minister. Their daughter many years later received the reins of power.

In India, Jawaharlal Nehru was not really martyred except metaphorically through his military humiliation at the hands of the Chinese. After Nehru died in 1964 there was a brief succession by Shastri and then Nehru's daughter, Indira, entered the scene. She turned out to be even tougher as a politician than her father.

In Pakistan Zulkifar Ali Bhutto is widely regarded to have been judicially martyred by an alliance between the military and the judiciary in Pakistan in 1977. His daughter Benazir Bhutto lived to fight another day and to become

Prime Minister of Pakistan twice. She is still a powerful force in Pakistan, though under siege.

In neighbouring Bangladesh, Begum Khaleda Zia and Hassina Rahman-Waleda have both been Prime Ministers — female successors to martyred husband and father respectively.

In the Phillippines there was the phenomenal Corazon Aquino as a female successor to her martyred husband, Benigno Aquino.

In Burma (Myanmar) the Nobel Peace Laureate Aung San Suu Kyi is a kind of female successor to a martyred father.

But in Africa there has not been much female succession to male martyrdom. Although the son of Sylvanus Olympio of Togo has tried to succeed him as President, none of Olympio's female relatives were in the running for succession. Not many have heard of the widow of Patrice Lumumba or the widow of Murtalla Muhammad let alone voted for their succession.

Mrs Anwar Sadat had been highly visible as First Lady but rapidly retreated into obscurity after Sadat's assassination. Neither the widow of Thomas Sankara nor the widow of Thomas Mboya of Kenya became politically significant.

If South and South East Asia have had such a striking series of female successors to male martyrs, why has Africa lagged behind so abysmally? Some good things in Africa have adverse consequences for female empowerment.

For one thing African cultures are less dynastic than most Asian cultures. Therefore the power of heroic succession in Africa is weaker because there is less of a dynastic pull.

A related problem is that African traditional systems of inheritance are often lateral rather than vertical. In Africa nephews sometimes have stronger rights than sons and daughters; uncles may have more authority than parents. This makes political succession less neat.

Thirdly, African rulers and even African Presidents, are more likely than Asian heads of state to leave behind children by several different mothers. Big men in Africa are, on the whole, more polygamous than big men in Asia.

Indeed, Chief Moshood Abiola, widely regarded to have been elected President of Nigeria in June 1993, left behind several widows upon his death in July 1998. When he took me to his home in Lagos once he introduced me to two vastly different wives — one was relatively traditionalist and the other was a professional woman with a Western Ph.D.

Yet, paradoxically, it has been Moshood Abiola's family that has come closest so far to producing potential female successors to male martyrs in the Asian sense. When Moshood was still in jail one of his wives became increasingly politicized, so much so that Kudirat Abiola was herself martyred. She was assassinated in 1996.

Abiola's children are also getting increasingly politicized. Kudirat's daughter Hafisat, a Harvard graduate, has already revealed considerable leadership and eloquence skills as a youth-leader in the US. She is a potential female successor to the martyrdom of both her father and her mother. In the 1980s in Southern Africa Winnie Mandela was a different kind of female successor to her husband's (Nelson Mandela) martyrdom in jail. She did become a symbol of the anti-apartheid struggle in her own right.

But apart from the Abiolas and the Mandelas, Africa has not been a fertile ground for this kind of female empowerment. And even in the case of the Abiolas and the Mandelas, the women have yet to attain the kind of pinnacles of power (super-heroes?) attained by such Asian women as Benazir Bhutto, Seremavo Bandaranaike or Indira Gandhi.

In the eye-shadow of colonialism

The golden age of more authentic super-heroes in 20th century African history was indeed the time of the struggle for independence against white minority rule. The unsung super-heroes were often women who took great risks. Frantz Fanon tells us that in the Algerian war of independence women exploited the fact that the oppressor underestimated them. The women turned their very weaknesses into skills of combat. Fanon tells us that Algerian women used their Islamic veils as camouflage to hide grenades for the struggle.

In the 1980s Winnie Mandela became the most famous African woman of the decade. She was harrassed, banned, detained, and humiliated by the apartheid regime but she kept the flame of struggle alive. Winnie was by no means an unsung hero but her heroism was often celebrated more abroad than at home.

More obviously unsung were most of the women of Zimbabwe. In the bush and forests of Zimbabwe during the struggle against Ian Smith there were many women liberation fighters. They did not pass unnoticed but they often passed unrecognized.

More recognized than Zimbabwe fighters, but less visible than Winnie Mandela, was Nontsikelelo Albertina Sisulu, who became President of the Federation of South African women in 1983, and President of the United Democratic Front in the same year. She was married both to the super-hero Walter Sisulu and to the liberation struggle. She still managed to bring up five children. It is no wonder that many observers feel that, whether or not women are heroes, the gender injustices of this world always ensure that they are indeed martyrs.

In 1998 a Moroccan poet and novelist responded to questions (real and anticipated) from his ten-year old daughter. His book was entitled *Racism as Explained :o My Daughter*. Tahar Ben Jelloun's book, ostensibly answering questions from his daughter about what racism is, has taken France by storm. It is a didactic book for both children and adults.

Under colonial conditions cultural and racial domination sometimes made the colonized admire super-heroes from those who had oppressed them. (See a report in *International Herald Tribune* (Paris), July 28, 1998).

There were days when Black children in southern Africa were taught to admire the adventures and exploits of Cecil Rhodes. Two whole countries were named after Rhodes; a greater achievement than that of even Christopher Columbus, who has only one country named after him (though many cities and streets). In what is now Zimbabwe young Black school children used to say proudly 'I am a Rhodesian' — a concept celebrating Cecil Rhodes.

I heard young Zambians in the old days repeat the formula that David Livingstone discovered Victoria Falls. Livingstone was a super-hero partly because he had discovered something which the young Zambian ancestors had known about for centuries. Colonialism used to invert and racialize super-heroes convincing many of the colonized to worship the heroes of their oppressors. (Livingstone was a kindly hero but Cecil Rhodes was decidedly not.)

The dialectic is a search for unity of opposites. Super-heroes are dialectized and inverted when Black Americans name their sons after heroic slave-owners of the past, including Thomas Jefferson. But heroes are also racialized and inverted when native Americans cheer the cowboys against the Indians and today's American Indians want John Wayne to annihilate the Apache warriors on the screen.

Heroism begins at home

For Africa, as for many other parts of the world, the 20th century is the first century of books *by* children. Recently we have had the Kwela books for young southern African writers, or the compilation of children's literary pieces by Linda Rode — award-winning anthologies of writing by children.

Such books include *Another Kind of Young Nation* and *Stories South of the Sun*, both collected by Cape Town-born Linda Rode. The second book in the series of young South African writing is *I, a Living Arrow*, compiled by

Linda Rode and Hans Bodenstein (Cape Town, 1998).

As we have indicated, there are areas of overlap between children's heroes and heroes of adults (like Nelson Mandela). Because a child's imagination is less restrained than that of an adult, the child may have other heroes who defy the laws of nature. Such heroes may travel on flying zebras or survive in the stomachs of dolphins or sharks.

A child's imagination does two things. On one side it tightens relations between humans and the rest of nature, so that rabbits speak Kiswahili and a baobab tree can keep Ndebele or Banbara secrets, friend to friend. On the other hand, a child' s imagination breaks loose from the constraints of nature even more completely and lets us as humans traverse the skies. The child's imagination can be both transnatural and supernatural

Books written by adults for children is a much older tradition. Adventure stories go back to the *Arabian Nights* and beyond. Fantastic tales of flying carpets and genies in bottles have entered mainstream adult language. Today, when talking about whether Iraqi nuclear expertise can ever be ended by UN weapons inspectors, some of us ask if the nuclear genie can ever be put back into the bottle. Is it too late? The language of the genie and the bottle takes us back to children's stories in the style of the *Arabian Nights*.

The English expression, 'Who will bell the cat?' is another illustration of how everyday adult metaphors often betray their origins in children's stories — such as those about cats and mice.

While adults derive their transnatural stories from religion, children derive them from the powerful pool of the imagination. Christianity has St Francis of Assisi in communication with birds and animals. And one of the most powerful hymns (Qasidas) on the birthday of Islam's Prophet refers to Muhammad as the Messenger of God who had a conversation with a gazelle:

Allahu ma salli alaNabii -
Ma Jaa naa bi Risaala -
Tahaa Muhammad wu Alihi -
Man Kallamathul ghazala
Let us call upon God to bless the messenger who had a
conversation with a gazelle.

Religion with transnatural imagery is what we have here.

Heroes and super-heroes are not just among the grown-ups. Even in real life children attain levels of exceptional heroism against adversity. At considerable risk to themselves children may rescue a dog from a burning farmhouse. In many parts of Africa children are forced to be soldiers to fight the wars of grown-ups. Sometimes they become immature accomplices, killing or maiming others on orders from grown-ups.

But there have been children who have revolted against this, and found ways of helping others to escape from savagery and war. Heroism in war may sometimes consist in refusing to fight for an unjust cause.

Then there are children who have overcome more ordinary adversities with a remarkable sense of purpose and resilience. The children I personally know best are my own. Heroism, like charity, often begins at home. Two of my children suddenly went blind. One was only 10 years old; and the other was at the otherwise boisterous age of 16. It was a shattering experience for my family. The family consisted of both those who were with me in the US and those who were at our ancestral home in Mombasa, Kenya.

The 16 year-old was initially shaken by his loss of sight. As teenagers often do, going back to *Romeo and Juliet* and beyond, Jamal even contemplated suicide. Jamal was my afflicted first-born. But Jamal did not succumb to despair. Instead we went to a summer camp where he and his younger brother were the only visually handicapped vacationers.

One morning at the camp Jamal expressed the wish to ride a horse. Considering his new disability, I swallowed hard and tried to understand. The camp agreed to make arrangements where Jamal could engage in horseback riding. That was accomplished.

However, that night Jamal had an additional aspiration. He wanted to clear an obstacle on horseback. This time I was triply worried but I knew he was having a debate with himself about how far he had really been disabled by his blindness.

I negotiated with the camp authorities about Jamal clearing an obstacle on horseback. They got him their best trained horse. And as Jamal approached the obstacle, the instructor was to shout to Jamal 'Now!' I held my breath at this additional self-imposed test. The horse galloped towards the obstacle. The instructor shouted 'Now!' and Jamal and the horse sprang across.

By the time Jamal got home, he had made up his mind that his eyes, were much less important than his will. He reorganized his entire approach to schoolwork — rapidly learning the new culture of books on tape rather than on the printed page, new skills of listening and of retention, and eventually learning braille as a new alphabet of touch rather than vision.

He did better at school blind than he ever did sighted. By the time he finished high school almost every major university in the US wanted him to go there — Princeton, Harvard, MIT, Stanford. He finally went to Princeton with an interest in engineering and ended up learning a lot about computers. He later went to Harvard and took a Masters in Public Policy from the Kennedy

School of Government. He then worked as a professional at Harvard for a number of years before transferring to Washington D.C. to help fellow blind people learn the skills of the computer age under the U.S. Federal Governments programmes .

This boy who had become blind in the middle of his teenage years could have thrown in the towel and cultivated a culture of dependency on others. In some cultures he might have become a street beggar. But instead Jamal turned his physical adversity into a challenge and a stimulus for achievement.

As for his younger brother, Kim, who became substantially but not completely blind at the age of 10, he lived to rise literally to be the top student in Law School at the University of Michigan, one of the best in the US. Indeed, he turned down an offer of admission to Harvard Law School. Kim is now a Professor of Law at the university established by Thomas Jefferson, the author of the US Declaration of Independence — the University of Virginia at Charlottesville.

Am I just a proud parent? Maybe. But did these kids also illustrate heroism in everyday adversity? The boys refused to accept defeat from an accident of nature and transcended it. Should some author write their story for other children?

There are no medals for such heroism, no flags flying, no trumpets of hero-worship except from parents. There is only the silent satisfaction of children triumphing over adversity. To paraphrase the dramatist John Drinkwater:

> What matters is not that vast mutability which is event, the pits
> and pinnacles of change, but a wounded child's will and
> valiance, that range all circumstance, and come to port unspent.

Yes, those two kids born in Mulago Hospital in Uganda, finally came to port unspent.

2
Developing a
Science Culture

Among Contemporary African Children

THOMAS R. ODHIAMBO

The economist, Robert Solow, won the Nobel Prize in 1987 for his theory on economic development which states that the key factor in economic growth is science-led technological applications, within the contextual background of other important factors such as education and the development of human capital.

As has been demonstrated again and again this century, the creation and adoption of new, problem-solving technologies can make up for the lack of natural resources and even make up, to a large extent, for deficiencies in financial resources. Japan, South Korea and Switzerland are remarkable case studies in this respect. Africa, on the other hand, in its history of the last 500 years dominated first by the slave trade and then by foreign suzerainty until barely three decades ago, demonstrates overwhelmingly that the possession of a rich, diversified wealth in natural resources alone, without the intervention of an endogenous capacity in science-led, problem-solving, innovative technology does not necessarily lead to economic growth.

Yet, in discussing science and technology in juxtaposition with the notion of economic growth and national wealth, we should not become overwhelmed with the instrumental view of science and technology as being concerned solely or even largely with providing the possibilities for enhancing the material comfort of humankind. Science is very much part of a nation's culture and, in this context, it is intimately concerned with the pursuit of truth, using science's own principles and paradigms for doing so. In a very real sense, science takes its cue and spirit within the socio-cultural fabric of that nation, with its singular value systems, including its ethical standards of compassion, righteousness and love. One of Africa's most illustrious medical research scientists, the late Aklilu Lemma, has emphasized this view with these perceptive words:

> Science and technology are not ends in themselves. They are both the product of the genius of a given culture as well as an instrument for the advancement of the welfare of man as

understood by that culture. Science, therefore, is not necessarily always universal, nor is it absolutely neutral. It is intimately linked to value systems and to a specific vision of the world. (p. 185)

With Africa having completed the century-old struggle for political independence across the continent four years ago, political space has now been generated for Africans to become creators once again. The continent can now, in freedom, develop a culture which recognizes that science is an integral part of African culture.

This is a weighty statement, as contemporary African culture is devoid of science. Africa has kept science and technology out of the economic development arena except in patches such as in South Africa and Egypt; and in its education systems, Africa has kept science as merely a subject in the school curriculum. Indeed, science has never been encouraged and nurtured to become a living theme in the life and play of the household, the workplace, and the body politic. The national project at the dawn of the 21st century ought to be the creation and nurturing of an enabling environment for scientific discovery and technological innovation, as part of the pro-active re-integration of science and technology into African culture. Science and technology had always been an integral part of culture in the heroic history of Africa before the cataclysmic onset of the 16th century, with its evil aftermath of the dehumanization of Africans through the large-scale slave trade.

The essence of science

One of the most profound recent statements about the nature of science, and its integrity within the larger reality of culture, was made at the Vatican City on 4 October 1991, when the Holy Father gave a Solemn Papal Audience at the end of a study week at the Pontifical Academy of Sciences. He described culture as:

. . . a concept which embraces everything of which man is at once the centre, the subject and the object. It includes all his capabilities, both as an individual and as one who lives in society.

Culture humanizes people, manners and institutions. On the other hand, science, instead of being in competition with culture, is actually a fundamental and now indispensable element of all culture. In most diverse fields, scientific and technical progress aims to guarantee better lives for individuals who can completely and more readily fulfill their specific vocations. The Holy Father stressed the need to promote the ethical dimension of science and technology so as to ensure that science-led progress is genuinely human; and he ended his Audience with this moving testament:

> Men and women of science, men and women of culture, the world needs you, your witness and your personal commitment, so that ethics may enlighten science and technology, so that the primacy of the person over things may be respected, and so that science and culture may deserve to be called human. (p. 26)

Science is characterized by open knowledge. It is not simply a collection of facts. It is a discipline of thinking about rational solutions to problems, through the establishment of basic facts, derived from objective observation and experimentation; then hypothesizing from the basis of what is known to what might be; and attempting to test the hypothesis through further observation and experimentation. Science is, consequently, a way of persistently approximating the truth, as seen through the spectacles of rationality.

In this manner, science by itself can never fully give us a comprehensive understanding of anything; but it can provide us with a progressively sharper working hypothesis of natural phenomena and many everyday events. As the astrophysicist, Martin Rees, has said several times, the levels of explanations that we can realistically seek, and what we can predict from our present state of scientific knowledge, is fairly limited. Indeed, our current knowledge of the universe, now roughly 10 billion years old, informs us that a much vaster timespan is still ahead of it, and that the universe as it is now is merely at the early start of its cosmic evolution.

This humbling conclusion should spur on our awareness that every day is a new day for learning and that there are layers upon layers of frontiers of possible knowledge still to be uncovered, if we can only continually sharpen our curiosity and ever provide a prod to our creative spirit, whatever our particular socio-economic circumstances might be at any time.

The essence of education

All people are born with an ever questing spirit to wonder, to explore, to tinker, and to find fulfillment in solving the immediate problem they began with. This is the essence of learning at whatever age, and at whatever level of the educational ladder and the universe, including our own immediate environment, has become the arena of enquiry and knowledge seeking.

In this context of learning, the learner becomes the centre of the learning process. Yet, in the inherited formal school system in Africa, the classroom and the laboratory have become the universal learning arena; and the teacher has become the central mover and arbiter of knowledge — relegating the student to being merely a receptor of knowledge, a recounter in national examinations of factual information that has been repetitively learnt, and a faithful observer of how others have explored old frontiers of knowledge. The bane of contemporary Africa is that the quality of education is generally measured by the student's prowess in recounting what he has learnt from the teacher and textbook, rather than what he has struggled to discover for himself, or what he has innovated or created because of his own enquiring mind. When, therefore, the student does not have the propensity to regurgitate this kind of factual information in competitive examinations, he is pronounced a failure.

In this event, despair sets in in people who are naturally hopeful. In his recent book, *Schools In Need of Education*, Professor Gerard Bennaars incisively characterizes despair as a lack of faith in humanity, if not in the realm of the divine. Hope, on the contrary, is a constant affirmation of faith in both. We agree with the author's new paradigm in African education, that what the continent urgently needs is an 'education of hope'. Hope implies expectation and desire — a looking forward to something good, and our expectation that it actualizes itself. Rather than persist with the present system of education which concentrates on the mechanical acquisition of factual information as prescribed by the syllabus and as required by the national examination board, a system that disregards the frustrations of the learners and thus deprives them of any hope for the future, the 'education of hope' that we promote focuses on creativity, placing the learner in the position of 'constructively acting upon problematic situations, and thereby creating a new world and a new hope.[3] Consequently, the learner takes charge of the learning process — he becomes a problem-solving agent, guided by the teacher, who ceases to be a preceptor, a master instilling sanitized information into his pupil, but who instead presents knowledge, skills and values that truly become liberating to the learner.

This is the intellectual and social environment in which the Foundation for the Promotion of Children's Science Publications in Africa (the Foundation) set itself up in November 1988, as a pan-African non-profit institution. The Foundation for the Promotion of Children's Science Publications in Africa's main objective is to promote the development, growth and delivery of children's quality publications originating in Africa in any language whatsoever, with particular emphasis on science and technology.

The essence of CHISCI in science

The key mission of the Foundation for the Promotion of Children's Science Publications in Africa is premised on the conviction that the future development and competitiveness of Africa lies in her children appreciating who they are, and their unique place in the universe and, in this process, intimately reintegrating modern science, technology, and mathematics into the African culture.

The success of such a re-integration process requires an interactive climate of enquiry, innovation and wonder within all possible arenas of life and living — the home, the workplace, the playground, the school and even the environment of out-of-school. The maintenance and renewal of such a nurturing environment in our life-long journey demands that every African child's unique talents and human creative potentials — regardless of gender, economic circumstances and ethnic or religious particularities — be vigorously fostered throughout one's biological life, by the home, the community, the general public, and the state.

This fundamental intent has been translated into the Foundation's strategic mission directed towards three specific goals:

To stimulate, promote and assiduously cultivate a reading and science and technology culture among children from a very early age — at home, in the village or community, at school or out-of-school, at play or at the workplace.

To stimulate, promote and sponsor the design, development, production, marketing and the distribution of quality and relevant children's publications, culturally relevant toys and games, having an innovative, socially-sensitive science, technology and mathematics content;

To promote the ownership of reading materials at the home and community level, and nurture a life-long book-buying propensity among children and their families — siblings, parents, grandparents, and guardians.

In experimenting how best to implement this far-reaching transformational programme for the learning environment of the knowledge-seeking African child, the Foundation has been implementing, over the last four years, a truly novel initiative — the so-called Non-Formal Interactive Learning (NFIL) Programme. This Programme has three components, which the foundation invented and pioneered:

Developing a Science Culture

The Children's Mobile Reading Tent provides a learning arena for all children, whether in school or out of school, economically disadvantaged or economically affluent, to read, be creative, solve scientific puzzles or problems, tell stories, take part in debates, or play with innovative toys, and in general realize their potentials in a fun-filled, interactive, diversified environment, with several empathetic experts and eager volunteers to guide them.

The Children's Creative Science and Technology Workshop provides opportunities for stimulating scientific experimentation, ingenious technological activities, and remarkable natural history objects, under the watchful eye of an expert.

The Children's Readers Club, which has been established in each of the foundation's campuses. The Club mobilizes members for individual and group reading sessions, for poetry reading competitions, for special events (such as music sessions, creative art learning, and theatre), and from time to time for doing sketches for the radio.

The principal effort of the foundation supervisors of these activities is to guide, to stimulate and to nurture. In such an environment, the natural ebullience, inquisitiveness, and creativity of children easily cascades into the interactive learning arena.

In contrast, the formal classroom, with a commanding teacher and the threat of national examinations, often leads children to feel intimidated, and to acquire a fearful disposition towards the entire contemporary educational process.

Undoubtedly, the Kenyan public is taking notice of the Foundation's Non-Formal Interactive Learning approach; and the Foundation is due to make it into a major campaign around the East African Lake Victoria basin as from the year 1999. Then, the end of the separation of science from the African culture will have begun in earnest — from a populous region in the very heart of Africa.

References

Lemma, A. (1991), 'Science and Technology in Africa: Some Reflections on Lessons Learned and Prospects and Challenges for the Future', in *The New Challenge of Science and Technology for Development in Africa*, p. 185, ICIPE Science Press, Nairobi.

Marini Bettolo Marconi, G.B. and P. Poupard (eds) (1993), 'Science in the Context of Human Culture', Vatican City, Pontifical Academy of Sciences.

Bennaars, G.A. (1998), *Schools in Need of Education: Towards an African Pedagogy*, Lectern Publications, Nairobi.

3
The Condition of the Child in Africa

Academic Seminar at University of Zimbabwe 30-31 July 1998

TERENCE RANGER

For some years many of those connected with the Zimbabwe International Book Fair noticed how few African or Africanist academics attend the Fair . Last year it was decided to launch an African Scholarship Initiative at this year's Book Fair. The Southern African Book Development and Education Trust (SABDET), working with Professor Paul Zeleza, convened a meeting during the 1997 Fair where it was agreed to have an academic seminar immediately preceding the 1998 Fair devoted to discussion of its theme 'Children'. Professor Ngwabe Bhebe and Dr Alois Mlambo of the University of Zimbabwe undertook to organize such a seminar. It was agreed that the results of this seminar should be reported to the Indaba. And it was agreed that SABDET would organize a practical workshop for young scholars during the Book Fair week. SABDET has organized a workshop on Review, which takes place on Wednesday 4 August 1998. On Friday 6 August there will be a meeting to consider the African Scholarship programme for this year and to plan future programmes. It is already plain that an academic seminar on some aspects of the theme of 'Women', will be held probably between the Indaba and the Book Fair ; that more effort will be made to link the seminar to the rest of the Book Fair proceedings; and that SABDET will organize another workshop, possibly on the methodology, financing and presentation of research. There will be a Round Table at the US African Studies Association in Chicago in November 1998 where a report will be made on the African Scholarship Programme. The panel will consist of Professor Paul Zeleza, Dr Alois Mlambo, Margaret Ling of SABDET, and Professor Terence Ranger, visiting Professor at the University of Zimbabwe and Honorary Trustee of the Book Fair.

The first academic seminar, on 'The Condition of the Child in Africa', has just finished at the University of Zimbabwe. It has been a great success and Professor Bhebe and Dr Mlambo plan to publish a book based on its papers before next year's Fair . The seminar was distinguished by the range of countries and disciplines represented. In addition to many Zimbabwean presenters, chairpersons and commentators, there were scholars from Kenya, Malawi, Mozambique, South Africa, Ghana, Britain and the US. Presentations were made by anthropologists, political scientists, historians, sociologists, doctors of medicine, educational psychologists, social work practitioners and others working with street children or orphans.

It offered a great challenge to academics. Yesterday in this group we had a presentation by women academics describing a multi-volume project for the publication of women's texts and voices. It was said that these volumes would demand a totally new kind of historiography of Africa. Of course much more needs to be done to give African women a proper place in the study of Africa. Nevertheless, over the past twenty years many books have been written on women in Africa. A much greater challenge to the field is the demand that it take seriously the voices and agency of African children. I have undertaken several projects of field research, in which I have interviewed women as well as men but it had never occurred to me to interview children.

Indeed, the whole emphasis of oral historians has been on seeking out the oldest available holder of tradition — a representative of those 'living books in danger of dying'. Those who have studied more recent nationalism or guerrilla war or agricultural change have tried to interview the adult men and women who led these movements or who felt their impact. This focus on the owners of tradition and on makers of events has excluded children. As the seminar was reminded, in many African societies it is accepted that a child does not speak when adults are present. Yet it is obviously an important question whether, and if so how, 'the tradition' is transmitted to children; how far they construct local identities through their riddles and games; how they have experienced war and political transformation; and what experiences and attitudes they will bring to adulthood and eventually to eldership.

Some of the discussions at the seminar, therefore, were about the ways in which scholars can recover children's voices. It is not too difficult to interview child refugees and to present the voices of victims. What is more difficult is to recover the voices of children who have been or are acting within African societies.

Yet it is possible to go back into the past and to reconstruct the experience of children in social context. Charles van Onselen's remarkable book, *The Seed is Mine* (James Currey, Oxford, 1996) reconstructs the history of the Maine family of black sharecroppers in the northern Transvaal. The central figure is the patriarch, Kaas Maine, but around him van Onselen groups a constellation of sons and daughters, and sons-in-law and daughters-in-law.

All have been interviewed; all recall the experience of childhood vividly. The book presents the past experience of childhood and youth within an African family.

Participants in the seminar revealed their various techniques for hearing the voices of children. Some of them — like the Zimbabwean anthropologist Linda Dube — have used the classical participant-observation method. Dube lived among and interacted with the street children of Harare and has emerged with an extraordinarily rich picture of their organization into different activities; their hierarchies of prestige and power; their slang; their perceptions of themselves and of society. Pamela Reynolds, author of *Dance, Civet Cat*, a penetrating study of child labour in the Zambezi Valley, and of a recent study of the healing of child trauma after the Zimbabwean liberation war, has deployed the same technique, as has Alcinda Honwana in her work on child soldiers in Mozambique.

Others spoke of making use of the expressive products of children. Michael Bourdillon, who presented a paper on 'earn and learn' schemes on the tea plantations, described how he had set an essay competition for the school children. He was able to quote from the very revealing results. Jack Mapanje spoke about child riddles which in all their brutality and often misogyny were ways of confronting the rigours of life. The seminar heard of the technique used by the anthropologist Tim Allen, who in his work on refugees and violence in East Africa, tapped child perceptions by setting school drawing competitions. The drawings which resulted were enlightening in themselves and still more so when explained by the child.

In all these ways one could begin to hear African children. But what happens when you do? The results are often disconcerting.

Children's preferences are often not those prescribed for them by humanitarian international or national agencies. The seminar heard forceful papers on child workers, child soldiers and street children. World humanitarian opinion is pressing for the abolition of child labour (child being defined as everyone under 18); for the rehabilitation of child soldiers; for the rescue and institutionalization of street children. Yet when one listens to children these policies seem less straightforwardly admirable.

Children in Africa often say that they want to work for wages and have chosen to do so. They want to earn money to meet school fees or to buy clothes or to help support families. They prefer to work for wages rather than to contribute to equally, or more, demanding domestic labour (which is not proscribed or even condemned by international opinion). They feel they have more autonomy as wage workers. The government of India has passed a law recognizing the child's right to work and at the same time setting up protective measures against exploitation, defining the ages at which types of work become permissible and laying down conditions of employment. Pamela Reynolds, while telling the seminar a horror story of the way in which one white South African farmer exploited children's hunger for waged work, also recommended that the hunger should be met by properly controlled employment. A total ban on child labour would merely make it easier for exploiters to operate under cover. Others pointed out that the global demand for a ban on child labour coincided with interventions by the World Bank and the International Monetary Fund which made it impossible for African governments to pursue social welfare policies. Withdrawal of the possibility of children earning wages at the same time as welfare provision for families collapses would be disastrous.

Alcinda Honwana told the seminar that some children in Mozambique had taken up arms to help protect their families; many more felt empowered by having done so. Rudo Gaidzanwa talked about the agency of children during the liberation war in Zimbabwe — the possibility of them going over the border to join the guerrillas in Mozambique; their role as messengers and intermediaries between the guerrillas and the civilian population; the new sexual freedoms for some young girls. It did not make sense in either case to regard these children of war simply as victims. The seminar was reminded of the work of Sarah Gibbs in northern Mozambique, where she found that adults stressed the special resilience of children rather than their greater peril. When the bush was burnt out the old banana trees die but the young shoots continue. 'Their parents are dead but they will survive, alone'. But, of course, just as child workers need to be protected so child soldiers and *mujibas* and *chimbwidos* were at great risk during the wars and there are great problems of reintegrating them into society when the violence is ended.

Gaidzanwa spoke of the 'terrifying agency' of Zimbabwean children during the liberation war — of their fears and of the agonies of parents who saw their children vanish into Mozambique or suddenly ordering adults about as delegated by the guerrillas. It was emphasized, however, that social reintegration had to be achieved by the mechanisms of African societies themselves rather than by international schemes of 'rehabilitation'. Honwana described the processes of spirit possession and exorcism which served as healing mechanisms in southern Mozambique. The spirits of those unjustly killed, either in the recent wars or in one of the past violences of the 20th century, return to possess and threaten the living. They are appeased so that the possessed child, and the whole community, make their peace with the past and lay foundations for the future. Pamela Reynolds, who has studied similar rituals in Zimbabwe, emphasized that what was going on was not merely the reinsertion of children, who had exercised their agency, back into the patriarchal system, where they would be defined once again merely as children. After violence nothing could be the same again.

The same dialectic of agency and danger was stressed in the presentations on the street children. Linda Dube revealed the complex society of children on the streets of Harare and their sense of self-motivation and self-worth. Father Shanahan, who has worked for many years in the streets of Accra, and who deals with street grandchildren there, took the argument further. Urban life in West Africa was the real Africa and represented the future of most Africans. We should abandon our pastoral dreams and focus on the towns rather than the 'traditional' countryside. Children on the streets of West African towns constituted a sub-culture, an ethnicity, even a culture, which needed to be treated as seriously as any tribal society. In Accra the street children had chosen to be where they are; given the choice to reside in a well-provided institution, only a handful wanted to do so. Such children did not need to be rehabilitated.

But, of course, like child workers and child soldiers they did need protection and assistance. Shanahan described how dozens of African social workers went out onto the streets of Accra to live with the children and to respond to their needs. He described some of these workers holding literacy classes at night under the street lights. They were making alliances with the culture of the street rather than seeking to 'redeem' it.

Something of the same pattern emerged from discussion of child refugees. Cassandra Veney spoke about children as refugees in East Africa, making fascinating distinctions between the layout and structures of the various camps and the way in which this affected the fate of the refugees. In some of the camps there were large numbers of boys gathered together without their parents or other adults. The seminar was told of the research of Mario Aguilar who studied such a group of Boorana boys in a camp in northern Kenya. Aguilar showed how these boys, first in their games, and then in more formal dramas, acted out their own version of Boorana culture. Even in the agony of the camps, where they need food and clothes and teaching, children can exercise agency.

Brian Raftopolous stressed that African children exercised their agency only within the constraints imposed by power relations. To modify Marx one might say that children make their own history but they certainly cannot make it just as they choose. But this was true also of African adults and one should not stress the dangers and suffering of children without remembering how much adults share these dangers.

In addition to discussions of child workers, child soldiers, street children and child refugees, the seminar examined international and African statements of child rights; the problem of orphans; sexual abuse of children; corporal punishment; child sexuality. Finally, conscious that it was a seminar preceding a book fair, there were regular comments on publishing needs.

Jack Mapanje stressed how important child riddles are. They stimulated reason and imagination — unlike the deadening games played on computers. Yet it was very difficult to publish them except in expensive 'African Texts' series. Pamela Reynolds complained that it was very difficult to discover what other researchers on children were doing. She asserted that publishers did not want to carry books on children. Her recent study of the healing of children in Zimbabwe has not been published in Africa and will not have a second American edition. Robert Muponde attacked the damage done to children by many of the imported books bought for them. Father Shanahan asked that when the street children of Accra became literate they should have something interesting to read. The seminar wished these suggestions to be presented to the Indaba.

The presenters of papers to the seminar were, in order, Welshman Ncube (Law, Zimbabwe); Ken Kalonde (Art, Malawi); Robert Muponde (Literature, Zimbabwe); Pamela Reynolds (Anthropology, South Africa); Neddy Matshalaga (Development Studies, Zimbabwe); Alcinda Honwana (Anthropology, Mozambique); R. Mupedziswa (Social work, Zimbabwe); Cassandra Veney (Politics, US); I. Chitsike (Medicine, Zimbabwe); G.M. Powell (Medicine, Zimbabwe); S. Nyandiya-Bundy (Child Psychology, Zimbabwe); Linda Dube (Anthropology, Zimbabwe); Father P. Shanahan (Case Worker, Ghana); E. Kamaara (Religious Studies, Kenya); Rudo Gaidzanwa (Sociology, Zimbabwe); Michael Bourdillon (Anthropology, Zimbabwe); Jack Mapanje (Literature, Malawi); Terence Ranger (History, Zimbabwe).

Chairs and discussants were drawn from the University of Zimbabwe and from Sapes Trust.

4
Panel Discussion:
Piracy and Photocopying

The Threat to Authors, Publishers and Readers
of Books for Children and Students

SUMMARISED BY MONICA SEEBER

The focus of the panel discussion on copyright was on the negative effects of copyright infringement on publishing, and on copyright licensing as an effective means of balancing the rights of copyright owners with the legitimate needs of users in the African context.

The panelists were:

- Olav Stokkmo (Chairman), the Secretary-General of the International Federation of Reproduction Rights Organizations (IFFRO), based in Brussels. Before taking up this appointment he had for some years been Deputy Director of KOPINOR, the Norwegian reproduction rights organization or collecting society.

- Gerard Robinson, Executive Director of the Dramatic, Artistic and Literary Rights Organization (DALRO), the South African reproduction rights organization which is based in Johannesburg.

- Olalere Oladitan of the Department of Foreign Languages, Obafemi Awolowo University, Ile-Ife, Nigeria, representing the newly-established reproduction rights organization of Nigeria, REPRONIG.

- Greenfield K. Chilongo, Executive Director of the Zimbabwean reproduction rights organization, ZIMCOPY, which is based in Harare.

- Janetta van der Merwe, Project Director in the Publishing Liaison Office of the Adamastor Trust in Cape Town.

- Monica Seeber, Publishing Consultant based in Johannesburg, and the APNET Representative in South Africa.

The panel was representative of several perspectives since panel members representing reproduction rights organizations had the knowledge, insights and experience to explore copyright licensing in some depth: Janetta van der Merwe (who channels licensing requests on behalf of five tertiary institutions in the Western Cape) was fully cognisant of the users' perspective; and Monica

Seeber (who had just completed an 18-month term as Copyright Officer for the Publishers Association of South Africa) was able to represent the perspective of rights' owners.

The panel members agreed to limit the duration of their presentations in the interests of allowing as much time as possible for questions and comments.

Olav Stokkmo's presentation, which led the way, was entitled 'Piracy, scholarly publishing and youth literature'. He touched on the following topics:

- The economic importance of the copyright industries in countries where intellectual property rights are adequately protected.
- The importance of textbook and scholarly publishing and of youth literature.
- The threat to creative industries and economic growth posed by piracy (the unauthorized reproduction of copyright material for profit) and by unauthorized photocopying.
- The value of licensing where a user needs to copy only a portion of a work, for internal use within an institution or organization. In these cases Reproduction Rights Organizations (RROs) have in many countries been set up by rights' owners (authors and publishers) to licence photocopying and collect remuneration for distribution to rights' owners. Authors and publishers receive payment, the user gets access to copyright works, and a win-win situation is established.
- IFRRO, which represents national reproduction rights organizations in some 45 countries world-wide.
- The need to stimulate creativity by respecting copyright, for the pirating of scholarly publications, textbooks and youth literature has a destructive effect on the creation of intellectual property, the publishing industry and the economy of a nation.

In rounding off his presentation, Olav Stokkmo said:

> The primary task of the author is to create, and of the publisher to produce and sell the creator's product. Libraries produce services to the creative industries. Pirates produce problems, and later excuses when they are caught. Legislators and reproduction rights organizations search to offer adequate solutions to both users and rights' holders. Thus one might say that we are all producers — of goods, services, problems, excuses or solutions, but only goods, services and solutions help to bring the economy forward.

The three representatives of national reproduction rights organizations spoke on collective licensing systems in their respective countries. Of these,

DALRO of South Africa is the longest-established, and Gerard Robinson was therefore able to draw on his extensive experience in administering and protecting reprographic reproduction rights to expand on good principles and practice, such as the need for a reproduction rights organization to be properly constituted and to be accorded credibility in the international copyright arena. It needs to be mandated by a representative body of authors and of publishers and can then, through membership of IFRRO, become a fully-functioning part of the ever-growing family of reproduction rights organizations in developed and developing countries. He also explained the difference between the transactional licence (a one-off permission for predetermined reproduction of title-specific works) and the blanket licence (in terms of which the user is permitted to take copies from works in the reproduction rights organization's repertoire within pre-defined limits but without seeking permission each time).

ZIMCOPY has only recently been established and is not yet fully operational, and Greenfield Chilongo mentioned some of the difficulties he has encountered in persuading a society to treat intellectual property with respect, taking the positive view that there was definitely potential for progress in Zimbabwe.

Olalere Oladitan's position was at the same time more philosophical and more analytical, examining, *inter alia*, the definitions of 'children' and 'students', the use of texts in learning situations, the law in Nigeria, and the threats of piracy and photocopying — and then going on to assess who the 'true villains' are and how a culture of reading can be sabotaged by pirates and infringers. This was a fascinating and original approach but unfortunately time contraints allowed for only a tantalizing glimpse of his full paper, which was subsequently circulated.

Janetta van der Merwe was well placed to speak about the user's perspective in the academic community, since her job is to liaise between users and owners of copyrighted materials. Citing the need to create an awareness of copyright law, to facilitate compliance with the law and to negotiate reasonable fees for photocopying licences, she mentioned the problems of time (most academics require permission in a hurry) and cost (many students struggle to pay their tuition fees, let alone copyright fees). On a positive note, she believes that there is a growing awareness of copyright in South Africa's educational institutions and a general willingness to remunerate authors and publishers for their creative efforts and investments. She concluded by urging the different role-players — publishers, reproduction rights organizations and users — to balance their interests to secure the dissemination of information which will benefit society in general and children in particular.

Monica Seeber reflected on some questions that African publishers ought to be asking themselves in order to be better armed to respond to the threat of copyright infringement. These questions concern the adequacy of national legislation as regards both copyright protection and enforcement, and the need for self-education and lobbying for public awareness campaigns. African publishers have to face the challenge of educating people to respect copyright in the face of the needs and demands of information-hungry but cash-strapped readers, and should therefore support copyright licensing:

> A licensing scheme will offer publishers some returns on their
> creative and financial investments, and it will also enable users
> to fairly gain access to the information they need.

It was possible to reply to only a few of the many questioners who raised their hands after the panelists had spoken, especially since the questions varied in range and depth, and time was limited. As a sample of the diversity of the questions and comments:

— Jay Heale of South Africa sought clarification on what a teacher may copy for his class, and how a school could get permission for copying in excess of what the law allows. Gerard Robinson replied that a reproduction rights organization could grant permission transactionally, but a blanket licence taken out by the school would be better.

— Margaret Crampton of South Africa raised the issue of academic authors not receiving compensation for their contributions to scholarly journals, and journals often 'taking' their authors' copyright. In reply, Monica Seeber said that this was a 'multi-pronged' question that could not be fully answered in the particular forum, but that authors needed to become better educated as to their rights.

— Henry Chakava of Kenya pointed out that while he subscribes to the principles of copyright protection, much of what is being protected in Africa is not of African origin. Monica Seeber responded that her own presentation had indeed touched on this dilemma, but that surely Africa should not become a 'rogue' continent, protecting only its own, since respect for intellectual property is a universal principle.

The interest shown in the copyright panel session was an indication of the need for a fuller discussion next year.

5
Children and Books: Kenya
A Decade of African Publishing for Children
(1988-1998)

HENRY CHAKAVA

M y involvement with publishing for children dates back to the late 1970s. It was one of the ways I responded to the Great Literature Debate of the University of Nairobi, which raged in the late 1960s and 1970s and about which much has been written. It evolved as a result of many hours of discussion with Ngugi wa Thiong'o. He had just served one year of detention and was having difficulty reacquiring his university teaching job. I gave him a desk at our offices in 1979, and during the three years that followed he was able to complete three books, *Detained: A Writer's Prison Diary*, *Ngaahika Ndeenda* (I Will Marry When I Want), and *Caitani Mutarabaini* (Devil on the Cross). It was during this period that he swore never to write his novels in English again.

In those days, there were hardly any locally published children's books. Nairobi bookshops were full of beautifully illustrated children's books imported mainly from the UK. The challenge was, how were we going to make African literature the basis of study at university when our children were being brought up on foreign literatures? We decided to launch a series of children's books in Kenyan languages. Ngugi agreed to write the books and I undertook to publish them. We also adopted a strategy whereby I would approach all established Kenyan writers and invite them to write at least one children's book in their own language. Ngugi was keen that these readers should not appear inferior in any way, lest readers associate inferiority with mother tongue publishing. In the first five years, I had published three books by Ngugi, *Njamba Nene na Mbaathii Mathgu*, *Bathitoora ya Njamba Nene* and *Njamba Nene na Cibu King'ang'i*, *Kaana Ng'ya* by David Maiilu, *Ogilu Nungo Piny Kirom* by Asenath Odaga, and *Lialuka lia Vaana va Magomere* by Francis Imbuga. Although we could not afford to print on art paper and bind in boards, we at least used a generous layout, good paper and full colour illustrations on the cover and in the text. After the initial five titles, I was unable to continue with this series because sales were poor. None of the books has ever been reprinted.

In 1987 when I chaired Chinua Achebe's keynote address on Children's Literature in Africa, I had little to recommend me for the job. I was still smarting from the disappointment narrated above. I had also developed a Kiswahili reading scheme, *Visa na Mikasa*, which had not done well in spite of being recommended for use in schools by the Ministry of Education. Achebe called upon serious African writers to save African children from the 'beautifully packaged poisons' that are imported children's books by making a commitment to write at least two stories for children. Encouraging them to draw from oral tradition, he continued, 'Africa has an infinite treasury for those writers who want to and can exploit it' but was quick not to be restrictive, 'But there is room also for entirely new creations'. Achebe went on to say how oral tradition can be made to yield contemporary meaning, and recommended publication in 'simple and inexpensive booklets'. Quoting one story from oral tradition he also warned against 'locally brewed poisons', saying that he was as opposed to the racism contained in foreign children's books as much as the sexism in folk-tales. He concluded by appealing to African artists to take up the problem of illustrations, which are generally poor and unimaginative. Achebe's speech was a real inspiration to me.

The discussion that followed was even more illuminating. For a moment I feared there might be a confrontation with Ngugi (who was in the hall) over the language question. Achebe's simple response to this question was, 'people should be allowed to write in the language they are most at home in'. I thought about Achebe's paper for a couple of days and before he could leave Harare, I asked him if he could give me rights to his two children's books, *The Drum* and *How Leopard Got His Claws*, so that I could start a children's series with them. I also asked him if he would come to Nairobi as my guest to launch the series and he agreed.

Buoyed by Achebe's words, I began to reconstruct my concept of a children's book in an African situation. There was no room for imperfect imitations. The question of language was important but there had to be a national policy giving these languages a place in the educational process. The message too was important but it had to come through naturally. I was not going to discriminate against folk-tales, especially those who had been adapted to convey messages which are 'wholesome and appropriate', to quote Achebe again. The books I would publish would be simple, modestly designed, and illustrated in black and white, printed on ordinary paper and affordably priced at less than US$1. They would be written in English. With this the EAEP Junior Readers Series was born, and was formally launched by Achebe in Nairobi in November 1988.

Today EAEP has 127 titles in print (see chart below). As the series continued to grow, a need arose to grade the books fairly roughly, to give some idea about the level at which they could best be used. Four levels were introduced — Sunbird series (for up to age 7), Sparrow series (7-9), Junior Readers (10-13), and Secondary Readers (14-15). To enrich the series and give it variety, we have acquired titles from publishers in other African countries, including Uganda, Tanzania, Zambia, Malawi, South Africa, Namibia, Zimbabwe, Nigeria and Ghana. Further, we have cautiously introduced a comparable series in Kiswahili, at three levels: *Vitabu vya Paukwa Pakawa* (up to age 7), *Vitabu vya Nyota* (7-9), and*Vitabu vya Sayari* (10-13).

EAEP readers

MOTHER TONGUE READERS

Gikuyu	—	3
Dholuo	—	2
Luhyia	—	4
KISWAHILI READERS		
Visa Na Mikasa	—	9
Paukwa Pakawa	—	4
Vitabu vya Nyota	—	9
Vitabu vya Sayari	—	13
ENGLISH READERS		
Sunbird Readers	—	10
Sparrow Readers	—	17
Junior Readers	—	46
Secondary Readers	—	10
Total		127

With an average sale of at least three thousand copies per year, per title, our children's publishing programme can be said to be modestly successful and to compare favourably with sales of other children's books in the Kenyan market. This success can be attributed to several factors:

- The work of CHISCI (The Foundation for the Promotion of Children's Science Publications in Africa) in sensitizing children to books and reading through organizing the annual Pan African Children's Book Fair, and the monthly Reading Tent.
- The National Book Week in carrying similar messages to the provinces.
- The Kenya Publishers Association, which has used every opportunity to promote Kenyan books abroad, especially at book fairs and to lobby government for support.

- DFID, CODE and other non-governmental organizations such as Plan International and Action-Aid, which have been buying children's books and supplying them free to schools.
- The African Books Collective which continues to order regularly from us for sale outside Africa.
- The African Publishers Network which has exhibited these books at international book fairs.
- Finally, our promotional efforts which have included innovative ways of selling to schools in library boxes and discount packs, promotional visits outside the country, and exhibitions at book fairs in Africa and beyond.

At this point, it may be a good idea to consider why my attempts to publish children's books in African languages failed and why my second effort succeeded. It should be noted that all the books originally published in mother tongue have been translated into English and are selling alongside the others.

Why did our children's books in mother tongues fail?

1 The books did not support any curriculum, therefore were difficult to promote.
2 We did not give the books a series image but tended to promote them individually.
3 Our imitation of Western children's books was not complete. We fell in between two stools and ended up with books which were expensive but not attractive; poorly designed with rigid illustrations.
4 Our insistence on didactics and contemporary stories was overstretched. Instead of avoiding folk-tales, we could have re-rendered them to convey contemporary messages.
5 Both language and message may not have been properly graded and were perhaps too adult.
6 We may have been ahead of our time.

Why did our second attempt succeed?

1 The books were incorporated into the curriculum to strengthen the teaching of English in primary schools.
2 They were given a series image and a standard design, and could therefore be promoted as a series.
3 They were cheap.
4 An attempt was made to grade the language and the message.
5 Their publication came at the right time.

The next ten years

EAEP's children's publishing programme is the fastest growing part of our business and is likely to remain that way for some time to come. The field will become more and more competitive as other publishers develop their own lists, but more attention will be given to quality of both content and presentation. Therefore, EAEP's children's books of the future will be:

* less folk-loric and more contemporary in storyline,
* more professionally designed and illustrated,
* more colourful — employing colour in the text and moving gradually from duotone to full colour, costs permitting,
* more carefully graded; although this is a particularly difficult task in Africa,
* printed on better quality paper,
* better bound, using tougher boards, if not case-bound,
* affordable in price,
* distinctly African.

To maintain their competitive edge, other Kenyan publishers will likewise improve the quality of their children's books.

As for imported children's books, I believe they will continue to come to Kenya in large numbers, given the liberalized state of the market. Their publishers will respond to the taste of an increasingly discriminating readership by producing more appropriate books. The interplay of local and foreign children's books will be good for the industry. In the final analysis, it will be the reader who will benefit most from these developments.

6
The Longhorn Experience
A Decade of African Publishing for Children
1988 -1998

JANET NJOROGE

Longhorn Limited is a wholly Kenyan-owned publishing house that came into being in 1994, when the Longman Group of the UK divested fully from their Kenyan subsidiary. Longman Kenya Limited had been established in 1965 as a sales and marketing outlet. By the 1980s it had developed into a fully-fledged publishing house.

The change of name and ownership brought with it both challenges and opportunities that impacted on publishing programmes, including publishing for children. My presentation traces the metamorphosis of the company over the last ten years with particular reference to publishing for children.

1988–1989: Keeping pace

Longman Kenya Limited, like its parent company, was almost exclusively an educational publisher. It was active in publishing primary school textbooks in specific subject areas. Up to the mid-1980s, primary school textbooks were procured centrally by the Kenyan Ministry of Education and there had, in time, developed a situation where publishing houses were identified with specific subjects. (Longman Kenya was particularly active in Geography, History and Science).

The situation changed abruptly in 1985 when the education system was restructured. The 7-4-2-3 structure that had been in existence was changed to 8-4-4. This necessitated syllabus changes from primary through secondary to university levels. For Longman Kenya, the challenge was to publish textbooks that were in line with the new syllabuses in time to beat the competition. This was at a time when publishing policy decisions were made in Harlow, although the management of the company was wholly Kenyan. Differences of perception of priorities had to be overcome.

Competition assumed a new meaning when new players ventured into publishing to cash in on the opportunities offered by the new system.

Specialization by subject became less pronounced and state-owned publishers became major competitors against private enterprises.

For Longman Kenya, the years 1988–1989 were a period when the company was striving to keep pace at various fronts: completing new courses and competing with other players, the most threatening being the state-owned publishers. During this time, publishing for children was exclusively in the textbook area.

1990–1994: Diversification

Longman Kenya celebrated its Silver Jubilee in 1990. A series of children's readers — the Anchor Readers — was launched as part of the celebrations. Three titles were launched at the celebrations and two others followed soon after. This was Longman Kenya's first serious attempt to publish children's readers as a series. Prior to that, individual readers for children had been published in both English and Kiswahili, and a Science-cum-English series called the Puzzle Crackers (with four titles) had also been published.

It was also during this period that four Animal Activity books were published. This series gives children the opportunity to have great fun as they learn about the diversity of East Africa's animals.

Between 1991 and 1994, Longman co-publishedwith the British Council three collections of poems by Kenyan children. The collections consist of winning poems from National Poetry Competitions sponsored by the British Council in 1991, 1992 and 1993.

In many ways, therefore, this period was the most productive of the last decade as far as publishing for children is concerned. Educational publishing continued as Longman Kenya ventured into other subject areas and upgraded existing titles.

The diversification into non-educational titles coincided with further divestiture by Longman Group (UK) and greater participation in decision-making by the local management.

1995–1998: The transition

As part of a multinational publishing house, Longman Kenya's publishing programme had to be complementary to the parent company's overall programme. Consultations with Harlow were therefore necessary before decisions were made.

The change of ownership of the company shifted the responsibility of making publishing policy decisions wholly to the management in Nairobi. At the same time, there were some Longman UK educational titles that were no longer available. One of the priorities for Longhorn, therefore, was to publish alternative titles and to revamp others in line with changing market needs.

These last four years have also seen the entry of Longhorn into the Ugandan market. We have opened an office in Kampala and published textbooks in line with their primary school syllabus. Supplementary textbooks have also been launched.

In many ways, therefore, publishing for children has recently been concentrated on educational titles. However, we have recently embarked on a project to publish children's readers to expand the Anchor Readers (re-named Weaverbird Series) and also launch another series for younger children. Parallel series in Kiswahili are also planned, in addition to translating the well-known Longhorn Reading Scheme into Kiswahili.

The future

Educational publishing will remain the mainstay of Longhorn's business. With expected changes in the education system, more resources will have to be directed towards this since new courses will need to be developed.

Financial resources are scarce for publishers in Kenya at the best of times and conditions are particularly difficult at present. However, Longhorn is determined and committed to participate effectively in publishing non-educational books for children.

This is in recognition of the need to nurture the reading habit in children by providing suitable reading materials. It is also a prudent business strategy that will help us reduce our reliance on textbooks and hence our vulnerability.

7
A Decade of Publishing for Children
Uganda

Publishing for children in Uganda encompasses two main areas: textbooks and supplementary books. Most of the primary school textbooks are published in the four examinable subjects: mathematics, English, science and social studies. The textbooks are tailored to a specific curriculum and most publishers in Uganda — most of whom are the usual British-based international companies — have restricted their publishing programmes to textbooks that answer the needs of the examination syllabus. I would be re-inventing the wheel if I concentrated on textbook publishing. Suffice to say that publishing of textbooks in Uganda picked up in the early 1980s to coincide with a World Bank funded project. The books were mainly adaptations of textbooks from other African countries and were supplied by two international publishers. But the quality of the books and the methods used by the two publishers to win the tenders became targets of intense criticism from the public, sections of the government and even donors, to the extent that a book policy that created a level playing field for all publishers — both local and foreign — was put in place in 1993. Since then, ten publishers are active in Uganda, publishing books for children, but nearly all of them textbooks.

One of the few exceptions, however, is Fountain Publishers, an indigenous publishing house which has ventured into publishing supplementary reading books for children. This decision was taken in the knowledge that, 'Textbooks are studied, not read'. It was, therefore, necessary to publish books that could be read, rather than studied by Ugandan children, hence the launching of our children reading series.

The Readers' Project

For most of the 1970s and 1980s, Uganda's publishing industry was in limbo, having suffered greatly under the pressure of internal strife and economic decay. During that period, Ugandan children had to do with the little they had in terms of books that were filtering in from Kenya and occasionally the UK.

By 1998, when Fountain Publishers was established, there was a widespread book famine in all sections of society. Whereas it is true that the Ugandan government tried to import books from the UK and India to fill the vacuum, the quantity and appropriateness of these books left a lot to be desired. For a book-hungry child, however, this far from ideal situation did not matter. They read the few books that came. But whether they appreciated the contents, or whether the reading skills of these children were improved by those books is another matter. The complete absence of children's books by Ugandan authors, which were based on local ideas and experiences, was none the less not lost on us.

It was, therefore, on the basis of wanting to provide more culturally appropriate reading materials that Fountain resolved to launch the first children's story books under the general title 'Our Heritage Series'. The general title was appropriately chosen as generally Africa's, but more specifically Uganda's, answer to the foreign children's story books that had dominated Uganda's schools.

The Our Heritage Series was based on Uganda's popular folk tales, legends and animal stories that have always been told to children over the generations but which have never been written down and published. The stories were solicited through a newspaper advert placed at intervals in various newspapers. An experienced teacher was assigned to work as the general editor for the series.

She selected the stories on the basis of clarity of language, simplicity, moral and cultural appropriateness, regional balance and the potential to interest children. The first ten selected typescripts were graded broadly from levels 2 to 7. The books were then edited, illustrated and eventually published in 1993. The usual promotional techniques were used to launch this new set of books — the first lot of indigenously published books to be launched on a grand scale.

A number of trade inquiries started coming in, but so did questions and criticism: 'Who says that kids of these days want to read about antiquated stories in this active era of the TV?'; 'How can children relate to illustrations that depict Ugandans half-naked in simple robes when they are nowadays used to people in modern clothes?'; 'Illustrations hamper children's imagination, you should let their minds conceive the characters themselves', said one newspaper reviewer. Then came issues of production: 'Why are the books thin?'; 'Why are the covers weak?'; 'Why are they single colour?', And then price: 'Why are the books three times the price of Ladybird books?'

These, I am sure, are some of the challenges and questions most publishers in Africa have to face when it comes to launching a new series of children's books — especially in a country that lacks a precedent of children's publishing. Indeed some of these challenges are still with us more than six years after we launched the books.

We may not have answered the questions, but public interest in the books started to grow and six years after launching the Our Heritage Series, a number of the titles have been reprinted more than five times.

The number of titles has also doubled from 10 to 20 in just over five years. Some of the donor-supported procurement programmes have taken them on, and local teachers are in many cases showing great enthusiasm for these books at the expense of imported ones. And although originally intended for the local school market, the books have done just as well outside Uganda.

An ODA (now DFID)-funded programme for lower primary school readers in Malawi schools in 1995 procured 10,000 copies of each of two titles from the Heritage Series. The African Books Collective (ABC) in London especially under the IABS scheme has also been a good customer for the Our Heritage books ever since Fountain became a member.

From this modest beginning Fountain Publishers have been inspired to publish more titles for children. These include a set of five books on environmental protection using stories under the general title, *What a Country Without Trees, Birds, Grasslands, Wetlands, Animals*. We have also embarked on other books like the *Read and Learn* series, *Learning to Read*, plus a few local language books.

Challenges

Like all other lines of publishing in Africa, publishing for children presents major challenges which Fountain Publishers has faced, and will continue to face in the future just like other publishers in Uganda and Africa in general. These include:

- Lack of a reliable marketing network: Most of the children's books sold by Fountain have been through donor-funded projects. This is a very unpredictable marketing outlet. The absence of a bookshop network in Uganda makes it difficult to sell books to the public and to test the popularity of new titles.
- Limited purchasing power: The development of a bookshop network is partly hampered by lack of purchasing power for books other than those on the recommended textbook list. This shortage of cash is particularly

felt in rural areas. Any modest sales of children's books tend to be restricted to urban areas where incomes are higher.

- Emphasis on textbooks: Excessive emphasis on textbooks in core subjects by the government and the entire education system leaves little room for children's books which in most cases are supplementary readers. Government, donors, schools and parents all consider textbooks a priority and children's books a luxury. For example, out of about US$20 million spent by the Uganda government on books over the last five years, only about $3 million has been spent on children's readers. This policy has the tendency to restrict creativity and willingness to develop non-textbook reading materials.

- Competition from external books: Due to small print runs, children's books published locally in Uganda tend to be more expensive and less colourful than those published abroad like the Ladybird series. This makes the foreign books more attractive than the local ones even when the local ones are more culturally appropriate.

- Inadequate skills: Shortage of editorial and artistic skills is a major hindrance to the development of children's books. There are no special training facilities for book authors and illustrators in Uganda, and few talents are attracted to the profession largely because the publishing industry is not a lucrative one.

Prospects

In spite of these challenges, Fountain Publishers still believe that publishing for children is a worthwhile venture and that it has a bright future in Uganda and Africa. There are a number of favourable factors that account for this.

- Low capital requirements: Unlike textbooks which require extensive capital investment to develop, children's books often require less investment. For a publisher who has little money to invest, children's publishing was our most obvious first choice.

- Easy production: Non-textbook children's reading materials are technically easier to develop. The books are usually small, and therefore require less editorial person hours. Even at printing stage, the small books are more easily handled by the less sophisticated printers that we have in Uganda and the region.

- Numerous themes: For a creative publishing house, children's publishing can provide a rich outlet for ideas. Unlike textbooks that have thematic restrictions, general books for children can be based on virtually any theme, published in different sizes and shapes and can be made exciting to the children.

- Unrestricted markets: Children's books are far less sensitive to curriculum boundaries than general textbooks. In Uganda, it has been easy to buy children's books from Kenya, Tanzania, India, and of course the UK. Similarly, we at Fountain have been able to sell our children's books to Kenya, Malawi, Sudan, Rwanda and through African Books Collective, to many countries in Africa.

Conclusion

Like all industries in Africa, publishing is still struggling to find its feet on a shifting ground of political reforms and economic restructuring. Stiff competition from international publishers, limited book purchasing power of the population and the generalized poor reading culture of Ugandans make the road to successful publishing rather bumpy. But the enthusiasm generated by the few books that we have managed to publish has been encouraging enough for us to continue. A lot of this encouragement has been derived from interactions and exchange of ideas with publishers both local and regional and development agencies. This has brought many positive results, for example:

- The launching of the Uganda Publishers and Booksellers Association (UPABA) in 1991. This created a voice for local publishers in their quest to level the playing field with multinationals who were taking the lion's share of the funds meant to purchase books for schools.
- The result of Uganda Publishers and Booksellers Association's dialogue with the government was the National Book Policy which enabled local publishers to sell books for the first time ever to donor-supported projects.
- Membership of regional and international organizations like the African Publishers Network (APNET), African Books Collective (ABC) and others, opened a forum for Fountain and other publishers to exchange ideas through book fairs and create a market — albeit modest — for books outside Uganda. These have also helped in exchanging useful information in the publishing industry, and occasional training through seminars and workshops.

Our publishing programmes which have produced local books bearing familiar local Ugandan names and themes, have demystified the book to many Ugandans. A number of publishing companies are coming up basing their operations on our model. This is proof that publishing for children in Africa is not just possible, but that it has a future if the right environment is maintained.

8
The Future of African Publishing for Children

PAMELA N. KOLA

B ook writing and publishing are two sides of the same coin, and our starting point is to treat them as equal partners in the book industry. Publishing is the profession, trade or business of producing and making books available to the book industry, with the writers providing the manuscripts. So we need to develop a rich cultural, creative and enabling environment for writers to produce manuscripts for publishers.

The history of the written word as recorded in the ancient Egyptian literature can be traced back to 3000 BC but the invention of printing came much later in the 15th century. The book industry as we know it today was established in the 19th century.

In Kenya, publishing is a much more recent phenomenon, dating back to the arrival of the Christian missionaries nearly a century ago. They set up printing facilities mainly to print evangelical reading materials. These were strengthened by the establishment in Kenya of the East African Literature Bureau, and the introduction of multinational publishing companies. The multinationals set up offices locally and with strong capital bases, and the growing demand for quality education, they monopolized the publishing activities in Kenya.

In the late 1950s and early 1960s, the movement towards African independence created patriotic feelings which found expression in books, and this was the beginning of indigenous publications and publishers. Books written by Wole Soyinka, Chinua Achebe, Ngugi wa Thiong'o, Okot B'tek and Micere Mugo fall into this category. They were generally received with a lot of enthusiasm and helped to inspire other African writers.

This period also saw the establishment of indigenous publishing companies. East African Publishing House, the first Kenyan publishing company, played a big role in mobilizing the publication of children's books. From its foundation in 1965 the company produced and made available for schools and general readers African fiction and children's books written by, among others, Asenath Odaga, Cynthia Hunter, Grace Ogot and myself.

The policies announced by the government which were geared towards localization and curriculum reviews provided further opportunities for local authors and publishers.

Today Kenya boasts of having many publishing firms, one-third of which are owned by indigenous Kenyans. They produce some school textbooks, adult literacy materials and children's books, both in English and local languages. But it is also worth nothing that the Jomo Kenyatta Foundation and the Kenya Literature Bureau, the two government-owned publishers, dominate the school textbook market to this day. At the same time very substantial book requirements are still imported.

Given the Kenyan scenario I have outlined, and focusing on the non-curriculum sector of the book industry, I would now like to highlight two main factors which I believe will determine the future of African publishing for children:

1   Indigenization of the publishing industry to encourage local participation and mobilization of more interest in local writers.
2   Inculcating reading habits and interest in writing at an early age.

Governments and stakeholders should concentrate on these major factors so as to design policies that foster the development and promotion of a progressive and sustainable book industry and, by extension, publishing for children as a distinct and viable component.

In this particular regard, adequate consideration should be given to the following observations:

Writing of children's books

Success in publishing children's books can be guaranteed through a deliberate effort to encourage writing by both children and adults.

To encourage writing, creative writing, essays, poetry and storytelling competitions should be introduced in schools and prizes given to motivate the teachers and the pupils; and the winning pieces published.

In addition, regular workshops and seminars should be organized at community and institutional levels to develop writing skills.

Illustrations are equally crucial, and illustrators should undergo the same training and exposure as writers, since illustrations make the reading more appealing and help in interpretation of the text. Cartoonists, for example, capture the imagination of children; this needs to be adapted in the publishing process for children.

A lot of attention should also be paid to design. Often the preference for imported children's books is based purely on the design rather than content. More specifically, the cover and the colour scheme have a great deal to do with the ultimate choice.

Books for children should have strong covers, be interesting, and colourful. They should be localized so that the children see themselves in books and can identify and empathize with characters in the books.

To capture the attention of different readers, publishers should consider providing books in local languages.

Readership

The only way to meet the increased demand for children's books, given demographic factors which put the population of children at close to 60 per cent of the total African population, is to formulate policies that will lead to a vibrant indigenous publishing industry. Incentives such as tax exemptions and rebates on equipment and material should be considered and access to credit facilitated so that local entrepreneurs can be attracted and encouraged to make publishing a viable commercial proposition.

Policies on education should encourage reading for leisure, in addition to merely reading for examinations. This will enhance the market for non-curriculum books.

In order to make books affordable for the largest portion of our population who are basically on the poverty line, book-production costs will have to be minimized; initially through subsidies and eventually through economies of scale.

Where international aid is sought, the donors should be encouraged to provide funds for locally purchased books to promote the local publishing industry.

Distribution and marketing

To create a supply-driven publishing industry, distribution and marketing strategies are crucial. In Kenya, as in other African countries, distribution forms the weakest link between the publisher and the reader, and this problem should be addressed seriously if more children are to have access to books.

Apart from lack of infrastructure and poverty, particularly in the semi-urban and rural areas, there is need to establish home and community-based libraries and widely distributed library services. Alternative ways should be found of reaching communities with books — donkeys, horseback, camels, bicycles and even handcarts could be used.

Publishers need to strengthen their sales, marketing and public relations departments to give adequate publicity about the books available, their suitability and desirability. They should organize book launches, previews and reviews, book trades, book fairs and exhibitions. They should take it upon themselves to organize field-sales teams to visit bookshops and schools. The publishers ought to pay royalties to their authors promptly as a means of encouraging them to submit more manuscripts to boost the production of children's books.

Faced with daunting poverty, a high illiteracy rate, low incomes, large extended families, poor infrastructure and an insurmountable debt burden, the future for African publishing for children poses a big challenge and it is incumbent upon this gathering to devise specific strategies to meet this challenge.

Non-curriculum reading time is being encroached upon and is in fierce competition with other leisure options including the electronic media and computers, resulting in limited reading and publishing output. It is imperative that African publishers use the new media to promote reading and publishing for children.

It is gratifying to recognize the formation of various organizations in Africa such as book councils, writers, publishers, booksellers, librarians and other book-related associations — all of which have accepted and made children's books a major area of concern. This includes the African Publishers Network.

In line with the current move towards regional economic blocks within the continent, these associations should adjust and realign their constituencies so as to harmonize their book policies and operations to take advantage of the enlarged regional markets.

Finally, efforts should be made in this region to translate and publish children's books in other languages to reach a wider readership.

References

Kola P.N. (1986), 'Why Write for Children?', Paper presented at a Nairobi Workshop organized by YMCA for nursery school teachers.

Mugiri E. (1991), 'Publishing a Child's Book', Paper presented at a seminar, Writing for the Child, organized by CHISCI, Nairobi.

UNESCO (1982), *Towards a Reading Society: Targets for the 80s*, UNESCO, Paris.

9
Books and Children

O.M. LAWAL-SOLARIN

> Books are one of the most vibrant and effective weapons in our
> campaign to liberate African nations from poverty and ignorance
> (Ansu Momoh).

It must be clear to everyone that unless our children are properly and well educated, the goal of a developed society will be extremely difficult to achieve in Africa. Books for children are the most important tool with which we can achieve this objective. We need to 'catch them young' and educate them thoroughly not only through formal education but also by cultivating the habit of reading for information and pleasure. When this habit is inculcated, it will be mutually beneficial to our children and society at large.

However, it is still a daunting task to publish children's books in Africa today because of infrastructural difficulties, poor economies, a dearth of authors and illustrators of children's books, poor distribution facilities and (the most difficult of all for the publisher who must recover his investment) poor reading habits. If we take Nigeria for example where there are at least 20 million children between the ages of six and eighteen in the school system, probably not more than 5 per cent (one million) read for pleasure at one time or the other.

What can we do?
We hope that by sharing our experience, and learning from each other, we will be able to tackle this problem of providing books for our children and inculcating the reading habit which is so important to our future in Africa.

Publishing books for children

Authors
Many authors prefer writing textbooks for children rather than the creative writing of story books. It is a difficult task many authors are unwilling to contemplate. The writer needs to keep the interest and action alive in the book as well as use simple and direct language. The vocabulary must fit the age

level of the intended readers, and the subject matter must also be carefully considered. The contents of the book must deal with objects, facts and situations that the children are familiar with, especially the very young. For older children, writing books about the cultures and varying vegetation and climate in a diversified and multi-ethnic country like Nigeria, and indeed in Africa, will widen the horizons of the children and inform them about their country and their continent. Folktales that teach morality and stories that fire the imagination of children are of great benefit in the development of the mind and spirit. Weaving stories around heroes, famous men and women, good manners, simple cleanliness, common ailments and life-threatening ailments like Aids will educate children and set standards of behaviour they may not be able to learn at home. Teaching science subjects, history and geography can be made easier by an imaginative storyteller. Adventure stories and nursery rhymes can be recommended for would-be authors of children's books.

Design and Illustrations

If finding authors for children's books is a difficult proposition, finding good illustrators and designers in Nigeria is like looking for a needle in a haystack. You can never employ illustrators on a full-time basis, and if you find a good illustrator, he wants an arm and a leg for illustrating the book. Sometimes, the artist wants a large advance payment, apart from negotiating for royalty payment. He is not prepared to wait like the author for returns on the sales of the book. We have managed to strike a balance by negotiating a price we consider reasonable per page of illustrations in our children's books.

The whole essence of children's books is the design and illustration of the book. It is the only way the children's interest can be engaged. It will really be unthinkable to publish children's books without ample, attractive, vivid illustrations. Hear one young critic at the seminar/workshop organized by Children's Literature Foundation in Accra (February 1996):

> The illustrations were horrible, this put me off. If illustrators cannot give us good illustrations, they should not illustrate at all.

To reduce costs, apart from the cover illustration which must be in full colour, one may be able to get away with good black and white or single colour illustrations in the text. When you can find an illustrator who also has design skills, the production of a well illustrated book is easier, otherwise, you need a collaboration between the author, illustrator and the designer.

Production

Large print runs is the easiest way of bringing down the cost of production of children's books, so that the books can be reasonably priced. Every publisher knows that the cost of production can go down as far as 12 per cent to 15 per cent for a 10,000 copies edition compared to about 20-25 per cent for a 5,000 copies edition depending on the multiplying factor.

The choice of materials for the production of a low priced edition is also important. Using newsprint or recycled bond instead of high quality art paper will bring down the cost of production tremendously. In Nigeria there is import duty of 10 per cent on paper as well as 5 per cent VAT and virtually all the paper used is imported, whilst foreign books are imported free of any import duty so producing children's books affordable to a largely impoverished population has to be carefully considered. The average selling price of glossy foreign children's book is at least S500,00 to S1,200,00 for a hard cover edition. We have come up with a low price edition of a maximum S100,00 per book. Even with low per capita income, and poor reading habits, a large population is still a market for a print run of a minimum of 10,000 copies of any edition of a book.

Marketing

Where is the market for children's books? The obvious answer is through schools and libraries. Parents rarely go out of their way to buy books for children unless they are prodded by their children or forced to by the schools. Every commentator on children's book publishing in Africa has decried the poor returns on children's book publishing due to poor reading habits, poor economy, and poor per capita income which makes purchase of books the least of people's priorities. Yet every experiment in reaching children through various innovations like children's reading tents or special children's book fairs have shown that children are avid readers, they show interest in books but sadly, we fail our children. The books are often too expensive, as observed by Mary Bugembe:

> You could see the tremendous interest in a particular book, but
> a look at the price always puts the children off. They dare not
> ask their parents to buy them the book.

No matter how low the income is in any developing country, there is a market for children's books. But how do we tap the market? We at Literamed are experimenting with Children's Book Clubs in private schools which has recorded a modest success. There are a lot of private schools in Nigeria with a population of at least four million children of parents with above average income. With our low priced books, we started a pilot project with selected private schools in Lagos. We encourage the children to buy at least three books a year, one per school term. Since we are selling the book directly to the children, we allow a 20 per cent discount on each book. The money is collected upfront. The rest of the books are promoted all over the country through schools and bookshops. It has been possible to sell a minimum of 10,000 copies per annum for each edition. Yet not all the children are members of our book club in the pilot study. We are trying to organize other publishers to join us so that we can offer a variety of books whilst we continue to build up our titles. We also want to try some mass marketing through bookshops in urban areas and through itinerant booksellers (a special Nigerian phenomenon). We will stock the shops with our children's books aiding sales by advertising on the radio and by placing posters at strategic public locations.

Distribution

Most developing countries have very poor distribution systems due to poor infrastructure. The cost of distribution in Nigeria for instance is enormous. Even when most large and medium-sized publishers have depots or branch offices in various parts of the country — north, southwest and east — the cost of moving goods is prohibitive. Publishers have to invest in costly vehicles for movement of goods on sometimes very bad roads with occasional losses through accidents. Until recently the relationship between publishers and booksellers was not very cordial but with virtual deregulation of the book market, the situation has improved now that booksellers get a minimum of 20 per cent discount from publishers. Hitherto, it was only 10 per cent. We are hoping that as the economy improves, a better distribution system through bookshops will lead to larger print runs and low priced editions.

Conclusion

Most of the difficulties of publishing books for children mentioned can be duplicated in all African countries with varying degrees. However, there seems to be light at the end of the tunnel because:
- Apnet membership through National Publishers Associations has helped and will continue to have impact on training, publishing, collaboration and interactions between African Publishers.
- The Zimbabwe International Book Fair contributes a regular forum for exchange of ideas and interactions between publishers of every hue.

The best way forward for improving on the quality and quantity of books for children in the developing countries of Africa will be:

- To collaborate on co-publications, and buying rights which will help in building up titles without incurring costs of origination for all titles in your list.
- By carefully choosing inexpensive but presentable paper combined with larger print-runs, low-priced editions of children's books can be manufactured. Books for children manufactured in India are good examples of what can be achieved. When books are affordable, many more people will be able to buy them, thus encouraging reading habits.
- Various methods and techniques employed by various organizations to improve reading habits on the African continent are to be commended, for example, children's reading tents, specialized children's book fairs, mobile libraries and children's book clubs.
- A collaboration between school authorities, ministries of education and parents in a scheme that prescribes one book (not a set literature book) per term per child between the ages of 7 and16 years. It does not necessarily have to be the same book, which can then be exchanged with other children after reading. This will go a long way in cultivating the reading habit. Low-priced books are possible because of larger print runs. Distribution costs will be minimal and the viability of publishers will be enhanced, because of a guaranteed market.
- To aid distribution, the development of bookshops in urban and rural areas, encouraged by publishers will go a long way in sharing the burden borne mainly by publishers. More itinerant booksellers will also promote the sale of books in the rural areas (booksellers who sell books during the schoolbook season, then reinvest their profit in selling other commodities until the next book season). They are usually everywhere — mostly in the rural areas or set locations in urban areas. Sometimes they are market women or unemployed youths who sell books in traffic hold-ups.

References
Bugembe M. (1996), 'Children's Reading Tent', *African Publishing Review*, March/April Vol. 5 No. 2.
Dekutsey Woeli A. (1996), 'Children's Publishing - The Child's View', *African Publishing Review*, May/June Vol. 5 No. 3.
Lawal-Solarin O.M. (1996), *Creating a Conducive Environment for Book Publishing*, Nigerian Book Foundation, Lagos.
Smith D. C. (1990), *A Guide to Book Publishing*, University of Lagos Press, Lagos.

10
The Publishers Association of Tanzania

ABDULLAH SAIWAAD

In the period between 1983 and 1987, the future of publishing looked very bleak. The government's financial situation was not good, primary school education was controlled by the government and so was school textbook publishing. Only three publishing companies, which were semi-government, were allowed to publish school textbooks. But the price structure was decided upon by the Ministry of Education. The ministry based their purchase price on a percentage of the labour cost for printing. In 1986, the big publishers who had weathered the storm since 1983 began to feel the pinch. Many of the small publishers had already gone under.

In 1986, Eastern Africa publications managed to secure funds from UNESCO to run a workshop on 'The Role of the Publisher in the Development of Education'. At this seminar the small and the big publishers got together and decided to create an association which would provide a forum for discussion. A steering committee did the groundwork and in September 1987 The Publishers Association of Tanzania was inaugurated.

Membership and types

In the period between 1987 and 1990 PATA had 28 members. Of these 12 are still operational today. In between 1991 and 1993 there were 50 new members of PATA; of these only about 14 are still in operation. To date the membership on the roll books stands at 78. Of these only 30 are actively engaged in full time publishing.

There are four types of publishing house which are members of the Publishers Association of Tanzania (PATA). These are the small, private indigenous commercial publishing houses which number about 20 today. Then there are the public companies. There were three but will soon be two as one is in the process of liquidation. There are two indigenous companies with multinational backing and there are three religious publishing houses which are members. There is an associate member which is a branch of a multinational publishing company.

Book weeks and book fairs

Since 1988, the Publishers Association of Tanzania has been organizing National Book Week Festivals which incorporate the Dar es Salaam Book Fair in September. Publishers (members and non-members) exhibit and sell books at this festival. At these occasions, the association invites distinguished guests to visit the festival to learn about the book industry.

This year the Seventh National Book Week Festival will be held between 15 and 21 September. This year this festival is being organized by the recently formed National Book Week Committee. Book weeks provide a good platform for publishers to market their books.

Government control of textbook publishing stunted the growth of publishing in Tanzania. Publishers are thus small entrepreneurs, some with education backgrounds and even fewer with editorial and marketing skills. To participate in these Book Weeks enables these publishers to see what other publishers (even some multinational companies) do in book promotion and marketing.

Marketing and promotion

Despite these efforts, the Publishers Association of Tanzania felt there was a need for sustainable marketing promotion for its members until such time as the trade has been stabilized and re-established. Thus in 1997, the association proposed a co-operative scheme for its members. The aim of this scheme is not to replace the publishers' marketing departments but to assist and strengthen them. In this scheme, a publisher is advised on how to prepare promotional materials which are then used by PATA's marketing officer in marketing the books. PATA then hands over all orders to the publishers to fulfill. PATA is willing to follow up payments by booksellers and other institutions. In this scheme the association will identify at least 20 viable bookshops in the region to take the central role in marketing and selling the publishers' books.

The Publishers Association of Tanzania also takes part in some regional book fairs and puts up a joint stand and assists publishers in their book marketing when required.

Children's book publishing

In 1988 the theme of the National Book Week Festival was promoting the reading habit. At one of the seminars that ran concurrently with the festival, the shocking situation of the unavailability of children's books was presented by the Head of the children's section of the National Library. The Publishers Association of Tanzania took up this challenge and in 1989's Festival the theme was Children's Books: Our Top Priority. One of the concurrent events was a workshop on writing children's books. Manuscripts had been secured from publishers and authors, editors and librarians assessed these manuscripts and commented on them. Four were found publishable but the publishers did not have the necessary working capital. The Publishers Association of Tanzania secured assistance from NORAD and for the first time in Tanzania, children's books for pleasure were published by three publishers. This success story made the association present a similar proposal to other donors. At the next fair CODE, which had a regional office in Dar es Salaam, decided to assist by bringing in a consultant to assess the publishing situation and present a proposal.

In 1991, another workshop was conducted and the first manuscripts were subsequently published under the Children's Book Project in 1992. The Children's Book Project is now seven years old.

Profitability

The peculiar situation of Tanzania makes children's books difficult to market and not very profitable. For the past thirty years parents have not bought textbooks for their children. As such even the customary one-time visit to the bookshop by parents is non-existent. Further, whereas in the early 1970s there were about 107 bookshops serving a 20 million population. Today we have less than 30, and about 10 of them are in Dar es Salaam. These serve a 30 million population.

Recently, the Children's Book Project for Tanzania has embarked on a reading promotion campaign. In the nominated schools, books and other implements necessary for the establishment of a school library have been donated. What has been surprising is the interest shown by the children. In some cases truancy has dropped and children are always queuing for books in the library. This project was only for some experimental classes but in many cases all classes demanded access to the books. This interest in books has made the association think again about accessibility. Are the publishers' prices wrong, and thus unaffordable? We know that there are a few retail outlets but children do not seem to be interested in buying books.

In Tanzania, children's book publishing has not been a successful undertaking. At the association, we have come to the conclusion that government assistance is necessary. By government assistance we do not mean the government actually buying books, though this might help. We believe there is a need for the government to have clear policies with respect to inculcating the reading habit. This can be done by introducing into the curriculum reading for leisure and changing the methodology from being teacher centred to resource centred which will mean an increased use of libraries, laboratories, study visits and so on. We believe that once the seed of the reading habit is planted, the publishers and other book sector people can assure that it germinates and flourishes.

11
The Kenya Publishers Association

Country Report

DAVID MUITA

The Kenya Publishers Association was established in 1971 to promote the book industry in its broadest terms in the country. We have had considerable success in this effort and the current membership stands at 44, and there are other publishers who have indicated an interest in joining.

Membership of the association is categorized according to the number of books a company has published. Those with 0-10 titles pay an annual fee of Ksh 5,000, those with 11-20 titles Kshs10,000 , and those with 21 and above titles pay Ksh 25,000. Most of the members are book publishers but several individuals have indicated an interest in becoming members. A one-off membership fee of Ksh 2,000 is charged for all new members.

The Kenya Publishers Association has been lobbying the government to level the playing ground as regards the development and provision of school textbooks. The school market remains the most lucrative publishing area and parastatal publishing companies (government-funded) have monopolized this market since 1985. Fortunately, recent developments indicate that the Ministry of Education is giving attention to the cries of the private publishers to set the market free. The market is slowly being opened up and hopefully it will not be long before full liberalization is granted. This is important if quality of content is to be achieved. A free market encourages competition with a resultant improvement in quality in content and all aspects of the book production process, including the retail price.

The Kenya Publishers Association is also keen to improve readership. There exists enough reading material in the market but readership is relatively poor. A big responsibility to improve this situation rests on the Kenya Publishers Association.

To achieve this and other intended goals, the Kenya Publishers Association has proposed to proceed as follows:

1 Links with government ministries

Work closely with government departments, particularly the Ministries of Education and Culture and Social Services, especially the Departments of Culture, Adult Education and the Kenya National Library Services, in the promotion of literacy and education through the production of relevant books, reading and learning campaigns, as well as lobbying for appropriate education policies. It is our intention to work closely with the Ministry of Education in its efforts to raise the academic standards and general readership of students.

2 Capacity building for publishers and booksellers

Publishers in Kenya depend on a network of booksellers across the country for book distribution. Because of the over-reliance on the school market, many pseudo-booksellers emerge in the month of January and close shop by March each year. The majority who remain are unprofessional in that they will sell a book in the same way they sell a tin of cooking fat. It is therefore crucial for the publisher to undertake the training of booksellers in collaboration with the Kenya Booksellers Association. This has never been undertaken before in Kenya and the Kenya Publishers Association intends to seek funds from donors and well-wishers to undertake this training.

Most publishing personnel also require training. The association hopes to have an elaborate training programme in line with the African Publishing Institute's Training Curriculum for publishers. It is the hope of the association that this training will in future be expanded to cater for booksellers as well.

3 Book fairs and book exhibitions

The Kenya Publishers Association encourages members to participate in local and international book fairs. We are currently very keen to tap the East African market in Uganda and Tanzania, and beyond.

The association supports the CHISCI in the organization and running of the Pan-African Children's Book Fair. It also plays a crucial role in the organization of National Book Week under the Book Development Council. Without jeopardizing the role of CHISCI and the Pan-African Children's Book Fair, or that of the National Book Week, the Kenya Publishers Association will launch the Nairobi International Book Fair to be held between 2 and 6 September 1998, at the Sarit Centre, Nairobi. The book fair will be run by members of the Kenya Publishers Association and will be basically a book trade fair. We are also assessing the feasibility of joint local book exhibitions across the country at the grassroots level — taking books to the people. This approach would popularize books for both adults and children. This will be a cost-shared venture between the association, publishers and booksellers.

4 Awards

Currently the Kenya Publishers Association administers two awards in publishing which are aimed at popularizing books:

The Jomo Kenyatta prize for literature
This is a bi-annual award given to the most outstanding new book published within the specified period (every two years). The aim of this award is to encourage good literary contribution from both the writers and the publishers.

The best publishing student award
This is given to the best final year student in publishing at Moi University. The aim is to promote high standards of training in publishing at institutions of higher learning. We should note, however, that this is the only university that teaches publishing at higher levels in the country.

We are looking into possibilities of establishing more literary awards. We would particularly like to give recognition to Kenyan Poets, Children's Literature, Kiswahili and other special areas.

Children's publishing

The book publishing industry in Kenya is one of the most vibrant in Africa and continues to make great improvements. Children's books publishing has been one of the fastest growing areas of publishing in the country. This is attested by the fact that most publishers have even ventured into full colour publishing for children. This area also has a ready market in the country, probably second only to textbook publishing. Publishing in colour has also meant that the books are more attractive and appeal to a wider international market. Books for children also move faster because they are low priced and are therefore affordable. They also offer a diversity of themes, subjects and styles of presentation, thus making them interesting.

There are at least two publishers who have specialized in children's books, Phoenix Publishers and Jacaranda Designs, and they have explored a variety of approaches to make the books as attractive as possible. Other publishers who publish children's books alongside other areas include Macmillan, EAEP, Longhorn, Oxford Press, Jomo Kenyatta Foundation, Kenya Literature Bureau, Focus Publications, Stantex and Horizon. Sasa Sema also publishes comics that appeal to children.

Unique ideas used by publishers of children's books
These include experimentation with colours that appeal to children, use of folklore as background to the stories, use of unique illustrations that are familiar to the child, and so on. This is mostly noticeable in books published by Jacaranda, Phoenix, Macmillan, Oxford, Longhorn, Focus and Stantex.

Collaboration with other organizations

We believe we cannot succeed on our own, and we are willing to work together with organizations interested in the improvement of the book industry. These include APNET, the British Council, CODE, SIDA, UNESCO and others.

The tasks enumerated above would definitely be impossible to achieve if the Kenya Publishers Association members were not committed. Every one of us has to be involved in one way or another. We have made sure this is possible by forming various sub-committees with specific roles, namely: the training committee, the publications committee, book fairs, exhibitions and awards committee and the national book policy committee. These committees have already achieved considerable success in their various operations.

One of the most crucial objectives of the sub-committees is to raise funds to carry out their functions and hopefully sustain the Kenya Publishers Association Secretariat.

The foregoing, however, might create the impression that all is well at the association. This is so as far as forward planning is concerned. But funds are the greatest obstacle. The establishment of a functional Secretariat has seen the improvement of the Kenya Publishers Association's performance. This can be argued to be one great achievement for the association. But the operations of the Secretariat pose a major challenge. There were no rents and salaries to pay in the past — this is now a monthly requirement. With our meagre resources, we are hard pressed to keep the Secretariat going.

Subscription fees are not adequate. It is obvious that ways of raising regular funds for the association must be put in place and this is one of our most challenging tasks.

We are thankful, however, to APNET for sponsoring our training workshops and for their support in other activities that we have been undertaking.

12
The Nigerian Publishers Association
Strategies for Promoting Trade in Books

DAYO ALABI

The Nigerian Publishers Association was founded in 1965. It serves as the umbrella and rallying point for people and organizations engaged in book publishing. One of the main objectives of the association is to promote national interest in the publishing industry — a vital tool for book development. The association maintains regular contacts with the following: state and federal Ministries of Education; government agencies and parastatals that have anything to do with book development and/or acquisition; the continental African Publishers Association (APNET); other international publishers' associations; and other international bodies that relate to or affect book development and copyright issues.

Membership is open to all those engaged in book publishing (as opposed to newspaper or magazine publishing). Members, which include small-scale, medium-sized and big firms (offsprings of multinationals), are drawn from all parts of the country, with a larger concentration in the south-west, where foreign publishers started their operations when they first arrived.

There are currently about 70 registered members while more are in the process of being registered. However, there are over 500 other publishers, mainly author-publishers, publishers of autobiographies and *ad hoc* publishers who have not shown any interest in joining.

The permanent headquarters/secretariat is located in Ibadan, Oyo State of Nigeria, and headed by a full-time Executive Secretary. The affairs are managed by an elected Executive Council made up of eight members. These include the president, three vice-presidents and four other members.

For effective operation, the association has three zonal chapters: West, East and North, with each chapter having a co-ordinating committee, headed by a co-ordinator. The zonal co-ordinators are the vice-presidents of the association at the national level. However, the northern chapter is yet to be formally constituted.

The association's activities

- Planning, organizing and executing training programmes for members in all aspects of publishing.
- Organizing annual conferences and the Annual General Meeting.
- Participating in international conferences on publishing.
- Organizing local book fairs.
- Participating in international book fairs.
- Carrying out active anti-piracy campaigns.
- Publishing its house magazine, *The Publisher*.
- Providing input to government in the formulation of policies that will affect book development or education in general.
- Co-operating with other bodies and associations concerned with the book industry or education in general.

To effectively carry out these activities, the Nigerian Publishers Association operates through committees which include:

Trade practices/Book league committee
Conference/Publicity/Book fair committee
Nigerian Book Foundation committee
Anti-piracy committee
Education and professional training committee.
Editorial committee (for the house magazine)
Joint action committee (with booksellers)
Audit committee
Secretariat committee
Finance committee.

Strategies for Collective Promotion of Books

While there are great opportunities for joint marketing of books, these have not been fully exploited because of various factors, including:

- The economic predicament (partly resulting from the political problems) which has bedevilled the country for a long period.
- Competition amongst individual members of the association.
- Strained relationships between publishers and booksellers as a result of mutual distrust.
- Lack of total commitment of some members to the ideals of the association.
  However, the major areas where the association has emerged as a cohesive body to promote the book trade include exhibitions and book fairs, dissemination of news and the Nigerian *Books in Print*.

Exhibitions/Book fairs

There is an exhibition during the annual conference and general meeting. This involves most members taking a stand to display their publications. Lectures or seminars are also organized with students from various schools and with members of the public participating. This is done in collaboration with other associations in the book industry, such as the Nigerian Booksellers Association, the Nigerian Book Foundation and the Nigerian Library Association, as well as television stations, ministries of education, and so on.

Dissemination of news

This is done through the official news magazine of the association, *The Publisher*. News about new books of members and other activities are featured.

The Nigerian *Books in Print*

This lists most books published in Nigeria, including the titles, authors, publishers, and so on. This is the boldest effort so far in a joint promotion of books published in Nigeria. The association, as a body, has not been involved with book promotion through direct launches, festivals, book weeks or literacy days. Individual publishers, though, on an *ad hoc* basis, participate in literary days or prize-giving days organized by schools.

Very few publishers launch their publications. The concept of 'launching' a book in Nigeria involves inviting a serving or retired but influential public/ military officer to write an autobiography which is 'launched' at a well organized carnival-like ceremony where those wanting to show gratitude for a past favour or look forward to a future one buy a copy or few copies with hundreds of thousands of Naira. After the launch the book may never be found on the shelves of booksellers.

Generally, book promotion in Nigeria has not been given the prominence it deserves, either collectively or by individual publishers. Some publishers concentrate their efforts on ensuring their books are adopted for use in schools by all means, including those that are not ethical.

However, the Nigerian Publishers Association in its efforts towards collective book promotion has the following plans:

1   To hold an annual book fair in each of the three regions.
2   To organize a book week jointly with the Nigerian Booksellers Association, Nigerian Book Foundation and other related associations.
3   To provide office space for the Booksellers Association, Library Association, Association of Nigerian Authors, Book Printers' Association,

Nigerian Book Foundation, and so on, in the newly acquired Permanent Secretariat of the Nigerian Booksellers Association. This, when fully developed, will be known as Book House.

Children's Books

Publishing

There are very few publishers in Nigeria who specialize in publishing children's books. Most publishers, particularly the offsprings of the multinationals, have concentrated on publishing textbooks for children rather than creative story books. This is either because authors find this area difficult or because during the 'oil boom' , it was cheaper and easier to import foreign books, for example, the Ladybird series.

One exception is Literamed Publications Limited: over 95 per cent of its publications are for children.

Marketing

Nigeria has at least 18 million children between the ages of five and twelve years in the school system. This offers an enormous potential market for children's books but, as a result of the decline in the economy, most parents cannot even afford necessities. This has significantly reduced access to and interest in reading for pleasure.

However, there still exists a large market for children's books in Nigeria. At least 15 per cent of the parents of the 18 million children can afford at least three non-academic, creative/story books per year at a cost of NS 100 per book. This translates into over NS 810 million (US$10 million). Publishers just need to know the characteristics of the markets.

The style of marketing children's books in the North is different from in the South. Sales efforts are directed at the government in the North which undertakes bulk purchases for public schools. Some sales are made through bookshops and directly to the few private schools.

In the South, the bulk of the sales is made directly to the large number of private schools. Bookshops still make a reasonable contribution.

Few publishers engage in activities like organizing book clubs in schools, promotional workshops for proprietors/head teachers of schools although some organize reading or essay writing competitions.

Apart from publishers' representatives moving from one school to another, there are no special promotional activities to boost sales.

Profitability

Children's book publishing is undoubtedly profitable. It remains the only aspect of publishing that attracts high volume sales. Out of anxiety a good percentage of parents buy all kinds of books for their children despite the harsh economy. The only problem is quality. To achieve a quality of production similar to that of the developed world means increased costs of production and higher selling prices, making the titles beyond the reach of an average Nigerian. This is responsible for the low quality of children's books in Nigeria.

The success of children's book publishing is confirmed by the wide acceptance of Lantern Books published by Literamed Publications.

Diversity, New Ideas and Innovations

The traditional areas of concentration by local publishers have been in this order: academic, primary and pre-primary, story books and finally picture books and cartoon books. However, several publishers are being innovative, for example, recently my company, CSS Limited, has been championing the publishing of children's science fiction books. This is a new series of children's books written, illustrated and designed to popularize science in Africa. This is the Early Learning of Science Series for Africa (ELSSA). ELSSA aims at:

- allowing children to cultivate the habit of reading.
- extending and reinforcing natural skills.
- encouraging children to learn science at their own pace.
- involving parents in the learning process.
- taking children ahead in a changing environment.

Conclusion

There is no doubt that there is a huge market for locally published children's books in Nigeria. All that is required is understanding the peculiarity of the market and producing acceptable books at an affordable price. The current situation of the economy notwithstanding, there is room for innovation. The fact that large quantities of imported children's books are still brought into the country is evidence of this market.

In general, however, publishers need to engage in more dynamic promotion to encourage reading, in spite of the economy. The economy is definitely going to boom in the future so we should ensure that the urge to read is kept alive for that day when most parents can afford to buy books for their children.

13
The Zimbabwe Book Publishers Association

Promoting Collective Strategies for Trade in Children's Books

IRENE STAUNTON

The Zimbabwe Book Publishers' Association (ZBPA) was formally established in 1983 after a burgeoning of publishing activity following independence and the sudden expansion in education provision. Today it has 16 members and three associate members. The membership has fluctuated slightly over the years as smaller publishers have come and gone.

All publishers pay the same annual subscription fee of Z$1,000 and all have one vote. Affiliated publishers, usually agencies for foreign companies such as Struik or Butterworths, pay a lesser fee and do not have a vote.

The larger publishers, College Press (a local company in which Macmillan has a shareholding), Longman, Zimbabwe Publishing House and Academic Books, focus on textbook provision. Mambo Press, the Literature Bureau and Baobab Books are the largest of the three general book publishers; the first is supported by the Catholic church, the second is subsidized by government, and the third is affiliated to Academic Books, and thus has the support of a textbook list.

The ZBPA functions through an executive committee which is elected annually. For the last four years we have used the secretarial services of the Confederation of Zimbabwe Industries for basic administrative tasks; from 1990 to 1994 we had a full-time executive secretary, a position we hope to revive as we recognize that only by having a full-time employee can we respond adequately to members' needs.

Currently the ZBPA's main activities are to:
- represent publishing issues and the concerns of the publishing industry to government;
- lobby for an increased per capita grant, for efficient and fair disbursement of donor funding, and against sales tax on books;
- liaise with the Curriculum Development Unit;
- represent the Zimbabwe publishing industry at book fairs;
- compile and publish *Zimbabwe Books In Print*;

- initiate the annual literary awards;
- liaise with booksellers;
- represent the publishers at trade associations;
- provide a forum to which publishers can bring their concerns;
- administer *ad hoc* projects, for example, paper supply.

Larger projects are generally donor-funded; smaller projects such as the annual literary awards are funded through the ZBPA and local sponsors.

The ZBPA was instrumental in establishing the Zimbabwe Book Fair Trust and the Zimbabwe Book Development Council, both of which now act independently; the ZBPA is, however, represented on the board of each. Both organizations are dependent to a greater or lesser degree on donor funding, and not on the publishing industry itself. Their objectives are to support the book chain, to support local publishing, and to network, and they do this successfully through a variety of complementary projects, the largest being the book fair, which provides a market place and a forum for discussion.

Book fairs

The Zimbabwe International Book Fair offers our members the opportunity to network, promote and launch books, and discuss ideas with other associations.

The Bologna Children's Book Fair is the largest children's book fair and although the ZBPA has often sent representatives, we believe we would be better represented by APNET. African publishers attending independently cannot provide each other with mutual support for the following reasons:

- We do not often know each other;
- We do not know each other's books;
- The stands or booths are very small;
- Africa is often under-represented;
- The row of stands is often tucked away and is not visited save by people with very particular interests (sometimes only to collect coins or other souvenirs);
- African publishing is not generally taken seriously (of course there are important exceptions);
- Requests for books tend to be somewhat stereotypical: folktales, for example;
- Most delegates are far more interested in selling to us, rather than buying, and we need to do more to equalize or reverse this trend.

We believe that one APNET stand which presented the best of children's book publishing in Africa, staffed by representatives who could provide each other with mutual support and backed up with good promotional materials, would do a great deal for children's publishing in Africa.

Zimbabwe Book Development Council

There are two projects initiated by the Zimbabwe Book Development Council which have a direct impact on the promotion of children's literature. The first is the reading tent which they organize at the book fair where children's books are displayed and authors read stories to children, giving them direct access to a contemporary storytelling opportunity. I use the word 'contemporary' because we so often bemoan the lost idyll of grandmother sitting at the fire telling age-old stories to the eager upturned faces of her grandchildren.

However, we need to acknowledge that something has to be done in its stead, that we need no longer rely on the spoken word and that children need stories which reflect their daily lives as well as traditional folktales. Parents and teachers can read stories to children every day if they choose to do so.

APNET needs to have a regional campaign which focuses not on children, but on the parents of those children. We cannot fully develop a regional market for children's books if we rely on the education systems alone. Parents tend to leave book purchase to schools, even when the schools cannot afford library books or supplementary readers; nor are they often aware of how children's chances improve if they are introduced to books and reading from an early age, and if they read for pleasure in their spare time.

Reading improves understanding of concepts, develops visual literacy, broadens vocabulary, introduces new ideas, stimulates the imagination, enables us to appreciate the experiences of others with greater compassion and provides fulfilling entertainment.

A second initiative taken by the Zimbabwe Book Development Council was to arrange a library support scheme in which libraries buy books from a general catalogue compiled by the council. The scheme, funded by Danida, has great potential, as long as people purchasing the books recognize the importance of trying to develop an extra-curricular reading culture.

The responsibility for developing a reading culture has been ceded to the Zimbabwe Book Development Council which was one reason why the council was established. A society that does not have a reading culture will not invest in books; in particular, it will not invest in children's books which have no obvious didactic purpose.

Promoting books and trade

The ZBPA has not taken many initiatives to promote and sell books into Zimbabwe or into the region. There are several reasons for this:
- We have no full-time executive officer, all the work being done voluntarily by individuals on the executive committee who have other full-time commitments;
- Few publishers have strong children's lists, and it would be difficult to justify supporting the few rather than the many;
- The smallest publishers have the smallest resources of finance and staff; they have the least access to the tenders which are being offered by international institutions such as DFID, the EU or the World Bank; and they have the fewest possibilities of promoting their books in the region.

However, although the ZBPA has had sub-committees to look at the needs of small publishers, the specific case of promoting children's books regionally has not been articulated; even had it been, the ZBPA does not have the resources to respond adequately.

If APNET were to take the initiative with the ZBPA to bring together all the publishers of children's books in a joint venture, this would be strongly supported.

However, trading within the region is going to remain difficult until various problems are overcome:
- Contracts and payments
  Whenever we have sold books or rights (referring to Baobab's experience) we have almost always had to spend a lot of time chasing payments, chasing contracts and contract renewals, and chasing royalty statements. Staff time, faxes and phone calls cost money and this unnecessary expenditure is a disincentive to regional trading.
- Standards
  We have sold rights to various publishers and sometimes the way our titles have been reproduced has resulted in numerous complaints from authors. While the difficulties of publishing in Africa — the need for low-cost productions and adaptations — there is little excuse for errors such as mis-spelling an author's name on the cover.

In view of this, a code of practice needs to be established, through APNET, under which companies agree to adhere to certain standards, principles and conduct.

Another set of inhibitions to inter-regional trade is that of a certain chauvinism and nationalism: the limitations of cultural exclusivity. Following independence, most countries in Africa needed to affirm their identities in a strong and positive way. But the downside of this — ten, fifteen, twenty years on — is that it can lead to a kind of cultural exclusivity. Certain books will simply not travel because the focus is perceived to be too different.

APNET should set as one of its objectives the need for an understanding of the different cultures, histories and experiences within Africa. We are, after all, only African in the same way that a Welshman is European.

Finally, there are the problems of tariffs, banking regulations, fluctuating currencies, complex trade routes, and so on.

Conclusion

Immediately after independence there was donor funding for books, new syllabuses and curricula were being developed and the publishers had a hey-day. The situation is very different now. Multinationals and their subsidiaries tend to have more resources in terms of staffing, capital and information but they are answerable to their shareholders and less likely to invest in non-profitable general books.

Smaller, independent publishers have more freedom and flexibility but fewer resources in terms of training, staffing and finance, and less access to information. It is often the small publishers who develop children's books (as opposed to school readers) but they do not have access to regional library tenders to make them viable. A survey carried out for this paper showed that all the publishers of children's books have consistently reduced the number of titles they published in recent years.

The challenge is to find ways in which the publication of general books can be supported by developing a reading community through the support of publishers' associations and regional and continental organizations such as APNET. At the same time, we should aim to achieve a parity of support to all our members, large and small, within an atmosphere that is mutually supportive, where competition is seen as a stimulus rather than a threat, and where no one is excluded for lack of information.

14
Booksellers and Publishers Association of Zambia

RAY MUNAMWIMBU

The Booksellers and Publishers Association of Zambia (BPAZ) is a voluntary non-governmental and non-profit-making organization for publishers and booksellers, institutions in related fields and individuals with a direct or indirect interest in the book industry in Zambia. BPAZ was established initially as the Booksellers Association of Zambia (then Northern Rhodesia) in the 1950s. It was only in 1974 when the number of bookshops and booksellers were dwindling that book publishers were accepted into the association as members — hence the current name.

The present government policy of liberalization has rekindled metropolitan and local businesspeople's interest in both bookselling and publishing. So the need to re-activate the activities of the association has again arisen.

The Booksellers and Publishers Association of Zambia constitutes a rare marriage between booksellers and publishers — an indication of the paucity of both booksellers and publishers that have operated since the 1950s and continue to operate actively in Zambia.

The main objectives of the association are to:
1 encourage the development of the book industry in Zambia
2 promote the consumption of books by the general public through book fairs and exhibitions
3 provide a forum for the exchange of information and ideas to its members
4 co-operate with government departments, local authorities and institutions in securing the furtherance of those objectives.

The association has a number of activities that it offers to its members:
- It organizes conferences, seminars and workshops for its members. These seminars have been sponsored by Finnida through the Education Sector Support Programme.
- It organizes and stages the annual Zambia Book Fair. The fair attracts a lot of participants from both local and foreign publishers and booksellers.
- It also allocates and manages the ISBN in the country, and provides an

enabling environment for the cross-fertilization of ideas on book publishing and selling.

- It disseminates information about activities in the region and outside, such as upcoming book fairs and book weeks, from various institutions like APNET and Book Aid.

Since the withdrawal of financial support from CODE in February 1995, the association has been surviving on its own resources. Small amounts are generated from the following activities:

- bookselling fees at the book fair;
- administering training courses and seminars;
- office activities such as DTP work on letterheads and reports;
- photocopying; and
- membership fees, the most reliable source of income.

The association has 53 members, out of which only about 20 are active members. These consist of publishers and booksellers with the majority being publishers.

Potential for joint marketing

There are many potential opportunities for joint marketing of books. Some of them are as follows:

- The Zambia Book Fair: This is the most significant opportunity. This event is held annually in Lusaka and is the best forum for accessing locally published books. Seminars are held on various aspects of publishing and co-publishing arrangements can easily be made.
- Displays: Individual publishers hold displays in various places as part of their own marketing strategies. These are usually held at educational institutions such as the University of Zambia.
- Schools Open Days: Private schools which have now formed the Independent Schools Association of Zambia hold open days for their schools and invite publishers to display and sell their books.
- Publishers using their own initiative usually travel from town to town to publicize their books and create awareness in the rural areas.
  We do not have book weeks or literacy days.

Trade fairs are not the best forum for marketing books since they mainly focus on the manufacturing industry. Publishers find themselves treated like an appendage of paper-making or printing companies and the participating fees tend to be high.

The publication of children's books

The publication of children's books can be described as scattered efforts here and there. The largest publishing house, Zambia Educational Publishing House, developed the foundation children's series which, however, has now stalled due to problems that the company is currently facing. The most successful and popular book produced by Zambia Educational Publishing House is *Lion the King*.

Zambia Printing Company developed the 'Watoto' series which are read-along books.

Maiden publishing house has published many children's books, the most popular, which are used by nursery schools, are *My Number Book* and *My Alphabet Book*.

Insaka Press in conjunction with Cambridge University Press have produced books in the main Zambian languages which are school supplementary readers. They are very colourful and popular with children.

15
The Reading Association
Swaziland Country Report

SEBENZILE Z. THANGO

Swaziland is a small country with a population of less than one million, children forming the majority. Three-quarters of the children are school-going at all levels, from pre-school up to university level.

While children form the majority, studies show that they are the most neglected as far as reading material is concerned. It is for this reason that the Reading Association was formed and the following are the objectives:

1 To alert the public about the lack of children's reading material in bookshops;
2 To encourage writers to produce material addressing concerns of the readers;
3 To create better relationships between writers and readers by coming together and discussing available written materials;
4 To provide an opportunity to meet writers of interest to readers.

The Reading Association has gone further in promoting both writers and readers by providing extracts of books prescribed in schools to our local newspaper. The nation benefits in that writers themselves have the opportunity to read other writers' work which strengthens their own skills of writing. It further provides an opportunity for isolated readers to gain more knowledge, both at school and at home.

The formulation of such an association was a blessing and an eye opener. We discovered that what we wrote was unknown to other writers. The Reading Association is a bridge from one writer to the other. Writers are able to reach each other and they are evaluated by readers through their critiques and literary appreciation.

A writer in this case also becomes a reader or a consumer of the material. There is networking as a result of the Reading Association. Writers, publishers and booksellers need to work in harmony in order to benefit in monetary and/ or promotional terms. The Reading Association becomes an indicator of what the writer and the publisher are doing and whether it is effective or not. Booksellers, too, play a vital role in conveying material from publishers to readers and at the same time they become indicators of whether readers are interested in the materials or not, through monthly sales on each book. Also, publishers may decide that readers do not like certain works, when the truth is that readers do not know it exists. The four participants, writer, publisher, bookseller and reader, belong to one body — they all need each other, therefore keeping constantly in touch is imperative. The association of writers is grateful to Professor Aruwa Aruwa for initiating and establishing the Reading Association.

16
The Publishers Association of South Africa

MONICA SEEBER

The Publishers Association of South Africa (PASA), founded in November 1992, strives to attract all South African publishers and incorporates large and small, educational, academic and general, indigenous and multinational, mainstream and alternative publishers and distributors of books under one umbrella.

The association believes that intellectual freedom is inseparable from liberty itself and that the freedom to write, publish and read is a fundamental human right. Publishers shall therefore have the right to publish and distribute works in complete freedom, provided that in so doing they respect all legal rights attached to these works within their own countries and internationally.

PASA is firmly committed to fostering and supporting a reading and book-buying culture in South Africa. It aims to encourage the growth and development of the local publishing industry by promoting and protecting the interests of all its members, by all lawful means.

PASA has some 130 full and associate members (the figure fluctuates) who publish in a variety of areas: religious books, fiction, children's books, schoolbooks, scholarly publications, poetry, drama, academic books, technical books, general non-fiction, and so on.

The national administrative office is in Cape Town and is governed by an Executive Committee comprising the Chairs of the various interest groups and an executive member holding the portfolios of copyright and international relations. The groups are: Academic; Development and training; Educational (with national and regional committees, and the sub-groups of Adult and Basic Education, and Technology 2005); and Trade.

PASA meets four times a year, rotating between Johannesburg, Cape Town and Durban. At each two-day meeting, the interest groups hold their own sessions, the academic group also devoting a special session to copyright issues.

Copyright has featured on PASA's agenda over the past two years. South African publishers, and in particular academic publishers, have been severely threatened by photocopying in excess of what the law allows. Although unlawful photocopying occurs in schools, governmental and administrative offices and the corporate sector, by far the worst offenders are tertiary institutions — the universities and technikons. Often the reason given is that books are too expensive but unfortunately sales of academic textbooks are dropping to the point where indigenous academic publishing may perish and publishers abroad may boycott South Africa. The photocopying 'plague' is endemic and the damage it does to publishing industries is well known.

After much debate, PASA members elected to join a collective licensing scheme whereby a collecting society administers their reprographic reproduction rights and issues licences to the tertiary institutions. This will not necessarily reduce photocopying in the short term but at least publishers and authors will receive some returns on their investments.

As PASA's copyright officer, I attended the International Publishers Association Fourth Copyright Symposium, held in Tokyo where I delivered a paper and I was invited, on behalf of PASA and APNET, to join the Copyright Committee of the International Publishers Association. The Committee's first meeting was held in Geneva in June, where it was decided to focus on:

- copyright awareness
- copyright enforcement
- anti-piracy strategies
- reproduction permission policies
- collective administration of rights (in collaboration with national reproductive rights organizations)
- encouragement of improved national copyright legislation
- arbitration for dispute settlement
- copyright policies within national publishers' associations.

Book promotion —working together

South Africa has no imminent plans to institute an international book fair and, although PASA does not have its own stand at ZIBF, numerous members exhibit and/or visit in their individual capacities. A prominent member of PASA said he saw no need for an international book fair in South Africa when South African publishers could achieve more by going to Harare (which already has an international reputation) than by starting all over again in Johannesburg. The South African Department of Trade and Industry organized a joint South African stand at the Frankfurt Book Fair in 1997, offering sponsorship to smaller publishers and 12 South African publishers were present. The venture is to be repeated in 1998. Unfortunately the Department of Trade and Industry declined to sponsor a South African stand at ZIBF98 on the grounds that it could only afford one book fair a year and the commercial potential of Frankfurt was greater than that of Harare.

Book weeks, book days and other book events take place annually, arranged, for instance, by the Johannesburg Public Library, the South African library and various shopping centres. PASA has worked with the Book Development Council of South Africa (BDCSA) and the Centre for the Book, based at the South African Library in Cape Town, to organize such events. The Book Development Council of South Africa was launched in 1994 with the objective of co-ordinating the book sector and formulating policy; at the moment, though, its future is doubtful due to lack of funds. The Department of Arts and Culture has worked with both the council and the Centre for the Book.

On the whole, collaboration between the various components of the book sector is sporadic. One of the legacies of apartheid is a fragmented society in which various sectors can be reluctant to work together and in which suspicion is common. Concerted efforts still have to be made to overcome the apartheid mindset. PASA has made commendable attempts to forge a good relationship with the Department of Education, and when their financial crisis is over, this will bear fruit. PASA and SABA (the South African Booksellers Association) are holding their Annual General Meetings parallel to each other this year with a joint awards dinner at which the winners of the Whitaker's Sefika Awards for best publisher and best bookseller of the year will be announced. The Centre for the Book plays a particularly important role in getting all the members of the book chain together, since it is a neutral and objective body.

The Publishing Training Project (PTP) operates under the auspices of PASA. Its focus is on assisting small publishing initiatives and non-governmental organizations. It offers short training courses and information and consultancy services in a range of publishing related subjects. The list for July-December 1998 includes: Introduction to the Finances of Publishing; Copywriting; Commissioning; Effective writing for the workplace; Producing newsletters and brochures; Introduction to book production; Copyright, contracts and co-publishing; and Writing in Accessible English.

In April 1998 the Publishing Training Project worked with the African Publishing Institute (API) of APNET to run a Training of Trainers course in Johannesburg. Participants came from South Africa, Namibia, Lesotho, Botswana, Zimbabwe, Zambia, Malawi and Uganda. This was a successful collaborative effort between APNET and PASA and it is hoped that more will follow. The Publishing Training Project, with the British Council, ran a copy-editing course at ZIBF98 with 25 participants from African countries.

Children's publishing in South Africa

Children's literature in South Africa has been inextricably linked to educational publishing, since profits were only made in selling fiction books prescribed as readers for class use. Almost all publishers producing children's literature only afford to do so through their profits from the sale of textbooks. Profits depended largely on sales to education departments with no more than 5 per cent of the output sold through bookshops.

But this year the schoolbook market collapsed when orders placed in 1997 were cancelled without warning in early 1998 owing to the provincial education departments' mismanagement or overexpenditure. Losses for some individual publishers have been estimated at R50 million in some cases, to say nothing of financial losses to authors and illustrators. Smaller publishers of children's books have either closed down or stopped publishing. As an example of the decline: in 1996, 108 English-language children's books were published in South Africa; in 1997, 88 were published; so far in 1998, 5 have been published.

For diversity in publishing children's books we have to look at the historical picture. Until this year South Africa had been producing over 200 children's picture books, early readers and youth novels a year. Of the PASA member publishers at least 50 published children's books during the last two years. The main local publishers of children's books are Tafelberg, Human and Rousseau, Maskew Miller Longman and Kagiso. Then there are small independent publishers such as David Philip, Gecko, Garamond and Ithemba! Many books for children written and published in South Africa have been praised abroad. The International Youth Library in Munich (which attempts to collect and catalogue all the children's books in the world) issues an annual recommended list; the latest list contains three South African books: *Jakey* by Lesley Beake, *Saturday in Africa* by Patricia Pinnock and *Matilda and Meggie* by Nola Turkington. A separate list of 'peace books' containing 41 titles includes *The Day Gogo Went to Vote* by Elinor Sisulu.

South African publishers have produced a number of picture books: first readers as part of the literacy drive; stories for readers with a realistic depiction of our fast-changing country; and a few (though not yet enough) factual books. Particular mention should be made of the Zebra series from Kagiso, individually designed books for first readers for whom English is not the mother tongue; and the Ster and Star stories from Juta designed for first readers in Afrikaans and English. Maskew Miller Longman run a Young Africa competition annually; the winning stories are published and form an exciting body of youth literature in English. Heinemann's children's publishing has an educational slant. It has published novels, poetry, anthologies, drama and short stories in all South African languages by established and new authors, emphasizing current issues and moving away from traditional themes. David Philip's series, 'They Fought for Freedom', published in conjunction with the Mayibuye Centre, consists of short, simple biographies of struggle leaders. The Early Learning Resource Unit has an anti-bias unit producing anti-racist and anti-sexist materials for children.

Why is the market for children's books so small? It is estimated that South Africa's book-buying public forms no more than 5 per cent of the population, and that 5 per cent consists mainly of affluent, English-speaking whites. The home reading habit has not yet taken root widely among black families owing to the legacy of apartheid Bantu Education in which reading outside the prescribed school texts was discouraged. As Professor Charles Dlamini, Vice-Chancellor of the University of Zululand, has said, reading 'is not a strong habit acquired by pupils by the time they [leave school] — the black public is not a reading public.'

Another problem is distribution. Of the many CNAs (chain stores selling stationery, magazines, gifts, confectionery and a few mass-market books), hardly any sell South African children's literature since the discount demanded is too high to make the publishers' effort worthwhile. Better bookshops do stock some South African children's books but they tend to be situated in upmarket areas and apparently their biggest sales of South African children's books are to tourists. Bookshops are virtually non-existent in rural areas. Potential readers in vast areas of the country simply cannot lay their hands on books even if they want to.

As long as books are associated with study and not pleasure the development of children's literature will be stunted. It has been suggested that if parents want their children to be readers, they need to associate reading with comfort and enjoyment in the home. However, attitudes are slow to change and most parents are themselves non-readers. The production of high quality children's literature needs to be accompanied by effective promotion and distribution. Efforts have been made, admittedly with little success so far, to organize book buses in townships and in rural areas and some discount retail outlets are beginning to stock a few children's titles. Book clubs and *stokvels* are catching on and, with more pushing by the print media, radio and television, could become a major force in the distribution of children's books.

Discussion Points
The Plenary Sessions

1 Reprints: A participant asked the panel whether they were able to do reprints of their children's titles. James Tumusiime explained that their better selling titles are reprinted annually but others only every two years. Books for the beginning years of reading tend to move more quickly but otherwise they occasionally have 'windfalls' in the form of funding for library projects, for example. Both Henry Chakava and Janet Njoroge reprinted annually.

2 Motivation for publishing children's books: A children's book publishing house was described as 'something between a cathedral and the stockmarket' in that there had to be an element of community service combined with the desire for profit.

3 New ideas: In response to a challenge from Miriam Bamhare, all those on the panel felt they were open to new ideas and techniques and were always willing to consider manuscripts and suggestions and new approaches to production.

4 Folktales and ideological correctness: A discussion initiated by a Ugandan woman writer debated the suitability of folktales which upheld outdated and gender-biased versions of the world — she cited the images of witches and nasty stepmothers. James Tumusiine felt this was overstated as there were just as many evil men in folktales. Henry Chakava, with reference to a paper written by Chinua Achebe, retold a folktale which upheld polygamy as well as son-preference and concluded that there was room for adaptation. Janet Njoroge suggested that you could be selective.

5 Copyright on folktales: It was only the particular written version which could be copyrighted but the story still remained public property.

6 A moral to the story: In response to a question whether there should always be a moral to a children's story, Janet Njoroge said certainly not as this would lead to stilted, unspontaneous texts.

7 Books sold outside Africa: A Senegalese publisher commented that they sold more books outside Africa than in their own area. He attributed this to good relations with their contacts in the North and the fact that the prevalent prejudice against adult books from Africa is not evident in books for children.

8 A revolution of books and reading: Mary Bugembe made a spirited plea for more books and more innovation to make children's books available — a revolution or even a miracle! A Ugandan poet called for the promotion

of storytelling as a route to a reading culture. One participant suggested that by approaching these issues of culture and conflict holistically, we could end the vicious circle of creating new problems by solving others. A librarian from a private school in Botswana, Ann du Plessis, pointed out that although she came from a wealthy school, largely catering for white, Christian, affluent children, there was still no reading culture. In a survey she carried out recently, she asked the children what they got for Christmas and there were only three or four children who got books. These books were either the *Guiness Book of Records* or Goosebumps, a popular series of horror stories for children. When she askled if any other members of the family received a book for Christmas, she had one response only, 'Yes, my grandmother, and she died the next day'!

9   Pamela Kola's presentation was different from the paper circulated and related her experience as an author. When she first published her children's books there was much enthusiasm and celebration — the whole community was proud to be associated with books but in the last decade this interest has declined. Now there is greater concentration on textbooks at the expense of anything else. A survey she did revealed that only 12 per cent of children in Nairobi were read to at night. She called for better quality, better designed children's books with an emphasis on 'non-curriculum' reading. She also pointed out that we need to nurture writers as well as readers — through essay-writing and creative writing competitions.

10   Legislators: A local MP, bemoaning the paucity of library books, suggested that there was a noticeable absence of policy makers at the Indaba. He felt that the Indaba should function like the United Nations and any deliberations needed to be taken seriously by those in positions of power. He suggested that all participants needed to ensure that reportbacks needed to be made to the policy makers in our respective countries.

11   The curriculum: A South African participant explained that South Africa is currently introducing an 'outcomes-based' curriculum which would make story books part of the curriculum. Eleanor Sisulu also felt that this dichotomy between curriculum and non-curriculum materials was misleading — stories are vital in education and education systems should be the consumers of children's books. This was supported by Charles Kalugula who felt a revolution in education was already underway in Tanzania with a move towards flexible, multi-book, resource-based, learner-centred approaches. The liberalisation of the curriculum would offer endless opportunities for publishers.

12   Indigenous language children's books: A Nigerian writer said that he felt

the 'Ladybird-reading child' was a minority, middle class, urban concept and that we needed to concentrate on village children who were looking for adventure stories set in their own exciting environments. A Ugandan publisher supported this view by calling for Africa to take the Indian-style route and produce more books of acceptable quality rather than try to compete with first-world style publications.

13 In summary Richard Crabbe described a competition to encourage reading which was held where parents were required to read four books with their children and respond to questions on them. The big prize was a trip to Disneyland. He suggested that competitions like this could be held with a trip to somewhere in Africa (even to ZIBF) and if publishers joined forces, they could easily manage to raise the funds. He called for African publishers to stop waiting for donor-funding and mobilise income and interest from within their own environments. He called for us 'big people' (in children's terminology) not to do things for children but to work with them. He ended with a quote from a Nike advertisement popular with children, 'It's time we just do it!'

Group One
Policy

17
ZBDC Strategies

Promoting Books and Developing Reading: A Summary

MIRIAM BAMHARE

The Zimbabwe Book Development Council, like most national book councils established under the UNESCO guidelines, has a dual role and responsibility. On the one hand, the reason for its existence and the impetus for its establishment rest in the needs of the stakeholders in the book Industry: the creators and manufacturers of books — writers, publishers, printers and booksellers. On the other hand, the reason for the existence of that book industry rests in the needs of the consumer — the readers who, by and large, were not instrumental in establishing such book councils.

In the light of the above, it is obvious that, although neither our stakeholders nor our beneficiaries can exist without the other, it often takes great balancing skills on the part of book councils to serve both masters. However, the approach of the Zimbabwe Book Development Council is to promote books by co-operating with and, wherever possible, assisting the manufacturers of books to improve the quantity and the quality of the books they produce, and to provide a link between them and our other master, the readers or consumers. In this category are librarians, teachers, academics, pupils, students and the general reader.

The projects which the Zimbabwe Book Development Council has established to promote books and develop reading can be characterized by three features. Firstly, they are integrated projects which all benefit both our stakeholders and our beneficiaries.

Secondly, they are institution-based. The institutional base consists of schools and libraries throughout the country. It is our deliberate policy, based upon analysis of our specific circumstances in Zimbabwe and upon research carried out in other similar contexts, to build up the capacity of schools and libraries as the only way of democratizing and maximizing access to books, information and knowledge.

The third characteristic of our projects is that they are participatory. The Zimbabwe Book Development Council recognizes that projects that do not respond to felt and articulated needs, and which do not allow beneficiaries the major say in their implementation, are doomed to fail.

The Zimbabwe Book Development Council has four projects running concurrently, constituting its Book Awareness programme: National Book Week, the Book Fund Project, the Children's Reading Tent and Youth Forum and the Children's Book Forum.

The National Book Week project

This was initially aimed at focusing the entire school-going population on the benefits of reading. Many of the ideas for promoting reading in schools emanated from the Zimbabwe Book Development Council, and competitions for the most interesting and innovative ways of encouraging reading during National Book Week, held during the third week of March, were initiated by the Council.

With the support of the government and the Ministry of Education, we have networked with over 7,500 primary and secondary schools. Long before the actual week of National Book Week, we start sending out letters to schools with suggestions for celebrating National Book Week and enclosing the National Book Week poster.

A programme of seminars for librarians and teachers is another facet of National Book Week. This year our seminars took us to three provinces only, although we had planned to cover all provinces, with the help of Colleges of Education and Regional Offices of the Ministry of Education.

The lively official Launch of National Book Week this year was held in Harare's heartland, Mbare. Harare High School and the neighbouring schools hosted the launch, which was officially opened by the Minister of Education, Sport and Culture.

Both schools and libraries are involved in this project and the enthusiasm which it has generated, especially in the rural areas, is most encouraging. However, it was not until this year that the Zimbabwe Book Development Council turned its attention to making the 51 weeks between the annual Book Week celebrations into reading and book weeks as well. Our National Book Week poster 'Carry On Reading' was intended to reflect this new direction.

Unfortunately, pressure on our human resources has prevented the follow up we intended to have had in place by this time. Similarly, our efforts to involve our stakeholders more directly in National Book Week, in spite of the obvious advantages that they would reap from such involvement, have not yet made their mark. Our experience over the past year has taught us important lessons, the most important being that unless key persons within the education system are brought aboard on these projects, no matter how much time, money and work we invest in them, they will not have the desired impact. Heads of schools, colleges of education and Ministry of Education officials all have to be individually converted to the importance of such programmes. They can be very diligent gatekeepers and can cause serious bottlenecks if they are not committed and involved.

The Book Fund project

This is the most spectacular and most easily measured of our projects. It is also the most integrated. Not only does this project serve to increase the consumption of books, thus creating an incentive for local writers, publishers and printers, as well as booksellers to produce more books; it requires them to produce books of better quality. Through our librarian training programme, the capacity of librarians to serve the needs of the reading communities through the provision of books and services, is set to increase considerably. The newly released *Book Fund Project Catalogue* of locally written and published books, even in this short period has had a dramatic impact upon the book sector.

With the publication and circulation of the *Book Fund Project Catalogue*, the Zimbabwe Book Development Council has administered a much-needed injection into the ailing book sector. Readers, librarians, booksellers, publishers and printers, writers and illustrators are involved; all have a part to play, and all have benefits to reap.

The Children's Reading Tent

The participation of the Zimbabwe Book Development Council in the annual Children's Reading Tent and the establishment of a Youth Forum this year represents two more initiatives to stimulate a love for reading and familiarity with books. Through our programme of seminars for care givers for children — teachers of pre-school and nursery school children, parents and librarians — we provide guidance for the development of good reading habits and a love of reading in the young. The reading-related activities in the reading tent are popular with children.

In the Youth Forum, apart from the provision of a forum in which youths can enter into dialogue both with their peers and with their mentors, the Zimbabwe Book Development Council has initiated a survey of reading habits and reading preferences among this age group. This is a very important strategy which we are developing to ensure that the providers of books for this group are aware of what the readers wish to read and what they would be prepared, therefore, to buy.

The Children's Book Forum

This programme is another integrated Zimbabwe Book Development Council project. It grew out of the recognition that there was very little relevant and interesting literature for our adolescents and young adults. Research has shown that this is the age when the lull in reading becomes most marked and when there is the greatest danger of readers lapsing into aliteracy.

The objectives of the Children's Book Forum (Literature) project are to add seven new titles to the literature available for adolescents and young adults. Through the Workshop for Writers and Creative Designers and the Illustrators' Workshop, we were able to bring together both our stakeholders and our beneficiaries. Some 97 manuscripts in English, Shona and Ndebele were entered for the Story Competition launched at the end of the workshop and from these we have seven manuscripts which are now in the final stages of publishing and will soon be ready for distribution to our libraries.

The Zimbabwe Book Development Council continues to support reading through its membership of organizations such as IBBY, the IRA, IFLA and through attendance at workshops and conferences on reading and related issues. Recently, during the launch of the Book Fund Catalogue, the Zimbabwe Book Development Council announced its new initiative to revive the idea of reading associations at both the local and the national levels.

It is our conviction that once the passion for books and the joy of reading are sufficiently stimulated, especially among the young, the book industry will have the incentive to produce the quantities and the quality of books required to satisfy the demand. However, the book industry will have to make sacrifices now and invest in the creation of that passion, if it is to reap the rewards later on. The Zimbabwe Book Development Council is doing its part and has worked out strategies and structures that are already having a significant impact on readership amongst the young.

18
Structures to Promote a Reading Culture
Nigeria

CHUKWUEMEKA IKE

N igeria does not have a reading culture. You hear this statement *ad nauseum* in Nigeria, uttered and accepted as an incontrovertible truth, as if it was a cultural deficiency inherent in our Nigerianness. The absence of a reading culture is seen as one of the distinguishing features of a Nigerian child from a European or American child.

The state of reading development in Nigeria

The claim that Nigeria does not have a reading culture has been debunked from time to time by the appearance of books with mass appeal. During the dying decade of colonial rule what became subsequently known as Onitsha market literature developed in the market town of Onitsha in eastern Nigeria. Written at a language level (English) accessible to its audience — schoolchildren, teachers, traders, artisans, civil servants, male and female — the pamphlets or books explored themes which touched on the everyday lives of their readers. Consequently, they were consumed as fast as they were published, their popularity spreading to English-speaking Cameroun.

Obasanjo's *My Command* (1980) and Madiebo's *The Nigerian Revolution* and *The Biafran War* (1980) gave Nigeria two instant best sellers. Written by commanders of the Nigerian army and the Biafran army respectively, the books contained very much sought after details of the 30-month Nigerian civil war, revealed for the first time. The nationwide stampede to buy and read the two books was remarkable.

The Kano market literature of the 1990s is also worthy of mention. Written in the Hausa language, the pamphlets or books explored issues of concern to their readers — about the same composition as for the Onitsha market literature. Its high rate of consumption is said to have alarmed the conservative establishment, afraid of 'contaminating' the youth with ideas!

Nigerian youths are known as avid readers of local magazines specializing in relationships between the opposite sexes as well as Mills & Boon, Enid Blyton, and similar foreign novels.

We have cited these sporadic developments to make the point that there is nothing physiological or racial in the low level of book readership recorded in Nigeria today. According to our findings, the low readership level is attributable to two major problems: the disappointing level of basic literacy throughout the country and the absence of appropriate and relevant books and other reading materials for the majority of the Nigerian population.

By basic literacy, I mean the ability to read a written language with ease, and to understand and appreciate what is read. Unfortunately educational standards have deteriorated so noticeably in Nigeria in recent years that many (if not most) of the pupils going through public primary schools are incapable of reading with ease and understanding either in English or Nigerian languages.

The unavailability of relevant books and other reading materials may be difficult to appreciate in a country with one of the highest publishing capacities in Africa. The truth is that at least 90 per cent of the titles published in Nigeria every year are textbooks for pre-primary, primary and secondary schools. Little conscious effort is made by government, publishers or authors to ascertain and provide for the needs of children, adolescents and adults of all ages and both sexes outside the formal education system. The developments cited earlier became possible only when publishers and authors broke free from the textbook syndrome.

We maintain that any attempt to promote the culture of reading books in Nigeria which does not address these two basic problems is doomed to achieve severely limited success.

Structures for promoting the reading habit in Nigeria

Different governmental and non-governmental agencies have at one time or another participated in the promotion of the reading habit in Nigeria.

The National Library of Nigeria mounted an elaborate Readership Promotion Campaign from 1981 to 1985. This included an annual National Reading Week in 15 states of the Federation, and in 1984 a National Seminar on Reading in Nigeria. It also included the wide distribution of a variety of promotional materials — book markers, car stickers, calendars, memo pads, posters, metal badges, and so on.

The Nigerian Educational Research & Development Council (NERDC), another Federal government agency, followed with an ambitious programme of organizing a Young Readers' Club in every state, with an organizational structure to co-ordinate them. It launched the readers' clubs in 20 states. However, by June 1996, only six out of the twenty were still functioning.

At the non-governmental level, the Children's Literature Association of Nigeria (CLAN) and the Nigerian Chapter of IBBY concentrated on encouraging the love of reading among children and the provision of suitable reading materials for them. Their activities included workshops for writers and illustrators of children's literature. Their efforts, along with the contributions of committed authors and publishers, boosted the publication of suitable reading materials for Nigerian children. A *Directory of Children's Books* (Nigeria, 1997) compiled by the Nigerian Book Foundation Reading Promotion programme lists about 300 titles of poetry, drama, stories, folk tales, readers, picture books, history, biography, information and music. Some titles are written in the Yoruba language, and smaller numbers in Igbo and Hausa languages. Most of the titles are written in English, which drastically reduces their usefulness among rural children who need children's books in the local languages.

Other non-governmental organizations which have participated in reading promotion in Nigeria include the Readers' Association of Nigeria (RAN), the Association of Nigerian Authors (ANA), the Network for the Promotion of Reading (NEP-READ) established in 1997 and Women Writers of Nigeria (WRITA).

Apart from the problems of basic literacy and unavailability of appropriate and relevant reading materials cited earlier, one other reason why the level of readership remains low in Nigeria in spite of the efforts at promoting reading is the fact that these efforts, worthy as they are, have been sporadic, unco-ordinated, and have not been part of a master reading promotion plan for the country.

The role of the Nigerian Book Foundation in promoting the culture of reading in Nigeria

Founded in 1991 as a non-governmental, non-profit book development organization, the Nigerian Book Foundation began to function in 1993. It is an umbrella organization bringing together the key participants in book development, to ensure that all components of the book chain function maximally and that the state provides a conducive environment for the book to flourish. Its mission is to facilitate the development of a vibrant book industry in Nigeria.

The Nigerian Book Foundation has a Board of Trustees, currently comprising ten Nigerian men and women of high repute appointed on merit to reflect the rich diversity of talent nationwide in matters pertaining to book development. It is responsible for the general superintendence of the policies, finances and physical assets of the Foundation. The Foundation also has a National Advisory Council as its professional arm, advising the Foundation on its annual programmes and activities, and providing a common voice for the Nigerian book community on appropriate occasions. Its membership includes the presidents of the national associations of authors, publishers, booksellers, printers and librarians, nominees of the two ministers responsible for culture and for education, the National Librarian, representatives or organizations relevant to book development and persons appointed on merit.

From its inception, the Nigerian Book Foundation had the following among its long and short term objectives: to encourage the reading habit among Nigerians and promote through books ideas and ideals that would enhance the socio-cultural development of the country. Its holistic approach to national book development and its status as an umbrella organization bringing together the key governmental and non-governmental stakeholders in the book industry make the Nigerian Book Foundation an ideal national organization to promote the reading culture and children's books.

Organization of the Nigerian Book Foundation reading promotion programme

Experience has shown that, for the size and population of Nigeria, it is unrealistic to attempt to promote the culture of reading nationwide from one location and hope to achieve significant success. During 1996 and 1997, the Nigerian Book Foundation set up three reading promotion pilot projects — one in the north, one in the south-east and one in the south-west of the country, with a National Co-ordinator in the south-west.

The current structure is as follows:

Programme Co-ordination: at Nigerian Book Foundation Headquarters, Awka

Reading Promotion Unit 1: to cover the south-east zone (located in Anambra State)

Reading Promotion Unit 2: to cover the south-west zone (located in Oyo State)

Reading Promotion Unit 3: to cover the northern zone (located in Plateau State).

Considering the number of states and the population to be covered by each unit, the number of units is grossly inadequate. The limiting factor has been funding. Each unit has rented office accommodation and is run by a Programme Officer and a Secretary, both of them on part-time bases (owing to limited funding).

Funds are released to each unit every quarter from the Programme Co-ordination Unit, to which regular progress reports and financial returns are sent. Co-ordination takes the form of correspondence, occasional meetings with Programme Officers at the Headquarters as well as monitoring visits to the units by the Programme Specialist and the Nigerian Book Foundation President, especially during each unit's major activities.

Major reading promotion activities

Annual National Book Week
The Nigerian Book Foundation has organized an annual National Book Week since April 1994, usually in the second half of April, to sensitize the government, organizations and individuals on the centrality of the book to national and individual development. The activities have usually included an opening ceremony, an exhibition relevant to the theme, a national workshop or forum on the theme and annual book development awards. The theme of the 1998 Book Week was 'Cultism and Drug Abuse: The Role of the Book in Human Development'.

Hitherto, the activities of each annual Book Week have been concentrated in Lagos. As from 1999, each reading promotion unit will organize activities in its zone, to widen the impact of the Week.

Children's Book Day
This was organized for two years in Lagos during the annual Book Week and was warmly received all round. The National Council on Education, comprising all federal and state Ministries of Education, welcomed the idea of a Children's Book Day but wanted it held nationwide during the National Children's Week in late May of every year. No funds were, however, provided for this, hence no special activity for children was organized in 1998.

Mobile Reading Centres
The major activity of each reading promotion unit is the mobile reading centres in various locations (according to an agreed calendar) each lasting three days, targeted at potential book readers — children (in primary and secondary schools) and adults of all ages, male and female, literate in English or in the

dominant Nigerian language of the community. It is also targeted at parents, teachers, religious leaders, community leaders, town union officers, adult education authorities, state education authorities and local government authorities.

The activities in each centre include the operation of a reading centre (a hall or a large room) open to children and adults for the three days. Each reading promotion unit has purchased children's and general interest books and other reading materials which are made available to readers. Donations for additional books are also solicited. Children are given the opportunity to interact with any available authors from the community, for an insight into the craft of writing. Quizzes are also organized to test how much the children have benefited from the books supplied. Books at the centre can only be used at the centre; they cannot be taken away.

Publishers and booksellers are encouraged to mount exhibitions of books for children and other general interest books during the period, to enable parents, children and adult readers to know what books are in the market and to buy them.

One of the three days is devoted to a workshop for teachers, parents, local government officers, community leaders and other individuals and organizations considered relevant, to enlighten them on their role in promoting the reading culture in their community. A video cassette developed by the Nigerian Book Foundation on the subject is shown, after which the programme specialist or another official makes a presentation, proposing ways in which the community could facilitate reading promotion after the foundation has moved off to another location. An open forum follows.

The period before the mobile reading centre is spent on intensive consultations with appropriate organizations or individuals in the community concerned.

Books for the family project

As its contribution to the provision of appropriate and relevant books for Nigerians outside the formal education sector, the Nigerian Book Foundation developed the Books for the Family project with the following objectives among others:

1   To involve fathers, mothers, and members of the extended family in the generation of appropriate reading materials for their children, thereby underscoring their relevance to the education of their children.
2   To generate, produce, trial and publish (in Nigerian languages and/or in English) reading materials which would serve as avenues for transmitting

to the young positive values and mores of the family and the wider community.

3   To generate from the cultural heritage of the community (through the members of that community, literate and illiterate), produce, test and publish in an inexpensive but readable format suitable reading materials for the needs of the entire family, in Nigerian languages and in English.

4   To arrange the translation of suitable publications already in existence into Nigerian languages and arrange to publish the translations.

5   To ensure effective promotion and distribution of the books published.

Each programme is to be built around one language community, the number of programmes to be established depending on the extent of funding available.

The project has not taken off, as all efforts by the Nigerian Book Foundation to obtain funds locally and from foreign sources have failed. Seven pamphlets developed in the Igbo language by Reading Promotion Pilot Project 1 in 1996/97 are currently undergoing external evaluation prior to publication.

When funds become available the reading promotion units will be involved.

Is the game worth the candle?

We are conscious of the fact that at the end of one year all three reading promotion units would have conducted the intensive three-day reading promotion programme in only twelve communities. For a country the size of Nigeria, this is no more than a drop in the ocean. There are, of course, other foundation activities such as the Book Week, the Children's Book Day, and the Nigerian Book Foundation fora. In addition, there are other avenues for the promotion of reading and children's books; by co-ordinating its efforts with them, the foundation could achieve a widening of the overall impact. All told, however, the total annual impact will still be relatively small.

The problem does not, however, lie with the Nigerian Book Foundation structure. It lies with grossly inadequate funding. Funding of the Reading Promotion Programme since 1996 has been by Heinrich Boll Foundation for which the Nigerian Book Foundation has been immensely grateful. The funds cannot, however, do more than what has been described and they terminate on 31 December 2000.

The Books for the Family Project, designed to grapple with the key problem of providing appropriate and relevant reading materials, remains on the drawing board because of lack of funds.

Substantial additional funding will ensure a tangible impact.

19
Structures to Promote Children's Books and Reading Development
The Malawi Case

JAMES L. NG'OMBE

This topic presupposes the existence of a normal distribution network, which is not the case in Malawi. A distinction must be made between the urban and rural setting. Urban areas have growing populations with greater buying power than the rural areas. As a result the tendency has been for bookshops and other related distributors to be concentrated in the towns because that is where book distribution is a viable commercial activity.

On the rural scene, the Christian Literature Association of Malawi is the only network still distributing books, although it too is cutting down on the number of outlets and keeping the few that have good track records as revenue-generating centres. Both Macmillan Malawi and Jhango have used the People Trading Centre (PTC) chain of supermarkets as book distributors but have not registered much success with these outlets.

Children as buyers or readers

In Malawi, as in most African countries, reading for its own sake is a strange phenomenon. Reading must have a purpose and pleasure or information-seeking has never been a sufficient motivation even for university graduates. So development of a reading culture has suffered. Parents or teachers often do not pass on good reading habits to the children, be it at home or school. Books are bought only if they meet directly curricular or examination requirements.

Therefore the family must be nurtured into becoming a reading centre before schools and libraries can take over. The hunger for books in children is what the book industry needs in order to develop and grow. But because African governments have other priorities (such as feeding the voters) other structures are required to support or to guide, the limited government support for children's educational development.

The Book Publishers' Association of Malawi

The Book Publishers' Association of Malawi was formed in 1996 to bring together book publishers to tackle such problems as developing a reading culture, the need for a government book policy, and the absence of a proper distribution network. The following has been achieved:

1997 — National Book Fair

This was the first fair organized by the Book Publishers' Association of Malawi. A reading tent was erected and the first Jhango-Heinemann story competition prizes were awarded. These awards are to continue for ten years.

Following the fair, UNESCO convened a workshop to discuss the formation of a Book Development Council involving all the stakeholders. The most important outcome was the formation of a Steering Committee to oversee the evolution of a book policy under government auspices.

For the first time the Distance Education Centres were involved in a book procurement pilot exercise in which books were provided from a revised, multiple-textbook-based list. This project is funded by DANIDA.

1998 — Regional School Fairs

The multiple-textbook approach to syllabus interpretation by the teacher was consolidated under the World Bank funding for secondary books. Under this project up to four teachers per school were invited to a regional fair where publishers displayed books from a pre-determined list. Schools were given a budget according to official enrolment figures and were free to spend their allocations according to their school needs. The books were sourced from the publishers by consolidators and delivered to schools direct.

Through negotiations between the Book Publishers' Association of Malawi, the Ministry of Education, donors and the Book Development Council Steering Committee, a textbook policy was prepared and has now been presented to government for adoption. The draft policy incorporates the school empowerment mentioned above.

One important feature of the draft policy is the creation of schoolbook funds which will enable schools to make further purchases, hopefully from booksellers, thereby helping develop the distribution network.

The National Library Service has so far been the main distributor of reading material to the rural areas. They have even produced booklets, with CODE funding, to promote functional literacy among school dropouts and new adult literates.

20
Reaching Out to Children
CHISCI's Vision for the Development of a Thriving
Publishing Industry in Africa: A summary

MARY H. BUGEMBE

The Foundation for the Promotion of Children's Science Publications in
Africa (CHISCI) was established in November 1988, for the purpose of
promoting a reading and science culture among children in Africa.

In order to fulfil its mission, CHISCI adopted the following strategies:

1   Children, as the primary target of its work, must play a central role in all
CHISCI's activities. This will ensure that they are directly involved, and
that CHISCI and all other key players can have direct feedback on the
impact of their work for children.

2   An Africa-wide forum bringing together key players in the creation and
dissemination of children's literature has been established to give focused
and continuous attention to the reading needs of children so as to work out
strategies that would facilitate a speedy increase in the provision of
children's literature in Africa.

3   Parents and guardians, as fundamental mediums for children, must be
embraced in the campaign to promote a life-long reading and science culture
emanating from the home.

4   The right environment must be created that allows children to enjoy reading
and experimenting. Apart from the traditional libraries, other avenues of
reaching out to children within their own environments must be explored.

5   The role of the media in sensitizing the public on the importance of reading
is critical to the success of our programme activities.

CHISCI's activities have included the organization of the annual Pan-
African Children's Book Fair since 1992, management of three Children's
Community Libraries (two in Kenya, and one in Uganda), organization of a
Mobile Children's Reading Tent, running of a Children's Discount Book Store
and Book Club, as well as the running of the Children's Science Press.

A pictorial exhibition of CHISCI's work is available to demonstrate the
highlights of this summary of their activities.

21
Reading Skills Enhancement Project

MERVIN OGLE

Most of my concerns about the official, professional and public attitudes to reading are born of my experience in English teaching and teaching development over the last 30 years. These concerns are confirmed by an article entitled 'Let's not marginalize adolescent literacy' by Richard Vaca in the May 1998 issue of the *Journal of Adolescent and Adult Literacy*. A major point made in the introduction to the article is the following:

> While not questioning the paramount importance of early literacy development, we hear much less about a parallel crisis in adolescent literacy development — the magnitude of which is yet to be fully measured, let alone confronted and addressed. In many urban and suburban and rural schools in the US, large numbers of adolescents rarely engage in reading and writing that promotes growth.

This criticism of educational policy and its implementation in schools is valid in most countries and more so in developing countries with very limited resources.

Whenever people talk of literacy they mainly refer to the basic skills in learning to read and write. They are referring to either the reading instruction that occurs in the first three to four years of school or to the remedial adult basic education for people who are completely illiterate.

The other level of reading takes in the whole idea of the study of literature which usually occurs in the last three years of schooling and is often painfully and frustratingly linked to examinations and invariably kills what little interest in reading there is.

The intervening years, which offer rich possibilities for reading development and for the fostering of a love for reading, are sadly neglected. This narrow perception of literacy Vaca says 'is manifested through educational policy, school curricula and a public mindset on literacy that doesn't appear to extend beyond learning to read and write in early childhood and elementary school.'

It would be interesting to compare the amounts of research and development funding that go respectively to basic childhood literacy and adolescent reading in a given country. With the more basic needs more acute in third world countries and with their paucity of resources it is understandable but equally disappointing that so little attention, both in terms of the provision of resources and classroom time, is paid to adolescent literacy.

A major problem is that most funders, both public and private, preoccupied with performance indicators as they are, are more likely to fund those programmes which lend themselves more easily to quantitative evaluation — the numbers game comes into its own here, when applied to basic literacy. On the other hand, more advanced reading skills that include inferencing, prediction and elaborating meaning in texts are less easy to assess. This neglect of reading skills at the higher primary and secondary levels extends to government education officials. When they talk of books they mean textbooks, they rarely include books of fiction and other supplementary texts.

Thirdly, many teachers also unfortunately show the same indifference to supplementary reading programmes.

If there is some reading development reaching beyond the early years it is restricted to either unimaginative round robin reading of the class reader, the study of decontextualized comprehension passages or the intensive study of literature texts prescribed for the school certificate examination. In all three examples reading often becomes a chore and any latent interest in reading in the child is lost.

Another disabling factor in this neglect of reading beyond basic literacy is the high price of books in developing countries. An average grade 5 reading book of 5000 words or 25 pages costs about R 20 in South Africa. Given a class size of 40 you would require as much as R 600 for one set of readers. A good reading programme would require at least four readers per year. In addition if you include a set of supplementary readers you are looking at a cost of about R 2,400 per class or R 60 per pupil. A lot of money in South Africa but really miniscule in pound or dollar terms.

The strict application of market forces also restricts the provision of books to poorer schools because it is cheaper to pulp or recycle books than to distribute them to schools. Allied to this is the fear of flooding the market and thereby reducing sales.

All these factors — external funding norms and preferences, educational policy and curriculum planners, imperatives, teachers' shortcomings and false priorities and the high cost of books — militate against the implementation of reading programmes that will help children not only in their own language learning but also learning to negotiate meaning in life generally and in the way they cope with literacy in all aspects of the curriculum.

It was for these reasons that English Language Educational Trust (ELET) embarked on a reading skills enhancement programme with a generous grant from the Department of International Development.

Background

The English Language Educational Trust in close co-operation with the KwaZulu Natal Department of Education in the Vryheid region is implementing the reading skills enhancement project.

At present the project involves five subject advisors and 43 teachers in the Vryheid region of KwaZulu Natal. It is being funded by the Department for International Development (DFID).

Rationale

Developing learners' motivation to read is essential in developing their reading skills and improved reading skills greatly assist learners in all fields of study and in life generally.

The English Language Educational Trust has considerable experience in reading projects in KwaZulu Natal's rural schools. This experience shows that a focused and well-organized programme of reading for enjoyment can excite students and motivate them to read. This also tends to spread through the rest of the school and community.

The use of structured readers both as sets of class readers and as part of a classroom library can lead to a variety of skills that address linguistic, literary and practical needs at school and in the world outside. To exploit and build on already acquired basic reading skills the project will focus on higher primary classes — grades 4, 5 and 6 — in 43 schools.

This book project addresses a major issue of social equity where the majority of children are being schooled in a second language.

What does it involve?

The project involves providing books and materials to 129 higher primary classrooms in grades 4, 5 and 6 in 40 schools in the Vryheid region of KwaZulu Natal. The teachers receive training in the use of the books and each project teacher is expected to train at least two other English teachers at her school in the effective use of the books.

The 43 project teachers attended two two-day courses held at a selected school. In all, 5,160 students and 43 teachers will benefit from the project. Each classroom will receive at least two sets of class readers, one collection of readers of different titles and a set of learner booklets.

The two main phases of the project are the class reader programme and the supplementary reader programme. In phase one a two-day training workshop on the use of a class reader will be held, class readers will be chosen and provided to the schools (two sets per grade) and the class reader programme will be monitored in ten of the schools. Of these the training workshop and the provision of one set of books per grade have been completed.

In phase two, similar steps are being taken comprising a training workshop, co-operative selection and distribution of the supplementary reading collections and the monitoring of the programme in a further 10 schools. Those schools that will not be visited for support and monitoring will be required to complete progress reports.

The rationale for the phased nature of the book provisioning is that there is a need to first create a taste for reading through a direct classroom-based approach whereby reading-related activities such as class discussions, role play, writing activities and silent reading are undertaken before catering to that taste through the provision of individual and possibly more demanding readers.

The supplementary readers will be organized to allow for about five copies of each of 15 titles across a range of complexity and interest so that readers can proceed from relatively easy books to more challenging ones.

The monitoring of the project in the sample of ten schools will include classroom lesson observations, an examination of records of reading-related activities, book reports, reading progress charts and providing of support to teachers in school training in the reading programme.

Implementation Problems

A project such as this involving collaboration between the service provider, the regional education department, the teachers, the publishers or booksellers and the funder (DFID), is bound to have some problems.

The first problem in a rural area, where postal and telephone services are inadequate by modern standards, is one of communication. The first workshop was attended by only 21 of the 43 teachers invited. Fortunately the department made amends by holding a second workshop at their expense at which over 50 schools were represented.

The second problem is of consistency of attendance.

The third problem which we are trying to address is that of book distribution. The first set of class readers were distributed at a workshop. I have not yet ascertained whether they all got to the schools until I visit the schools and receive reports from other schools.

As I see it all the above problems are parts of one big issue — that of ensuring that suitable books reach the children who should be helped by their teachers to gain the most value out of them.

Finally, the choice of books has been based on a number of considerations:

1 The one of cost has meant that we have chosen mainly local publishers. This has meant a cost saving of about 20 per cent on the price of books.

2 Local books with South African settings have a better chance of an African representation in the stories themselves. The benefits of this are obvious. The drawback, however, is that while most of the books reflect this Africanness, the writers themselves are predominantly white (but progressive) South Africans. Nevertheless, the need and necessity of children to see themselves in some of the books they read is being addressed.

3 A number of these books were workshopped with teachers and the selections were influenced strongly by their preferences.

Once this project has been completed, it will be used to advocate for greater attention to be paid to intermediate phase reading development — a sadly neglected area of educational development.

22
Sharing the READ Experience
Strategies:Children's Books and Reading Development

CYNTHIA D. HUGO

READ Educational Trust has been active in South Africa for nearly 20 years and its mission is to create a reading and learning culture in South Africa by improving the effectiveness of the educational process. Our emphasis is on language and literacy education in public schools and our strategies include training teachers in book-based literacy methods, developing and publishing children's books and teacher support materials, setting up school libraries and running national literacy campaigns.

READ's teacher training programmes target whole school communities and focus on effective classroom strategies for teaching reading and developing language, communication and information skills within the book- and resource-based approach. These include shared reading and writing, group and guided reading, books for language development, reading aloud, reading for information, reading and writing for real purposes and selecting books for classroom use. The training is accompanied by materials (books, posters and teacher support materials) and monitoring visits by READ trainers.

READ has developed and published an extensive collection of low-cost, high-quality books and other classroom materials, including Big Books, sets of group readers, story posters, read-aloud story collections and wordless books. Our materials are written for non-mother-tongue learners of English and are culturally sensitive, level appropriate, attractively illustrated and designed and affordable. All materials are tested in schools with active involvement of teachers and pupils.

READ initiates and organizes literacy campaigns and programmes like READATHON, Festival of Books (drama competition) and Festival of Stories (story-based materials development competition for teachers). We work in partnership with the private sector, tertiary level educational institutions, departments of education and other literacy and educational organizations.

READ's programmes have so far been adopted in 2,300 schools with nearly 12,000 teachers; they affect 650,000 schoolchildren each year. Children in READ schools double their gains in literacy skills compared to their peers in non-READ schools.

23
WOTAP's Strategies
Promoting Children's Book and Reading Development

TERESA SAMUEL IBRAHIM

With the escalation of the war in southern Sudan since 1983, it is estimated that over three million people have migrated to live a displaced life in northern Sudan. Of these, over a half million are re-settled in camps in and around Khartoum State, most of them women and children.

Most of the displaced women have rural backgrounds and they have been re-settled in an urban environment amidst desert climatic conditions. It was not easy for them to adapt to urban life and so supplement their relief food rations. Some resorted to making and selling local beer which is illegal, thus many of them became victims of flogging, fines or imprisonment. Some tried petty businesses like selling food, charcoal, dried fish, and so on, but their main problems were lack of capital and managerial capabilities. Most of them lacked skills for income-generating activities such as leather work, soap making and tie and dye. Exposed to congested camp life, children's and mothers' health became major issues needing to be addressed.

The situation is worse for displaced schoolchildren as the development of children's books has been neglected. The recognition of the importance of children's books is a reflection not only of changes of understanding and method but also of the appreciation that today's children are tomorrow's adults. The advantages and opportunities which reading offers will be secured if new generation grow up with the habit of using books. To produce children's books those in control of resources need to fully appreciate what will they achieve so they can motivate children's book writers.

WOTAP is administering four pre-schools which run a two-year pre-school programme for children in two major camps around Khartoum with a total enrolment of 800 children ranging in age from three to five years. These children are taught both English and Arabic, using national curriculum textbooks purchased by WOTAP. A similar situation exists in 'self-help' schools, set up by the southern and western Sudanese desperate to educate their children. In early 1997 WOTAP's pre-schools received children's books donated by Book Aid UK through WUS/UK and this was later reinforced by the efforts of the wife of the British Ambassador in Sudan, Dr Lilian Craig. The facilitator of the Women Action Group (WAG) and the English Language Foundation (ELF) also received some used children's books donated by the Diocese of Bradford for the displaced school children in Khartoum. WAG is a group based in Khartoum that brings together Muslim and Christian women for peace dialogue. It uses simple and attractive children's books for both mothers and children and is dedicated to preserving the English language as a Sudanese heritage. These two groups opened up some 25 libraries in Khartoum for both government and 'self-help' schools for the displaced children to use.

WOTAP was one of the beneficiaries which received 411 used and new children's books. We set up two mini-libraries in April and these open for two hours daily except on Fridays and Sundays. The libraries became a place of amusement when they first opened their doors — most of the children visiting were to be found busy in groups of two to three poring over the pages of coloured picture books in excited discussion. In the first week the librarians had to control entry, allowing a specific number of children to use the library due to the limited space. A borrowing scheme was later introduced for children above the sixth grade who are displaced and resident in the camp.

WOTAP is not planning to be dependent on children's books donated from abroad. It has put forth a strategy to encourage locally produced children's books that reflect the indigenous southern Sudanese cultures and traditions. These books should be in the form of illustrations, simple traditional tales, short stories, fairy tales, and so on. It has called upon talented southern Sudanese writers to translate some of the vernacular literature books. Those children's books donated from abroad will add to a body of knowledge for our displaced children now and will be expanded once peace is established.

WOTAP pre-school teachers were recruited from secondary school leavers among the displaced people and initially had no teaching skills. However, WOTAP produced a comprehensive up-grading training programme for these teachers and conducted them during school vacations using staff of the Teachers' Training Institute.

Lastly, WOTAP regrets that there is little prospect of the parents of these displaced children being able to purchase books and other educational aids for their children as long as they are living a displaced life. Unless the war in the Sudan stops we will remain dependent on local or international donors or on charitable organizations to support this noble cause.

On behalf of Women's Action Group (WAG) library stops I would like to take this opportunity to appeal to any donors locally or internationally who may have used or new children's books to donate them for the displaced children in Sudan.

24
Inter-African Partnerships

A summary of the ADEA Working Group Books Forum
Study on the Book Trade in Southern Africa

James Tumusiine introduced this panel discussion by explaining the background to the research into Inter-African book trade. APNET initiated the study after observations that it may be easier to procure a Kenyan book in the UK than to get it direct from the publisher concerned. After some time of inaction, the project was finally launched in January 1998, with the help of donor funding.

Ruth Makotsi is the major researcher in the project and she is assisted by a team of researchers; one from each country involved. The research is still ongoing but she made the following observations as her interim report.

The study focuses on southern Africa and includes eight southern African countries — Botswana, Zambia, Malawi, Lesotho, Swaziland, South Africa, Namibia and Zimbabwe and two other African countries, Kenya and Nigeria, which are valuable for comparison purposes. National researchers were appointed in each country.

The research was carried out in three ways:

- Through interviews with key players in the publishing industry in each country.
- Through questionnaires which were sent to key players in the industry, relevant government departments, shipping agencies, banks, donors and so on. Also, a publisher and a bookseller were selected in eight countries and book shipments were made between the eight countries: from South Africa to Malawi and vice versa, Nigeria to Zimbabwe and vice versa, Namibia to Botswana and vice versa, Zambia to Kenya and vice versa.
- Through research in archives or any other records which would give an historical perspective on publishing and trade. Some of the questions to be answered were: What does the country publish? Who are the publishers? What kind of publishing do they do? What is the publishing environment?

The findings are not complete but some issues have emerged. Most countries in Africa have very small publishing industries — usually less than 5 per cent of the economy. Consequently not much attention is paid to the industry. The publishing environments tend to be suppressive — poor infrastructure, poor reading habits and little purchasing power, particularly in specialised areas like children's books. Private indigenous companies have the biggest problem with very little access to credit.

However, the situation is not completely hopeless as statistics show there has been a growth of more than 500 per cent since 1983 when there were only 818 African publishers and 1998, when there are 4,000 publishers (at least 50 per cent of whom are commercial). Also, although the growth is largely textbook oriented, other areas are increasing, too, for example in the area of academic books and in children's books (in the latter there was no publishing a decade ago and the continent is now exporting).

At national levels, membership of APNET is increasing as more countries establish national associations and dialogue between publishers and governments is subsequently developing. Nevertheless most of the books imported into countries in Africa are imported from the US or UK — very little comes from other African countries.

There is still a reliance on textbooks which constitute lower risk publishing. Book production costs are high and publishers tend to do small print runs with high unit costs. The relevance of all the imported books is questionable but when funds are sourced through donors, these books are often sourced from the donors' countries. However, the ten countries in the study have all tried to do business with one another. When carrying out the pilot project shipments, the publishers and booksellers already had a working knowledge of the processes as they all tried to use them with varying degrees of success.

Ray Munamwimbu reported on the research carried out in Zambia. Zambia has population of 9.5 million with at least two million children at school. Although many of the books for schools and colleges are still imported, there is some growth in the local textbook industry — particularly at primary and, to a lesser extent, secondary level. The textbook situation was liberalised in 1991 and since then multinational publishers who had previously left, have returned and there is still unsatisfied demand in the schoolbook area.

Communication with other African countries is by road, rail or air. The physical infrastructure is in place but there are still limiting factors. DHL is the most reliable courier service but it is expensive. The post is much cheaper but it is unreliable, freight companies are cheaper still but there is a consolidation problem — they will not travel unless the truck is full — so it is only suitable for very large consignments. Also, there are no preferential postal rates for books in Zambia and with the enormous fluctuation in the value of the local currency the rates change frequently (upwards). There is no specific legislation about books and it is obvious that we need a national book policy to guide out legislators. The banking system offers a number of options for sending money out of the country and there are no problems in accessing foreign exchange.

There are also incentives to encourage small businesses, like no rates to begin with and so on. Export procedures are free and easy to manage.

Tsidi Moshoeshoe-Chadzingwa reported on the situation in Lesotho. The first people to do any publishing in Lesotho were the missionaries. Since they were not publishing for commercial purposes but rather to promote their religion, the infrastructure set up was never very sound commercially.

However, multinationals have now entered the scene and are concentrating on textbooks. They do not do much in the way of general trade or children's books as the market is so limited and the infrastructure for distribution is non-existent. Since Lesotho is so close to South Africa, publishers often publish in South Africa with Lesotho having only a 'skeleton' office. Lesotho tends to be obscured by South Africa.

The influence of APNET has already improved the situation in Lesotho as there has been greater exposure of books from Lesotho through APNET's promotional activities.

In conclusion, there is a great deal of invisible, informal and unregistered trade taking place in Africa because of the often cumbersome and time-consuming barriers governments have constructed against trade. This inevitably to the detriment of African governments. We need to be more creative in doing deals in Africa and take full advantage of some of the common elements in our cultures (rather than focusing on the differences).

A brief report on Botswana recounted the irony where a book written by a Botswana national is ultimately published by a multinational company and printed outside Botswana so it eventually appears in Botswana as an imported book. The publishing environment is not well developed. Taxes on royalties are between 30 and 45 per cent and, taking into account other taxes payable, the government ends up earning more than the author of the book! This is obviously a discouraging factor.

A brief report on Kenya revealed that there are 100 publishing companies in Kenya and also about 500 other companies involved in publishing materials. There are more than 200 booksellers. The main problem is how to market the books outside of Kenya. Transport costs are high but book fairs do provide a good opportunity to explore inter-African trade possibilities.

Malawi's publishing industry is in its infancy with very little knowledge about books and appropriate policies. Also, the existinmg trade in books that does exist is largely donor-driven.

In summary Ruth Makotsi suggested more trade should be encouraged in all forms — not just in printed books but using licensing, co-publishing, run-ons and joint ventures. Regions should start acting as a block — this is done very successfully in East Africa. APNET has made an impact on trade through their lobbying for recognition and deserves full support from all African publishers. Infrastructural problems need to be removed and governments need to develop sound national book policies. Reading needs to be promoted and the curricula widened. Banking facilities are adequate and although postal and shipping costs are high, the problems are not insurmountable.

Discussion Points
Group One: Policy

1   A participant asked for clarification of the relationship between the Zimbabwe Book Development Council and the publishers, the Curriculum Development Unit, government and the sources of funding. Miriam Bamhare explained that they were all stakeholders since the council's work complemented them. The council receives financial support from government and donors but the publishing industry itself does not contribute financially.

2   The question of conflicts was raised as there appeared to be divergent interests between promoting reading and promoting publishers. In response Miriam Bamhare agreed that the industry had not supported reading promotion and in practice, no common vision existed but the council's activities were not affected.

3   The possibility of the Zimbabwe Book Development Council at a later stage taking over some of the governmental functions was raised and Miriam Bamhare replied that government was already supportive. Certainly, some projects would need to be sustained, for example, once pilot projects like the Book Fund Project have been proved viable.

4   A Kenyan participant asked what the Zimbabwe Book Development Council had done to involve rural children and how successful this had been. Miriam Bamhare replied that the council reached them through schools and school libraries. Also, the Book Fund Project will reach a different audience. She commented that it was better to supply books to libraries than spend millions telling people to read.

5   Comments were made after Chukwuemeka Ike's presentation about the way relevant books do sell, so there is little truth in the myth of a lack of reading culture in this part of the world. This was supported by a participant from Botswana who pointed out the popularity of the *Pacesetter* series because the books reflect the lives of the readers.

6   A Botswana librarian asked what was being done about illiteracy in Nigeria. Chukwuemeka Ike replied that illiteracy rates are high and that there is a state agency to combat illiteracy funded by UNDP. Also, adult education centres exist but little is being done to meet the needs of new literates.

7   A Nigerian publisher pointed out that there are not enough bookshops in Nigeria. The people do read and buy books when they are easily available

but the distribution system is bad. So getting books to buyers remains the problem.

8 A Tanzanian participant said that Tanzania had similar problems since the infrastructure was rudimentary. How can they reach the people and especially those outside the school system? Chukwuemeka Ike suggested that the library needs to be integrated into the school system — just as the laboratory was integrated. The single textbook system needs to be replaced by the use of multiple books — creating a market for a variety of publishers.

9 A participant pointed out that we tend to confine ourselves to thinking about books but other stakeholders — those who package and distribute information, like television stations, newspapers, magazines and so on — may have something to contribute to the distribution issue.

10 An expatriate publisher and ex-teacher from Malawi said that there, the emphasis was on books for teachers. Shakespeare's plays were prescribed year after year but no copies were available except in the capital at an unaffordable price. Nevertheless people were very hungry for books, especially locally written, relevant material.

11 In conclusion Miriam Bamhare said that whoever promoted reading and books needed to ensure structures are in place to deliver them. Many stakeholders are not involved in the process — government, municipalities, families and church groups all needed to play their part, if too much was not to be left to too few. Finally, there was a political dimension — books for whom, for what purpose, for whose benefit?

12 In response to Mary Bugembe's presentation there was a discussion about the introduction of reading tents in other countries and how it had been popularized — for example, in Ghana it had led to a library being established and it had taken fire in Uganda. The reading tent idea had evolved into a mobile library in Nairobi which went out about four times a month to readers who could not otherwise access the books.

13 In response to Teresa Ibrahim's paper a participant commented that there are many displaced children who are not within reach of mainstream structures — street children and those out of the school system — and they should not be forgotten.

14 In summary, nine strategies for promoting children's books and reading development had been identified and documented: book fairs, book days and book weeks, book tents, mobile reading tents, mobile libraries, book festivals, books for the family, story telling and the involvement of the school system.

Group Two
Children's
Literature

25
Books and Children in Tanzania

ELIBARIKI A. MOSHI

The fact that it was necessary to establish a donor-funded Children's Book Project for Tanzania and that the project has continued into a second phase of five years says something about the publishing of children's books and the book trade as a whole in Tanzania. Publishing had been under government control for about 30 years and at the end of the 1980s the priority was to make textbooks available to schools.

This left the production of adult literature (we were meant to have a high literacy rate), general knowledge books and books for children unattended. Even the idea that children needed books other than textbooks was beginning to disappear.

In 1990, CODE (the Canadian Organization for Development through Education) conducted a survey to establish the feasibility of a Children's Book Project. This revealed the need for such a project and two objectives were identified: to produce books in Kiswahili for children to improve their reading abilities and to support and improve indigenous writers, illustrators, publishers, booksellers and printers.

The Children's Book Project for Tanzania was launched in January 1991 with enthusiastic support from publishers, booksellers, writers and illustrators who had long been frustrated. In its seven years the project has widened its objectives, in the absence of a national book council. The project has worked with publishers to produce about 130 children's titles. However, due to financial constraints few schools have received copies. Currently, a publisher of an approved book is obliged to produce 7,500 copies out of which the project purchases 5,000 and the publisher is expected to sell the remaining 2,500 copies in bookshops and other outlets.

Six schools in each of 117 districts on the mainland and Zanzibar receive six copies of each title. Each year each district selects another six schools to receive the books so that at the end of the fifth year 30 schools per district will have received some reading books. This is about 3, 500 (about one third) of the 11,000 primary schools in the country.

The project aims to re-kindle the desire to read and the appreciation of the importance of children's books other than textbooks. So the project has had to develop a national reading campaign. This is a new objective adopted after the first five years — once we had produced a good number of titles for children.

To conduct the National Reading Campaign the project visited Zimbabwe as guests of the Zimbabwe Book Development Council who explained their work in Zimbabwe. With the support of the International Reading Association (IRA), we also visited South Africa as guests of the READ Education Trust who are now our consultants on a Reading Pilot Project for six schools in Dar es Salaam and the Coastal Regions.

The project has received support from several donors and has adhered to good financial procedures. Our donors are SIDA, the Netherlands Government, NORAD and the International Reading Association (IRA).

We have planned and conducted several courses for illustrators, writers, publishers, editors and booksellers and arranged attachments for illustrators and editors in Kenya and Zimbabwe with the prime objective of improving the quality of books produced.

These efforts have borne fruit — the quality of books has improved so we are beginning to sell Kiswahili books in Kenya.

The gratifying thing about the project is the team spirit. We have a committed board of directors with members drawn from stakeholders — associations of authors, publishers, illustrators, booksellers, librarians and educationists. A technical committee known as the Children's Book Committee works closely with the executive secretary in implementing project activities.

The Children's Book Project came into being as a result of a need for children's reading books and to raise the performance of the book sector. It has made some progress but there is still need for more concerted work to achieve more — more books to reach more children and to build a reading culture beginning with the children.

26
The Children's Active Literature Project

GODFREY MOYO

An old man once told me that when the radio was first introduced in his village many years ago the people said they could hear the devil speaking. When television followed later, they said things had gotten worse, they now could not only hear his voice but see the devil's face as well. That is not a statement on television presenters, the majority of whom are wonderful people.

While everyone celebrated the advancement in technology the old man bemoaned the threat the electronic media posed to oral culture and the print media. Isn't it more fun to watch *Dallas* than to plough through Shakespeare, for instance? For many of us the choice is obvious.

However, used properly, the electronic media can become a tool to promote the culture of reading. It can be used to advertise books and indeed to promote reading for the sake of reading.

To develop children's literature and make it vibrant we need to create an environment that is conducive to books and reading. The question of promoting a culture of reading is broad but central to it is the economic situation of the nation. Someone who has only enough money in his pocket to buy a bag of mealie-meal will not opt instead for, for example, Marechera's *House of Hunger*. (Although this accomplished novel would satisfy literary hunger.)

The situation is more critical in the rural areas where libraries are rare and have very few books. Usually to be found in these libraries are books donated by a friendly foreign country whose language and culture is different.

Experts have said that indigenous languages play a crucial role during the formative years but in Zimbabwe, English is the most widely used language which has led people to feel that English stands for all that is superior.

Some years ago I was moved from being a reporter on a daily English newspaper to being the editor of a weekly paper that published in local languages. Before the end of the week, a concerned friend phoned to find out whether I had been demoted. Local languages are assigned such a lowly status that my friend did not think I was moving up in the world — despite the fact that I now had my own office and was in charge of a newspaper.

Until indigenous languages are accorded the status that they deserve, people will continue to suffer an identity crisis. Where is the democracy when vital matters of commerce, technology and other skills of survival are communicated in foreign languages? Maybe the task at hand is to give indigenous languages functional capability. It was refreshing to hear the Minister of Education, Sport and Culture say recently that it shall be the right of every child during the first years of education to learn in indigenous languages.

There is not enough reading material in local languages and publishers have been blamed for this but from a business point of view it is risky to invest in languages with a high illiteracy rate. If one walked through the stands at the book fair or through any bookshop in the city, it would be hard to find a book written in the vernaculars. Recently when an education minister received findings by a panel on how to formulate a comprehensive national language policy, he urged publishers to ensure the survival of indigenous languages.

He would be pleased to know that in Bulawayo the Children's Active Literature Project has dedicated the last three years to publishing books for children in their local languages. Also, we used to say: 'Publish books for children at affordable prices', but the cost of living proved us wrong.

When it comes to issues relating to children adults always speak for them but the Children's Active Literature Project, as its name suggests, actually involves children in the production of its books. The Zimbabwe Writers Union project (Bulawayo branch), initially funded by NORAD, has worked in close partnership with the NBU, a Norwegian union for children's authors who have been supportive and shared their experience generously.

The Children's Active Literature Project involves children, writers and illustrators in the creation of stories. An editorial team then takes over up to the production stage. The project has managed to publish five anthologies of folk tales, poetry, fiction and a picture book. Despite the difficulties in the trade and limited resources the project has had some success — some of the titles have even sold out. Our research has shown an alarming shortage of reading materials in local languages while demand is overwhelming.

The project has organized writing workshops for children who have included former 'street kids' now staying in a home. The workshops emphasized the importance of books and writing. At one such workshop children were asked to write on anything. It was remarkable that the children chose to write poetry rather than prose and that the favourite subject was that of death. Perhaps this spells the death of prose?

It is our moral duty to guard against the death of our indigenous languages by producing exciting literature for children in their own languages.

27
Reading Children

VIRGILIO S. ALMARIO

In 1995, in the introduction to his book *No Passion Spent*, George Steiner expressed for Western societies his own dark forebodings about the end of reading. He said:

> Mass culture, the economics of personal space and time, the erosion of privacy, the systematic suppression of silence in technological consumer cultures, the eviction of memory (of learning by heart) from school, entail the eclipse of the acts of reading, of the book itself.

He was referring to people who have no time to read in industrialized societies. And if they find time for leisure, it is spent on the latest diversions offered by modern technology. Nobody seems fascinated to discover what's inside the 'unopened book', to remember and to relish reading. Steiner himself was aghast to find that 75 per cent of adolescents in the US read against a background of blaring sound — from the radio, hi-fi or television.

Lack of reading materials is unknown in the US. Libraries full of books for all sorts of readers abound but the paradox is that Steiner feared for the 'eclipse of the acts of reading'.

In the Philippines, and most places in Africa, we cannot nurture reading because we do not have enough books or libraries. If we have libraries, they do not have books; and if they have books, the books are inappropriate.

We want to establish a culture of reading — to develop what most of our generation did not develop and to raise reading children who devote their free time to books. This is a big, though not impossible, task, notwithstanding the limited resources in our region.

The first step is be clear in our priorities and define the role of each member of society.

Books for all, all for books

Let us use, for example, producing enough books for children as a primary concern. It is difficult to start any reading education without books. It is doubly difficult to nurture the desire to read without a sustained supply of books and reading materials. But where do we get the finances? Many countries cannot even afford enough textbooks.

Let us begin with a plan — a national book production plan. This will tell us how best to use our limited resources, how to optimize available printing technology, and what kind of books to develop. Each step must consider the realities without losing sight of the needs of the children. Here are some pointers for the plan.

1   Control book imports
Foreign books open horizons and expand sensibilities but also bring in negative values. Limit imported books to those used in higher education and those which are impractical to produce locally. Continued dependence on imported books inhibits the development of a national book industry and local creativity.

2   Native is best
Children learn faster and more using their own language. Local talents are more sensitive to particular values and specific features of a national culture. Pride encourages writers and artists to be self-reliant and creative. A healthy book industry ultimately contributes to the stability of the national economy.

3   Let readers buy their own books
Parents and children must learn to buy their own books. Civic associations may be tapped to buy books for the most indigent communities. Subsidized prices or heavy discounts may be arranged for poor families. But a book becomes more valuable if it was paid for.

4   Produce affordable books
Supply affordable books. Any extra costs of production must be scrutinized and rationalized. Do we need full-colour inside? Must we import paper? Why not encourage the local paper company to improve the quality of its newsprint? Is local colour printing bad? Then, invest in young printers and send them to study modern printing techniques. Everything must boil down to the principle of selling cheap to sell more, which will mean reaching more readers and earning more.

Reading is a habit

When I started my children's book project, educators and businessmen told me I was wasting my time. 'The Filipinos do not like to read,' they said. Most developing nations in Asia and Africa are derided for being non-readers.

Reading is a habit. The child's liking for books is acquired and formed through a process of acculturation which must start at the earliest age possible. Thus, reading should not be taught only in school. In fact, this is too late — it must begin at home and be nurtured continuously and in co-operation with the community and institutions other than the school.

The second step is knowing the role of each member of society. Parents should buy books and be readers themselves in the eyes of their children. They do not have to build a home library. A few shelves for a modest selection will be enough. Providing a table or a corner for reading is ideal.

For those parents who cannot afford books, community libraries or the improvement of school library services is essential. These libraries are almost always unavailable in poor communities in Asia and Africa. Also, a child's interest in reading can still be awakened despite the absence of books in the home. One simple but effective way is storytelling. With or without a book, there is nothing more divine than a parent cuddling a child to narrate a folktale, an anecdote or a short bit of history.

Storytelling is not just a traditional way of transferring information, it is a means of showing affection. More importantly, it motivates the child to dream, to want to discover things and to ask questions which are preparation for reading.

The worst that could happen is a home's insensitivity to the child's desire to read. A couple who spend most of their time playing cards or a child who grows up in front of the television are not good beginnings for nurturing the love of reading.

Of course, there are exceptions. Many of us are exceptions — we did not grow up in a good environment for reading.

So, intensify the promotion of books and reading. Spend more money to advertise books and campaign about the importance of reading. Do not presume that people like to read and just do not have the capacity to buy books. A lot of the so-called 'poor' have money for their vices but will not save part of it for books. They must be convinced about the value of buying books for themselves and their children. Use all available avenues for selling books, convene more seminars, spend more on book launchings, ask celebrities to endorse books, organize bigger fairs, be more creative, and market books like pushing dope in the streets. Addiction to books will save the children from drugs, after all!

28
Unlearning Discrimination
The Early Years

BABETTE BROWN

Why am I, a white South African woman living in Britain (since 1963), writing about unlearning discrimination and why in a session on children's literature? For the past eleven and a half years I have been the Co-ordinator of the Early Years Trainers Anti-Racist Network which is a small but influential organization. I have also written a recently published book, *Unlearning Discrimination in the Early Years*.

Most British children between three and six years have been influenced by racism, sexism and other forms of discrimination. They express negative attitudes and feelings of superiority whether or not they have personal contact with, for example, black families, disabled people, people who wear different clothes or who speak foreign languages. Here are some examples.

In a nursery school in Manchester Jessica (three and a half) points at the new and only black doll and says to her teacher, 'That doll shouldn't be in the home corner. She's dirty and she smells'.

Tandi (five and a half) uses a wheelchair and Leroy (four) won't play with her because, 'She's a baby in a pram and I don't play with babies'.

Two four year olds ask Nandini, 'Why do you talk that funny language? Why don't you talk properly, like us?'

Young children use stereotypes even though they have no personal experience of the group they are stereotyping.

> Mary and Jean (eight) were working on the computer in the school library. Mary asked Jean to lend her ten pence so she could buy some crisps. Jean refused.
>
> Mary retorted, 'Oh you mean f . . . Jew. Stop jewing me.'
>
> The librarian intervened, 'What was that you said?'
>
> Mary stammered, 'Oh sorry, Miss! I didn't see you there. Don't tell I said that.'
>
> 'Said what?' the librarian asked.
>
> 'The f . . . word' was the reply.
>
> 'Do you know any Jews?' the librarian asked.
>
> 'No', they both said.

Young children also learn what society considers is the 'right' way to be a boy or a girl. Glenda MacNaughton recorded the following observation in an Australian nursery school:

> Brian and Rachid (five) were building a garage with bricks. Brian used gestures and language to tell Rachid where to place the bricks. Rachid placed each as directed. A Vietnamese girl, Soon Lee (five), approached them and asked if she could play too. Brian lifted a brick and waved it in the air and shouted: 'No bloody wog girls here!' Rachid imitated Brian's actions and words. Soon Lee ran off crying to the teacher.

Brian and Rachid had learnt that to be a boy means yelling and threatening girls and not letting them play. And Soon Lee was learning that she was being excluded from boys' games, not only because she was a girl but also because she was Vietnamese.

But activities can encourage young children to see themselves and each other through different eyes and to learn from one another. This activity was tried out by a teacher in a school in the UK:

> The children were asked to draw their very own dream ship in which they could travel wherever they wanted to. The teacher explained they should draw it so that everyone could see what was inside it — like a doll's house with the front opened. Not surprisingly, the boys drew guns and radar as well as engines or sails on their ships. One boy drew a fridge with beer in it. The girls concentrated on the living quarters, papering the walls, providing kitchens with appliances and food and one girl even drew a sick bay. The pictures were then put on the wall for the children to look at. During the ensuing discussion the boys poured scorn on the girls because none of them had provided their ships with engines and one had given hers wheels. They stopped laughing when it was pointed out that they would have had a very uncomfortable voyage because there was nowhere to sit or sleep in their ships and there was no food or drink so they would have died of hunger and thirst.

Many children's books reflect the attitudes and values of British society and shower children with blatant and subtle, verbal and non-verbal discriminatory messages. There are still too many books which feature positive white characters and images and which ignore the existence of black people or portray them negatively. But a growing number of authors, illustrators and publishers are producing books in which the central characters are powerful black adults and children, refugees, girls and women, disabled adults and children.

Books that encourage children to identify with characters who have been treated unfairly can encourage them to stand up for what they think is right and actively challenge discrimination. Even young children understand the concept of fairness — we've all heard the cry, 'It's not fair!'

As authors, publishers, parents and teachers, we need to empathize with children — by trying to remember how we felt when we were very young we can put ourselves more effectively into their shoes. We can then write, publish and select books that 'talk' to them.

Books such as *Someone Else* by Kathryn Cave, illustrated by Chris Riddel, confront important issues sensitively and appropriately:

> On a windy hill alone with nothing to be friends with lived Something Else. He knew that was what he was because everyone said so. If he tried to sit with them or walk with them or join in their games they always said: 'Sorry. You're not like us. You're something else. You don't belong.'
>
> Something Else did his best to be like the others. He smiled and said, 'Hi!' like they did. He painted pictures. He played their games when they let him. He brought his lunch in a paper bag like theirs. It was no good. He didn't look like them. He didn't see the things they saw. He didn't play the way they played. As for his packed lunches, 'You don't belong here', they said. 'You're not like us. You're something else.'
>
> Something Else went home. When he was getting ready for bed, there was a knock on the door. Something was standing on the doorstep. 'Hi there!' it said. 'Great to meet you. Can I come in?'
>
> 'Excuse me?' said Something Else.
>
> 'You're welcome', said the creature. It stuck out a paw, or maybe a flipper.
>
> Something Else looked at the paw. 'I think you've come to the wrong place', he said.
>
> The creature shook its head, 'No, I haven't. This place is perfect. Look!' And before Something Else realized what was happening, it walked right in.
>
> 'Do I know you?' asked Something Else, puzzled.
>
> 'Know me?' The creature laughed. 'Of course you do! Take a good look. Go on!' He walked round the creature from front to back or back to front. He didn't know what to say, so he didn't

say anything. 'Don't you see?' the creature cried. 'I'm just like you! You're something else, and I'M ONE TOO!' It stuck out its paw again and smiled. Something Else was too surprised to smile back. He didn't take the paw either.

'Like me?' he said. 'You're not like me. In fact, you're not like anything I've ever seen. I'm sorry, but you're definitely not MY sort of something else.' He walked to the door and opened it. 'Goodnight'.

The creature put down its paw, slowly. 'Oh', it said. It looked sadder and smaller. It reminded Something Else of something but he couldn't think what.

While he was trying to remember, the creature left. Then Something Else remembered. 'Wait!' he cried. 'Don't go!' He ran after the creature as fast as he could. When he caught up, he grabbed its paw and held on tight. 'You're not like me, BUT I DON'T MIND. You can stay with me if you'd like to.

And the creature did.

From then on, Something Else had Something to be friends with. They smiled and said, 'Hi!' to each other. They painted pictures. They played each other's games, or tried to. They ate their lunches side by side. And when something turned up that really WAS weird-looking, they didn't say he wasn't like them and he didn't belong there. They moved right up and made room for him too.'

In the book, something that really was weird-looking was a little boy.

We have a responsibility to encourage children to unlearn the stereotypes, prejudices and misconceptions that they have absorbed:

One morning Pauline and a group of black and white three and four year olds were enjoying story time in a nursery school in London. At the end of the session Pauline asked them what they would like to do next.

Emily:	Let's play Cinderella.
Pauline:	That's a good idea. Can I be Cinderella?
Emily:	No you can't.
Pauline:	Why not?
Emily:	Because you're black.
Pauline:	Why can't I be Cinderella because I'm black?
Emily:	'Cause Cinderella is white in my storybook and on my video.

Emily made a judgement based on her own experience. During the discussion that followed Pauline told Emily she was right — all the Cinderellas she had ever seen were white. But she helped Emily and the others to realize that Cinderella and all the characters in the story could as easily be black as white.

She later read them the book, *Amazing Grace*, by Mary Hoffman. Grace, a little black girl, loves listening to stories and acting them out. One day her teacher tells the class they are going to do the play *Peter Pan*. Grace wants to be Peter Pan but her friends tell her she can't because she's a girl and Peter isn't black. Feeling upset, Grace tells her Granny who convinces her she can do anything that she really wants to. At the audition she is the best Peter Pan and she gets the part.

The children loved this story and Pauline encouraged them to talk about their feelings and about the things they have done and the things they would like to do.

She could also have read them the story of *Mufaro's Beautiful Daughters* who react very differently to the king's search for a wife — the one aggressively and selfishly, and the other kindly and gently. This beautifully illustrated book is dedicated to the children of South Africa.

This is what President Nelson Mandela said when he accepted the Nobel Peace Prize in 1993:

> Children are the most valuable citizens in any society and the greatest of our treasures.

And from his summary of the first year of the Nelson Mandela Children's Fund 1996:

> There can be no keener revelation of a society's soul than the way in which it treats its children.

29
Tell Me about My Picture
Reading to Deaf Children — Learning from Deaf Adults

MARIA CHISWANDA

S tudy after study has confirmed that children who are read to from an early age develop reading skills earlier and at a higher level than their peers who do not have this advantage. Yet too often hearing teachers and parents do not read to deaf children because they do not know how to do so. Pictures, gestures, signs and drawings are children's own resource for the transition to representing their ideas in print. Deaf people are visually oriented and sign language is capable of expressing every idea, action and emotion.

There is little known about the reading achievement of deaf children in Zimbabwe. However, research elsewhere shows that deaf children have difficulty in reading. It is obvious that deaf children from hearing families will demonstrate specific difficulties in the process of achieving literacy.

Background

I am working with deaf adults in a small pilot project. One of them is mother to a deaf child. The deaf children I work with are between two and six years old They vary in their concentration on pictures but are interested in visual representations. They are mainly on Well's (1987) performative level of literacy.

Research on reading development
in severely and profoundly deaf children

Researchers have found that deaf children slow down in their reading at about eight years old. The causes for the low reading level and the difficulties in reading have been connected to a lack of fluency in the first language — sign language — by some and to the poor strategies used by hearing adults with deaf children by others.

For hearing children, learning to read involves abilities they have already exercised in understanding language at home or making sense of the visual world. Hearing children will see a picture and give it its label and for deaf children of deaf parents this would also apply. However, what happens to deaf children of non-signing hearing parents might be different. Children who understand spoken language and can distinguish between objects visually have already demonstrated sufficient language, visual acuity and learning ability to learn to read. About 90 per cent of deaf children are born to hearing mothers and developing communication between them and consequently the first language is not smooth (Meadow-Orlans, 1990).

Deaf adults use manual visual modality to communicate with deaf children. In addition, forms of communication such as non-manual expressions, eye contact and body posture assist the deaf adult and child to achieve meaningful interaction. Whether the deaf child uses signed language or communicates orally (through speech and speech-reading) the child will be predisposed to depend on visual cues. Bornstein (1989) concludes that it is therefore incumbent upon the deaf adult to visually focus the child's attention and, in turn, to attend to the visual signals from the child.

Based on the above, deaf parents and signing adults who are effective storytellers are said to demonstrate strategies that promote early reading in deaf children. The deaf adults use techniques that include appropriate visual attention and eye-gaze (tapping the child for attention) and signing only when joint attention is established (Scaife and Bruner, 1975). Bruner (1976), for instance, reported that joint attention to objects on the part of parent and child, along with the ability to hand objects back and forth (turn-taking), are pre-linguistic processes in the establishment of linguistic reference, a critical factor in narrative literacy. Adjusting sign placement (holding the child's hand and placing it on the appropriate place on the body) is another technique used.

Deaf adults demand that deaf children look at them as they sign/read (joint visual attention). They also model the deaf children's initiatives and signs (contingent responsiveness). Older children (four to six years) were encouraged to turn the pages when the adult stopped signing (turn-taking). They were keen to do this before the adult had finished reading. We also let them turn the pages if they insisted and only resumed after they had satisfied their curiosity. At some stages a child requested signs for the pictures in the sequence.

Researchers such as Bellugi (1988) and Bouvet (1990) propose that signing adults are successful readers to deaf children because it is easier for deaf children to recall (short term memory) manually and visually represented information than speech.

Encouraging the emerging literacy of deaf children

The children's reactions to newspaper pictures, child-adult made picture books, children's own drawings and magazines help in learning about deaf children's reading development. These visually-rich materials help them link signed language and the variety of forms in which ideas can be represented.

Family pictures were another source of interest. We used the pictures to find out at what stage the child could identify self and other familiar people. When the child did that, the deaf adult showed sign-names for the identified members of the family to encourage the use of names.

The deaf adult helped the deaf child to read pictures right side up and pointed at features that were recognizable as the top and bottom of the picture. Looking at pictures from left to right was done by modelling to the child.

Using pictures to understand feelings

Emotions are very difficult to explain — deaf adults work with deaf children using pictures to encourage understanding of feelings. In the video shown at the Indaba, the deaf adult pantomimed moods and the action in a given picture and encouraged the deaf child to imitate her. Developing reading and writing skills of deaf children effectively also requires creativity in bringing out the nuances of sounds, such as a dog barking or cock crowing to have the deaf child experience the story represented on paper. Another activity derived from pictures was identifying the moods of characters then drawing them. The deaf adult gave the sign for the moods.

Appreciating print

Children who were encouraged to trace drawings and letters eventually showed an interest in scribbling under (labelling) their drawings. The adult talked about the children's picture, expanded on it and gave sign vocabulary. One of the activities (on the video) done by the deaf mother was giving the deaf child the ZimSign alphabet and now and then manually helping the child to get the correct hand-shape. The children tried to represent the same ideas through scribblings which served as labels. The feedback that children receive about their writing (scribblings) gives them impetus to keep going and to improve. Sometimes the child asked the adult to write under the pictures or drawings. The deaf adult modelled by printing the label correctly.

Sharing experiences through pictures (deaf culture)

A feature that emerges when reading with deaf children using the visual modality at this early age is shared experiences. This may not happen naturally between the hearing adult and child. Children brought in photos or used drawings of family members or of special significance to make photo biographies. We stuck pictures on cards and wrote (following their signing). We are hoping to develop a sequence of activities that promote concept acquisition and literacy in deaf children through visual arts. One of the activities in progress is making a cumulative portfolio of pictures on which children can build various concepts like time, the weather, emotions, and so on.

Conclusion

Many deaf children lack the first language on which hearing children rely for developing reading and writing skills. Deaf adults provide models of the first language for the deaf children and can also model strategies that promote literacy in children. In the early reading development, visual arts accompanied by interaction through the visual modality could initiate literacy positively with deaf children. Most of all, reading to a deaf child demands that the adult shares the experience represented on paper, whether it be pictures or text.

References

Bellugi U. (1988), 'The Acquisition of Spatial Language', in K.F. Kessel (ed.), *The Development of Language and Language Research: Essays in Honour of Roger Brown*, Lawrence Erlbum Associates, Hillsdale, New Jersey.

Bornstein M.H. (1989), 'Between Caretakers and Their Young: Two Modes of Interaction and Their Consequences for Cognitive Growth', in M.H. Bornstein and J. Bruner (eds.), *Interaction in Human Development*, Lawrence Erlbum Associates, Hillsdale, New Jersey.

Bouvet D. (1990), *The Path to Language: Bilingual Education for the Deaf Children*, Multilingual Matters, New York.

Bruner J. (1976), 'Learning How Things Work with Words', in J. Bruner and A. Garton, *Human Growth and Development*, Oxford University Press, Oxford.

Meadow-Orlans K.P. (1990), 'Research on Developmental Aspects of Deafness', in D.F. Moores and K.P. Meadow-Orlans (eds), *Educational and Developmental Aspects of Deafness*, Gallaudet University Press, Washington DC.

Scaife M. and J. Bruner (1975), 'The Capacity for Joint Attention in the Infant', *Nature* 253: 265-266.

Wells G. (1987), 'The Learning of Literacy', in B. Filleoni, C. Hedley and E. Dimanrtino (eds), *Home School: Early Language and Reading*, Albex, Norwood, New Jersey.

30
Children's Books from South to North

HELENE SCHAR

S ince the beginning of European children's literature in the 18th century, novels and stories about people and societies from Africa, Asia and Latin America are among the most frequent subjects. Adventure books reflecting the conquests and experiences of the colonizers were glorified. It was important that the Europeans were portrayed as heroes and that the colonized people had a lot to learn from these heroes. In this fashion the children were obliged to strengthen their spiritual and nationalistic feelings.

The people from Africa, Asia and Latin America were often portrayed badly and condemned wholesale. Racist thoughts were thus encouraged. These clichés are still here today and they are deeply embedded and resurfacing in northern societies at this time possibly even through the influence of these books.

So-called colonial novels gave place to missionary stories, where the missionary brought the undeveloped people the right religion — the only way to be good and civilized. Civilizing them was the privilege of the Europeans. Later on in the line of secularization, novels about development aid to the colonized were produced. New techniques were introduced by Europeans emphasizing to children the importance of European standards. Again, they underlined the necessity of helping people from undeveloped regions to achieve development. Obviously, the so described cultures were never shown at the same level as Europeans were.

Until 1970 most of the books published clearly gave precedence to European thinking, knowledge and deeds. Often the European and North American authors still hold this position today.

During the 1970s when students in Europe went out into the streets and fought for a new order and a critical awareness, children's literature took a new orientation. The child had to be considered as an individual with his own will, needing to be developed without repression. Such thoughts have been reflected in children's books.

For the first time, research has shown that Eurocentrism in children's books causes racism. Children's books were systematically investigated through the images they transmitted, as to how the African, Asian and Latin American people were portrayed to the European child. The Council of Inter-racial Books for Children in New York and the Berne Declaration, a Swiss development organization founded in these times, established criteria by which these books could be assessed.

Through the analysis of these books, it was realized in the early 1980s that more than 90 per cent of all recommended books were written by European or North American authors about Africa, Asia and Latin America. This has been so since the beginning of European children's literature in the Age of Enlightenment. Children's books have always mirrored the society. It was obvious that experiences of new journeys, explorations and discoveries were reflected and the colonizing and Christianizing movements were well detailed.

Today what the European child reads about Africa, is about nature, about animals and white adventurers. If African people appear they live in poverty, they suffer hunger, distress and war troubles. On the other hand nearly every boy and man plays the drum and all females dance and there still exists strange and fearful superstition and witchcraft. All Africans live in rural areas. Very seldom do books show an African city life. Mass media helps to cement these impressions.

This perception has persuaded the Baobab Children's Books Fund that books, for example, from Africa, written by African authors reflect in a more spontaneous and original way the culture and the daily life of children and adults. Such an approach can help to diminish clichés and prejudices accumulated in the last 200 years and can help to promote understanding between peoples. The reader will have to face up to unfamiliar situations that may help him learn that there are different ways of living, all as valuable as his own.

That was the reason for the start of the Baobab Children's Books series with only authors from Africa, Asia and Latin America. With these books we aim to demonstrate that there is a children's literature from the developing countries worth being discovered and read also in Europe.

Nevertheless, the books do not sell as well as books from European and North American authors. In the literature for adults this has changed in the last 20 years. But in children's literature the educational and pedagogical aims of the Age of Enlightenment prevent experimentation and remain an economic and a moral handicap.

We can distinguish three different specific points to reflect about:

1   The fixed images of European readers

2   The economic situation of publishing and competition in the market
3   The expectation of critics and readers.

1   The fixed images of European readers

In my 18 years' experience in the field of children's books, topics about Africa, Asia and Latin America are expressed in fixed images which have persisted when it comes to writing about foreign cultures and societies since the beginning of children's literature. This is one of the main reasons for the reluctance in accepting texts from African, Asian or Latin American authors by Europeans. People are used to listening to the same expressions and are used to hearing about children that are actually European children in a foreign scene.

Since all these stories are told by Northern authors using their own cultural perspectives, and since they always interpret the values of foreign societies with their own perspective, readers are influenced to learn in a specific way about the life and customs of other societies. Often the descriptions give more about the authors than about the people in question. So most of the books about Africa, Asia and Latin America are still Eurocentric.

2   The economic situation of publishing and competition in the market

In addition to these circumstances, children's literature from Africa in Europe has no lobby. European authors have strong publishing houses and agents behind them that influence publishers or booksellers.

Children's literature from Africa needs a well functioning agency network. In Europe and North America this has worked for years. Books circulate across one border to another. It would be very helpful if this network could work in Africa so one country would know about well-written books from another country. Some steps in this direction have been taken between Zimbabwe and Kenya. It should be developed also among East Africa and West Africa with translations from French to English and vice versa.

If this can be developed it might be easier for African books for children to circulate also in the North.

The title *Adventure with Little White Man* written by Meja Mwangi from Kenya, for instance, has not sold as well as a highly awarded book written by a European author. This has nothing to do with the literary quality of the book but with the commercial relations between different publishing houses.

The Baobab series started with a very small unknown publisher in the children's book market. He was the only one prepared to start such a risky project as the Baobab series was in the eyes of all German children's books publishers. This situation after ten years of Baobab series has now changed. We could move over to a quite well-known publishing house for children's books and our books are better known and sold in bookshops.

Also, an already established children's author has more chance of publishing a book about foreign cultures that will sell well. Authors with difficult names (for a European) are hard to remember which makes the bookseller suspicious. Meja Mange's *Adventure with Little White Man* has been given the highest award that a children's book in Germany can get, yet he remains an unknown author — despite having written several books for adults that have been translated into German. His children's books have never had the same success that they would have had if the author was a European.

3 The expectation of critics and readers

Books from Africa are more rigorously criticized than ones from Europe. Very often publishing houses and critics question the credibility of the authors — the same people never have this scepticism when Northern authors write about Africa. They blindly believe that a European author has done his research.

Also, books from other cultures have to give much more information, for example *Chen Danyan, Nine Lives — Yumoto Kayumi, Kgespensterschatten/ Shadows of Spirits*.

It is unclear what is expected from African authors — exotic settings and information, unknown things but not too strange or too common things. At present, books from southern continents still require special support.

It still needs a specially interested group to convince people that books written by African authors for children can be good literature and help towards a better understanding of other cultures, generating more tolerance, respect and enrichment. Attitudes need to change so that books from the South can sit easily on the shelf among books from European and North American authors.

31
Selling African Children's Literature
Some practical experiences in Europe

CLAUDIA STEIN

I am at the Frankfurt Book Fair, trying to convince somebody of the quality of African (and Asian and Latin American) children's literature, earnestly suggesting a choice of promising titles I have read recently.

Those who haven't refused a meeting from the beginning, arguing that apart from books by German authors, they only publish licences from Scandinavia and the US ('Why don't you try Peter Hammer Verlag, they always do this kind of third-world stuff'), turn the pages of my list with a laconic smile, telling me this one is too short, animal-stories or traditional tales — no way; and the quality of those illustrations can't compete with German ones, but thank you anyway, we will have a closer look and let you know . . .

Change of scene: still at Frankfurt Book Fair, talking to an African publisher, trying to explain what kind of book I'm looking for, what might fit the German market: the story should take place in the present, young readers should find out about how youngsters live in other countries. The chances of selling fairy tales or animal stories are remote. And — this is very important — short stories are out of the question — no German publisher wants to publish short stories.

The publisher gives a sympathetic nod. He turns to his books and takes out some, telling me, well, they have this interesting short story collection and these excellent traditional tales — mostly animal stories, and they are all good, especially the one about the hare and the lion/turtle/hippo . . .

'Oh yes,' I answer, 'this is very interesting but don't you have anything set in the present, talking about people and not about animals and a longer text, no short stories, maybe a novel for young adults?'

'Well,' he answers, 'we have this very interesting collection of detective stories here.'

'I see.' I start losing patience. 'Well I think I'll take your catalogue to have closer look and let you know if I find anything.'

A minute later, I'm standing in the corridor, asking myself what am I doing here and who the heck had the idea of paying somebody for a job that absurd — trying to sell African children's literature to German publishers, trying to put things together which can't compete because they're so different in form, conventions, expectations and humour. Maybe I should stop trying to square the circle and leave.

Excuse the cynicism, but this is the dilemma I have. In spite of this description, in which I spoke about extreme cases, I do think it's worth trying. I will try to analyze which genuine difficulties arise when matching African children's literature with German market demands, and which result from prejudices and lack of creativity, flexibility and open-mindedness.

About the difficulties of selling African children's literature to the German market

Real problems
— Editorial conventions

One of the main reasons why many African children's books are not considered by German publishers is that the texts are too short for their editorial conventions. Sometimes publishers even reject texts they like a lot because they don't fit their overall scheme.

Collecting several texts in an anthology is out of the question because 'anthologies don't sell'. This may be fact or a persisting myth but it seems to be an unbreakable law.

— Expectations/motivation to publish a book from Africa

Even if the average German children's book publisher has better financial means than the comparable African one, any translated book represents an additional financial risk. There has to be a good reason to run that risk. One thing that German publishers expect from an African book they want to translate is that it informs about cultural or political characteristics. (Something which is not expected from Scandinavian or American books which usually sell because of their story line or theme.)

— Different sense of humour due to a different cultural background

Books may be difficult to sell because of a different sense of humour. An example is *Les Confidences de Médor*, a novel for young adults by Micheline Coulibaly from the Ivory Coast. In this novel, a dog tells the story of his wealthy human family which has recently moved to a hot-spot neighbourhood in Abidjan and which desperately tries to build up a European life-style. At first, a number of German publishers were interested but they all rejected it, arguing that the dog's perspective was too naive. I'm not sure if this is true or whether Europeans are simply not emancipated enough to laugh about Africans trying to act like Europeans — after all, they are also confronted with a caricature of themselves.

— Illustrations

The printing quality, far below European standards, is partly responsible for the slim chance of African illustrators being published in Europe. In addition, German publishers are conservative. French publishers, for example, are more open-minded — in French publishing conventions, it is not a problem to publish a relatively short text with full colour illustrations even for older children or young adults. There might be a better chance of getting something published there than in Germany.

The 1999 Bologna exhibition of African illustrations will help to make them more popular in Europe and also create new styles and standards in illustrations for the African market.

Excuses

— Fear of the 'unknown'

Publishers argue that African (or Asian or Latin American) books are too strange for young German readers, and that they wouldn't be able to identify with the world described. Strangely, nobody bothers about how strange books from Scandinavia or the US may be.

This aspect of 'strangeness' is overstated by adults. In their book about the 'unknown' in children's and young adults' literature, Hurrelmann and Richter state that children don't pay any attention to whether the book they are reading comes from England, Germany, Sweden or Brazil. According to them, there is always an inherent strangeness because children's literature in general mediates between the world of children and the world of adults (Hurrelmann and Richter, 1998).

If young people do notice 'strange' elements (foreign names or languages, different religions and so on), these have a generally positive connotation for young readers who are curious about 'strange worlds'.

Another excuse is that publishers claim they are unable to judge African literature on account of their lack of experience. The only answer is that they should use exactly the same criteria as for any other book, whether German, American or Japanese: the literary quality is what counts. Nobody ever asked a publisher to publish an African book out of pity — something which should be prevented rather than promoted.

— Language and communication problems

In the case of Latin American children's literature, the fact that publishers normally don't read Spanish or Portuguese is a problem because they have to pay for freelance reviewers, and they have to trust their opinion.

As most African children's books are written in English (which every publisher is able to read) or French (which quite a lot of publishers read), it is unlikely that language problems are responsible for the small number of African children's books published. A more probable reason might be the fear of communication problems: people fear long delays in the post and are usually unaware that African publishers are quite advanced in electronic communication — sometimes more so than European ones.

Recommendations and propositions

What African publishers should do
— Inclusion of the actual environment in African children's literature
Many African children's book authors, like Ifeoma Okoye from Nigeria or Genga Idowu from Kenya, postulate that the actual environment (social, political and so on) should play a bigger role in children's literature. (This is something that would at the same time meet the needs of African children and the expectations of the European market.)

A sign that more authors correspond to those needs and write more about current topics is the number of new African children's books talking about handicapped children, like Meshack Asare's story about a handicapped boy saving his village from a flooding (1988) or the stories about an albino boy or a deaf and dumb girl who frustrates the terrible plan of a witch to steal the smiles of all the children, published by Nouvelles Editions Ivoiriennes.

Even traditional tales could be more adapted to the actual environ ment of children — as in their oral form they often are.

As Genga Idowu pointed out in her *Bookbird* article (1998), the transition from oral to written form often results in a loss of quality. It is difficult to write down a traditional tale, keeping its charm. Not all people are writers, just because they write down the tales their grandmother told them by the fireside.

An example of good traditional tales is Charles Mungoshi's *Stories of a Shona Childhood*, published in the Swiss Baobab series which is a success in Germany.
— Networking and co-productions
A very promising development is the networking between French and English speaking African countries initiated by APNET and several language editions

like those by Nouvelles Editions Ivoiriennes. Co-productions allow better quality printing for picture-books.

What African publishers should avoid
— Over-adaptation to the European market
There is the danger of losing sight of the main aim of African children's literature: writing and producing for the needs of African children, not for the European market. In this context, Genga Idowu talks about profit driven publishing by companies that produce for the overseas market. However, this does offer finances to be invested into books for African children.
— Over-adaptation to the aims of western non-governmental organizations
There is another danger, less obvious and almost more serious: over-adapting to meet the aims of western non-governmental organizations, guided by political correctness and good will.

Employees of western non-governmental organizations often have a clear-cut image of what African children's books should look like. Talking to a publisher from Mali at the Bologna book fair, I told him how excellent I found this one new Malian picture-book series in the Bambara language and full-colour print. 'They are indeed very nice', he answered 'but there will never be any market for them, because people who can afford them live in the city and don't speak or use Bambara, and the kids in the villages who really speak Bambara are so poor they can consider themselves lucky if their parents can buy schoolbooks for them at least, which is not usually the case.'

There are many similar examples of well-intended projects leading to such senseless results or lost chances because the money could have been spent on a more useful project.

So, coming back to the initial scene, standing in the corridor of Frankfurt Book Fair, it is worthwhile my going to my next appointment and finding German publishers for African children's literature isn't that absurd after all.

32
African Children's Books in France
Distributing, Translating and Publishing

MARIE LAURENTIN

For almost a century, Africa has inspired children's books in France — a France strongly marked by its colonial past and its privileged relationships with numerous countries. A deeper study shows that if Africa is present in this way in children's books, it is essentially as an inspiration not as an author *per se*. (Except for the importance of traditional African tales which deserve special analysis.) But is African children's literature present in France today? We need to look back at history.

About the 1950s, a non-academic literature began to be published through a few African publishers. (Written works from religious missions were published earlier but with localized circulation). This literature emerged in the 1960s, during the first years of decolonization, undoubtedly stimulated by the development of education. But the number of titles was still low.

Up to the 1990s, publication was stagnant but now children — a large percentage of the population — have more access to education and books, and libraries — whatever their category — are essential in familiarizing children with written works other than school texts.

Despite their prohibitive cost, children's books are becoming more accessible. Book professionals are responding to the demand for African publications by Africans for African children.

Over the last six years, more titles for French-speaking children have been produced — the census for 1998 gives about 100 new titles, excluding publications in national languages which are also on the increase.

However, these books do not yet enjoy wide circulation in the Northern countries and more particularly, in France.

The distribution of African books in France

African books have limited distribution in France, even though the situation has improved. Potential distributors do not succeed, maybe because they do not believe in the product or there are too many practical difficulties. As for African publishers, they may not realize the importance of exporting their books or consider it too cumbersome.

A specialized bookseller-distributor

The bookseller-distributor Menaibuc is the only one who offers a catalogue of African titles. His privileged markets are libraries, book exhibitions and other cultural events. His service is now widely known.

Book exhibitions

Book exhibitions do allow the public, often in great numbers, to purchase written works from other countries. Thematic choices, or according to countries, can be exploited, like at the Children's Book Show (Montreuil), the Paris Book Show and the International Children's Book Fair of Bologna.

Some specialized shows like 'La Plume Noire' (literature from Africa), the Maghreb, Festafrica (Lille) and the Limoges Francophony Festival are meeting points at which the public — very demanding and very open — expects discoveries and the possibility of buying or getting to know what is not available elsewhere. Every effort is made to sell on those occasions.

Bookshops

Because of the lack of infrastructure and distribution, bookshops who take the initiative are most qualified to offer 'rare' books. Their approach is often militant (L'Harmattan), but this often pays off because the books they promote, ignored most of the time, arouse much interest. They can then identify books which were judged interesting and build up a stock.

Catalogues

A promising new initiative which is only limited by the number of titles distributed ,is a publishing house specializing in publications for Africa — African Classics. Their 1998 catalogue carries a selection of children's books published in Africa including titles from Akoma Mba Publishing of Cameroon, Les Nouvelles Editions Africaines from Senegal, the Cultural Centre of Niger, Edilis of Côte d'Ivoire and Haho of Togo. This initiative has had encouraging results so far (300 books sold in one month).

The direct order to the African publishers

This remains a last resort as with limited numbers and cumbersome procedures, it is not worthwhile. However, it functions in a satisfactory if minimal way.

Public libraries

The role of public libraries is indispensable in France because they often provide the only access to specialized books. They are indeed in tune with their public, generally well informed and able to guide readers. Their contribution as a buyer is also not insignificant.

The intercultural sector of Joy through Books

As a specialized documentation centre on the African children's books, we analyze, in particular through the magazine *Takam tikou*, all the French or bilingual African books. From this systematic survey, we develop bibliographies and thematic selections, market the books and organize days of study on a particular theme. It is an indirect contribution but essential to get the books known.

Translations

French translations of African children's books come exclusively from anglophone African countries (none from lusophone countries). Texts in national languages are not usually translated although they are sometimes published simultaneously with the French version.

Translations generally deal only with novels. The 'bravest' in this field is L'Ecole des Loisirs (School of Leisure Activities) — publishers recognized for their role in expanding children's literature and who carry a good number of translated works from famous African authors like Norman Silver from South Africa, Simi Bedford from Nigeria and Tsitsi Dangarembga from Zimbabwe. Also, a title by Meja Mwangi is published by L'Harmattan (a Kenyan author first published in Germany in English!). Two books by the South African author Sheila Gordon are published by Gallimard. Hachette has published a book from Beverly Naidoo of South Africa. Lastly, very recently, the Museum Dapper Publishing Company (specializing in African Art) just launched a collection of novels by an author from Ghana. The autobiography of Nelson Mandela is also represented at the Ecole des Loisirs.

An African Publishing House in Côte d'Ivoire, Les Nouvelles Editions Africaines has translated and published a Kenyan author, R. Ole Kulet. For all these examples, the quality of the texts is all important.

Beside the translations of novels (essentially for children about 12 years old), one should also quote the translations of a few tales and albums at the l'Ecole des Loisirs and at Circonflexe in particular. This remains quite limited: *Jafta* by Hugh Lewin: *The Lord of the Winds* (*Le seigneur des vents*) by

M. Pearson; *The Seeds of the Sun* (*Les graines du soleil*) by D. Stewart; *The Lonely Lioness and the Ostrich Chicks* (*La lionne solitaire et les bébés autruches*) by V. Aardema.

Access to French publishing for an African author

Another way to assess the fate of African books in France is to look at the possibilities for African authors and illustrators to be published in France.

'Specialized' publishing houses

Most French publishers are not keen on publishing African authors. On the other hand a certain number of French publishing houses, by editorial and commercial vocation or cultural commitment, choose to publish African authors (Les classiques Africans, Edicef, l'Harmattan, Hatier, Sepia). But in this case, most of these works benefit from almost exclusive distribution rights in Africa. So few of these books are known to French readers as very few are offered to bookshops and the catalogues are not usually available.

This position is starting to change under pressure from readers who are more open to foreign literature. Thus, among the houses with specialized catalogues, another policy is emerging: to publish African authors or books about Africa but to launch these publications in France — Sepia does this.

Non-specialized children's publishers

African books in the catalogues of non-specialized publishers remain quite limited and the origin of the book is not easily identified but it is still a contribution to a better knowledge of African authors in France.

The African tale published in France

African tales have always been the most accessible and exploited type of literature from Africa. They remain a source of inspiration.

In conclusion these would be ineffective if there were no readers; these books are wanted, perhaps because of historic links but also for other reasons like a personal African origin or a fascination with foreign cultures. Whatever the reason, people in France do want access to works from Africa.

In conclusion, in April 1999 the Children's Book Fair in Bologna will concern African illustrators who will be presented in a central exhibition, but it also concerns the entire publishing industry as the exhibition is a contribution of international significance in recognition of these publications.

33
The Development of Books for Children

Its Effect on the International Licence Business

GABRIELA WENKE

Wherever independent literature for children develops, the process happens according to the same pattern. Usually, the first texts for children are those teaching them to read and write — textbooks. That was the situation in Europe hundreds of years ago and over the centuries a diverse independent literature for children has developed, with a time lag compared to the development of adult books. Every culture appears to go through the same stages even if at a different pace. Given the differences with respect to languages, cultures and nations, the similarity in these stages is striking. They are not simply of scientific interest but relevant in international exchange — for the sales of licences and for co-productions. Development starts with school-books and learning aids, followed by educational books which contain a moral, to arrive at literary texts with no or no obvious claim or intention to educate. Differences between these stages are a bigger barrier than cultural differences. In a country where books have to satisfy the highest literary and artistic standards, there is no demand for the production of a book still oriented towards the textbook and traditional stories. Few licences will be sold.

Books like this will be produced but to produce conventional material, publishers will not follow unconventional paths.

Stage 1: Alphabetization

If you want to learn to read and write you need a primer — even if it is handwritten on loose sheets. But once the reading skill is acquired, you need material to practise your skill. Eleven years ago in Harare the need for authentic books for children, written by African authors, was repeated over and over to spare African children the fate of growing up on stories of the colonial masters that teach more about London fog than their own history. The discussion was summed up by the picture of African children in their kraal, reading about 'the air-conditioned child'.

Times of limited means require concentration on basics: short fables, tales and stories, primary level non-fiction about nature and the environment, encyclopedias and dictionaries. Orally transmitted material is written down, new ideas for books are translated from other cultures or languages and adapted to one's own needs. Books appearing in that stage are relevant for partners who face similar problems and have similar interests and aims. Tales and popular legends may be of interest to other cultures as well, yet they do not seem to be marketable in enormous numbers in the German speaking markets — Germany, Austria and Switzerland, for example.

This stage mainly concerns a certain age group: children learn to read at the age of about six or seven; consequently they need books. Juvenile books for children aged twelve and above are non-existant at this stage or at least are accessible or relevant only to a small percentage of children. For most of them, childhood is immediately followed by adulthood. At this stage, at times, the first picture books may be available for the very little ones.

When passing from one stage to the next, the previous one does not disappear, of course, but a new stage is added.

Stage 2: Education

This second stage produces a variety of very different books, and yet, even the seemingly most harmless adventure story always appears to hide a certain educational concept. Somehow, the child or adolescent hero ends up accepting that grown-ups are right. Boys survive adventures in the wilderness by making use of the experiences of the older generation. Headstrong girls are finally tamed, and are ultimately happy, of course, once they have married 'Mr Right'. Either the young convert the old to a more progressive lifestyle, or the old succeed in convincing the young of the advantages of traditional life. In a worst case scenario, stories become religious, ideological or political tracts: little heroines and heroes made into pioneers of the desired system.

In less obvious cases the stories offer the entire range of desirable ways of behaviour: diligent pupils, hard-working daughters. Decisions against drugs. Sex — if it is mentioned at that stage at all — only from a certain age onwards. Stories are woven around a problem which is ultimately solved.

Certain issues are taboo and thus not treated in books. Among them are sexuality, death and dying, physical or mental handicaps, nasty parents, drugs, crime or questioning the current political system.

There are also formal taboos: stories may only be told one-dimensionally, for example, or there are very specific ideas about the way illustrations for children are supposed to look. At a distance, provided by time, geography or cultural environment, it becomes easier to spot the moral index finger hidden in those stories. When, as a teenager, I read those typical books for girls, which had not changed significantly between the beginning of the century and the 1960s, it never occurred to me that things always started with a wild girl who ended up a tamed woman, or that handicapped people, girls, poor children or any kind of social outsider, always had to be particularly brave to succeed.

The offering becomes more and more varied: there are picture books for two-year-olds as well as more sophisticated books with longer stories for older children. And there is a variety of styles when it comes to illustrations. Ways and habits of looking at things change. Yet, whatever is considered ugly or repulsive never finds its way into books. Nor do abstract illustrations.

Ranging from the most basic story for first readers to complex children's novels, there is an unbelievable variety of texts.

I shall offer another simplification here: this stage is marked by the idea that, in principle, uniform educational objectives and their presentation in stories are possible. There is a certain consensus within the society on what is right for children and youth.

As far as non-fiction is concerned, which is also directed at numerous target groups in terms of age, an international approach seems to prevail at the expense of regional particularities.

Stage 3: Literature and Art

I recently re-read Tsitsi Dangarembga's *Nervous Conditions/Der Preis der Freiheit* (published in 1988). It was first published in German in 1991 by a publisher for books for adults (Rowohit, Series: New Woman) and is still in print today. It is an excellent book for young people. A book that shows a childhood and youth as they are and not as they should be. A book about a heroine who is not shown as an exclusively positive personality, but who has mixed feelings, who is torn between two worlds, a girl thinking rebellious thoughts, a girl whose world is no longer in order and who would not be helped by a happy end 'traditional style'. That is the stuff novels for the youth of today are made of. Novels which get awards and prizes and are listed as recommended reading in northern and central Europe today.

Similar criteria apply to the picture book (from one to eight years and above) and for the children's book (from six to eight years). Neither the young protagonists nor their adult environment are idealized: grown-ups as well as children have 'edges' and weak spots, irrespective of age, sex, race, social position (like teachers or politicians) and wealth. A case in point from Africa is *Da musst du durch, Lurch* (Don't Panic, Mechanic, 1996, Elefanten Press; Tafelberg Publishers, 1994) by Jenny Robson. It tells the story of a boy who is so cross-eyed that he can no longer keep up at school and he sets out to find a way out of his dilemma by being at once brave, funny, good-natured and ultimately cunning, too — after having been tricked by a crook.

When it comes to picture books, even with explicitly artistic, as opposed to blaring or corny illustrations, taste varies considerably with different cultures. And here too the perspective on childhood, on educational concepts for infants and young children has changed.

The trend in children's and juvenile literature is towards unique stories, either realistic or fantastic, or a mixture of both, which portray children as independent individuals, headstrong at times, and who grow up in societies that find themselves in constant upheaval, with family structures dissolving to be recreated in different forms.

Publishers' representatives, always in search of 'something special', hoping to make a good catch, will generally look for books of high literary value which do not raise the moral/pedagogic index finger. Publishers buy trivial mass productions or entertainment that follows a trend (mystery and horror stories being the current one) where they are already successfully sold, mostly in the US.

Conclusion

Irrespective of language and culture, three major stages of development of children's and juvenile books are relevant for the sales of licences to other countries.

1 Alphabetization level with primers, textbooks and teaching aids.
2 Educational level with books that have a more or less explicit intention to educate and a 'moral of the story'.
3 Literary and artistic level: expectations regarding quality are in no way inferior to those for books for adults; books at that level have (almost) no intention to educate.

In summary, There is (almost) no international markets for books from level 1; children's and juvenile books from level 2 are not bought even if they are of high literary value because ideas and images of education and childhood differ too strongly between countries and cultures. So licences from countries that are still fighting for recognition on the market for children's and juvenile books are of interest for buying countries only at level three.

34
The Jacaranda Experience
Kenyan Children's Books in America

SUSAN SCULL-CARVALHO

Great commotions arise out of small things,
but concerning small things. *Winston Churchill*

This story is about commotion — in Kenya and in the US — concerning our small company, Jacaranda Designs Limited. Our speciality is publishing for the children of Africa — and more recently, the design and delivery of client-sponsored socially responsible marketing and promotional programmes for children, youth and teachers.

Since our beginning in late 1991, we've enjoyed, experienced and learned a lot from commotion: much of it being intentionally created by us. Commotion is an interesting concept. It means either noisy excitement or an uprising or disturbance — even with violence. I prefer the former.

I will describe some of the commotion we have created or instigated — positive commotion and other commotion which we have not created or caused.

To avoid bringing you to tears, I will reveal only enough of the financial details to explain the results or benefits of our strategies of commotion.

The story of Jacaranda Designs begins in Kenya in January 1991 — fully registered but not yet operational. Up to July that year, a dozen individuals were hired to conduct in-depth market research among 600 families and over 200 educators. We also held focus groups with hundreds of children and teenagers, and interviewed publishers or agents, booksellers, reproduction and printing companies. Another 300 families were interviewed concerning children's 'edu-tainment' television programmes. This started some good commotion, as few other companies in Kenya had spent so much time asking potential consumers what they wanted.

This data was compiled, analyzed and used to draft our initial business plan and capitalization strategy. I went out to attract investors.

Investment is hard to get. Local investment was the hardest as publishing falls into the non-traditional investment sector. Most wanted to see products and results first. So, we started in October 1991 with only two investors secured and only partially paid up.

We began with some absolutes:

— Parents and their children want Africa-centred, quality reading material.

— Africa's parents strongly support education and both appreciate and understand the value of reading.

In 1991, about 95 per cent of locally available books for children, youth and adults, were imported. Including supplementary readers and textbooks, this figure held across Africa. Parents and teachers told us they bought or used imported or donated books, even though they wanted African-based, relevant material.

Significantly, they were not against imported or foreign-aid 'donated' books but against the imbalance owing to the lack of African-based publishing. They feared Africa's children might suffer instability if their cultural identities were not established.

We also began with an awareness of the abundant, largely untapped literary and artistic talent in Africa. Creating opportunities for this was important if African values and perspectives were to survive.

We chose to focus initially on children and youth, and respond through our many survey-based product suggestions.

This formed the basis of our first mission statement.

Money came in slowly from share capital and by draining what little I had left and from a highly supportive director, my husband. Our wealth was our combined talents and abundant enthusiasm.

Concerning our operating strategies, a couple of thoughts guided us:

The race is not always to the swift,

Nor the battle to the strong,

But you better bet that way.

And

Place your bet somewhere between

Haste-makes-waste and

He-who-hesitates-is-lost. *Robert Fulghum*

In two months, we produced our first three products, held a company launch among 200 friends and well-wishers, and watched ourselves on two television news broadcasts. It really helped. We started selling in Kenya and getting good, mostly free, press coverage mainly obtained by our created commotion: hosting special groups, special activities for youths, writing and spending many hours in interviews.

By early 1992 we started looking at the US trade and education markets, true to our original mission statement— our 'African cooking pot plan' (a three-legged pot) with one leg in Kenya, one in the rest of Africa (especially southern Africa), and the third in the US — but we had not planned on moving so quickly in export directions.

In early 1992, with the promise of Kenya's first multi-party elections, total uncertainty gripped us and the nation.We again encountered commotion — but of the disturbing type.

To hedge against downward trends in the economy, our company directors and investors (now about six people) and our staff decided we should enter the US market.

With little or no money, and thanks to the goodwill of my brother and a few friends in the US, we again started by research. We studied children's products on or about Africa, we interviewed parents, teachers, librarians and booksellers.

We learned there was a growing interest in Africa from those seeking multi-cultural children's publishing and intrigued by what authentic African books might offer.

We registered our branch office in California, sought volunteer support from my mother-in-law to manage accounts and distribution and hired a marketing and sales promotion manager at about $30,000 per annum, with partial trade-in for shares. She worked from home and we also hired an expert multi-cultural children's publishing publicist for six months.

We produced a colourful catalogue, filled with African motifs, bought mailing lists of booksellers, distributors and independent publishers' sales representatives. We made banners and displays, and went on the road to book fairs as well as teachers and librarians' conferences. Our first US book trade fair was in April 1993 — the American Booksellers' Association. The stand cost $300 and we paid about the same for airfares and lodging for a week. At that time, we had produced seven titles, a colouring book and two sets of children's colouring cards. We were just 18 months into the publishing business.

Our marketing manager and publicist were great. With articles, photos and telephone interview support from our team in Kenya, we created commotion. Quite a few journals, magazines and newspapers in the US ran reviews of our work and company.

But it hasn't been a smooth, easy road.

We had learned there was interest in our African children's books and we had received positive, created press commotion. We had achieved significant attention for our product but we were faced with an unexpected commotion. Africa was known in the US for bad business deals. No doubt there had been good deals but the bad memories are more lasting. As we entered the US book trade negotiations arena we found we already had three strikes against us:

Strike 1— Africa is not trusted: No money would change hands until the product was delivered.

Strike 2 —Africa is unreliable: No orders would be placed until our product was landed in the US. So we rented a small warehouse and shipped our books to California.

Strike 3 — Africa cheats and isn't quality conscious, especially for repeat orders. No money would change hands until the product was delivered and inspected. Again, we spent extra money to ensure topnotch quality.

Another shock was US buyers do not negotiate terms. It is a consumer-rich marketplace with limited shelf space. Certain booksellers only stock from certain distributors. Their terms are non-negotiable and I was trying to bargain, African-style!

To many US booksellers, we were simply too small. They liked our products (now bearing stickers with bar codes) but we were told to come back when we had over 12 titles, and preferably 24 or more.

I remember a telephone interview with a US-based newspaper reporter. About three minutes into the session he asked what colour I was what my ethnic roots were. This was followed by a pause, and then, 'Why would a white American be so interested in publishing African-based books for the children of Africa?' And, 'Do you feel qualified to do this?'

Another thought:

When you go out into the world, watch out for traffic, hold hands
and stick together. Be aware of wonder. *Robert Fulghum*

Wonder happens.

Again, our directors, investors and staff held meetings. This concerned increasing our volume of titles so as to reach accepted levels for the US market. Publishing is a risk-taking business — we decided to go for it, if I could sell more shares. Our company accepted loans of up to $150,000 which would be repaid with interest or converted to shares. We did, they did and we now have more shareholders, and unconverted loans have been repaid.

A positive lesson learned is that publishers can be competitors and market-building collaborators too. In sharp contrast to what happens in Kenya and elsewhere in Africa, we found our US publishing counterparts welcoming and eager to share information. We received contacts, tips and constructive criticism and their views on the most promising events. When we won awards, our US competitors actually wrote, called or in person congratulated us!

The US is a demanding and expensive marketplace and we are still in it but our growth has been slow due to our under-capitalization not lack of demand.

To make sales happen in the US requires more and constant promotion and special efforts. It demands high profile strategies: more promotional materials, a web-site, more Meet the Authors and Illustrators tours, more mailings, more hard cover productions, special packaging, special offers and lots more. The bottom line is capital.

In Kenya, from 1992 onwards too much commotion was in process. The bad type which disrupted our local economy. Two areas are most notable.

The first is the most damaging commotion: caused by corruption of public and donor funds. Projects intended to assist many only benefit a few.

Apart from infrastructure, power and health-related projects, our publishing sector was also affected by corruption. Corruption was within donor-funded children's book projects, library support programmes, textbook supply projects, local publishers' training support programmes and even book fairs.

The impact of corruption weakened our economy. Local book sales virtually halted, as households and schools had to go slow in book purchasing.

The second commotion was also disturbing commotion: the orchestrated unrest and violence which accompanies power struggles among emerging political parties as multi-partyism swept through Kenya. The violence drove away donors and caused the withdrawal of loans or grants.

We drafted and re-drafted business plans as the exchange rate fluctuated between Ksh 22 and Ksh 90 between 1991 and 1995 and back down to ranges between Ksh 38 and Ksh 64 between 1996 and now. During the 1993-1994 period, inflation reached 100 per cent.

The best years in the US were between 1994 and 1996 when we qualified for two donor-supported export promotion programmes for Kenyan manufacturers. Both provided a reimbursable scheme for the costs of certain export-related expenses like catalogues, travel and trade fairs. It enabled us to get 15 of our titles on the New York approved list for schools. This brought in some orders in 1996/97 but not yet the projected volume of about $250,000.

Strapped for cash, we still had to do something to boost our 'entry' into the US education market. So we hired a New York-based education expert to develop teachers' guides for our readers with classroom project ideas on Africa. These were free with purchases of classroom sets. We also developed our Afri-kit product line: Educational boxed sets, with a video and users' guide for participatory learning.

Our team stuck together — challenged to be even more creative, we had to generate new strategies and draft new mission statements.

In Kenya, we revised our business plans and production programmes. We added to our initial mission statement — our initial mission statement, with additions, could still hold true.

We've endured Kenya's first two multi-party elections; had droughts; and from mid-1997 the relentless *el nino* rains, wrecking telephone and power lines, and our roads. Faced with more unexpected commotion, and more cash flow struggles we had to re-examine our direction.

More adjustments were made to our mission statement in mid 1997.

Almost seven years on, we are a team of 20 talented individuals and have 19 shareholders. We have a total of 62 products including 32 titles, two each of video and audio cassettes, educational kits, posters, charts, art cards and gift-wrap paper.

From an asset base of one computer, printer and table, we now own a well-used music system, 10 Macintosh computers, four printers plus other creative equipment, and we all work from chairs on desks or easels. We own two vehicles and almost all is paid up.

We are still enthusiastic — from positive and negative commotion we've had to make changes and adjustments to survive and we've had to create other ways to sell our titles, and earn income.

Between 1994 and 1996 we produced under contract a weekly 8-page children's pull-out supplement with Kenya's largest newspaper, *The Sunday Nation*. This was read by some 1.2 million children every Sunday. *The Sunday Nation* paid us for printing rights, and we got free national publicity.

We have also designed and managed other socially responsible programmes which provide education and entertainment to our markets. We work with SmithKline Beecham to produce and distribute a children and youth magazine, involve school pupils, teachers and parents in a mural painting programme for children's wards in hospitals and we conduct competitions with our books as prizes. In addition, we have been invited to be on the instructional materials development team for the Personal Hygiene and Sanitation Education programme, sponsored by SmithKline Beecham and for all of Africa.

In late 1997, we were named the Kenya Distribution Agent for Heinemann Educational Publishers. This agreement justifies financially a deeper reach into the education and trade markets in Kenya.

We sought other income-earning activities and won a few contracts from other publishers to produce illustrations for an assortment of publications and titles.

Last year we were awarded the Interpretive Graphics Programme contract for the soon-to-open Nairobi Safari Walk of the Kenya Wildlife Service.

Our strength stems from individual talent, and thrives from our teamwork. We're known for quality. We have strong, gifted and skilled people; human resources which we have developed during the past seven years.

We've evolved. We've learned to practise enlightened self-interest. We appreciate our firm foundation and from it we have earned a good reputation based on publicly recognized quality work and steadfast business ethics.

More importantly, we have increased determination, desire and developed talents to do more, especially in this exciting new era of emerging, more liberalized and democratic nations of Africa. Kenya and all of Africa will also survive, evolve and emerge stronger. Positive changes are happening. Kenya, and Africa as a whole, offers tremendous potential, as an already growing market, and as a resource to be tapped for international partnerships in publishing! We are ready to do more in print and electronic publishing!

I quote Chinua Achebe, *Things Fall Apart*:

And the dog said: 'If I lay down for you and you lay down for me, it is play.'

We're seeking new partners for strategic business development — for the trade and education markets in Africa, the US and elsewhere. We seek to publish more books, magazines, and other print productions.

We especially seek partners to develop and produce for an identified unexploited frontier: 'edu-tainment' television and video productions, which can grow toward CD-ROM, inter-active media. Authentic African productions.

Change in Africa is imminent. We'll soon experience more commotion but this time mostly of the intended, positive, noisy, exciting type! And,we aim to be among the major players by forging important strategic business alliances, entering new partnerships and doing what we must. This will build business across Africa and within the US.

Jacaranda Designs still has a few shares for sale.

Some more thoughts:

About winning: it isn't important. What really counts is how you play the game.

About losing: it isn't important. What really counts is how you play the game.

About playing the game: Play to win!

Robert Fulghum

35
Fantasy and the Search for Reality

in Children's Literature

MESHACK ASARE

In a small seaside hamlet, a young boy is so fascinated by the activities at the beach that it becomes his most consuming dream to go fishing with the men, in their big canoes. So he spends his free time at the beach helping the men wrestle and manoeuvre their heavy vessels to the sea. But always, they leave him on the beach as they board their vessels and say to him: 'You are too small to go to sea'.

One day, after seeing the men off as usual, he sits in the shade of a coconut tree to watch them get smaller and smaller, then disappear on the horizon. Then his eyes fall on something on the ground. It is a dry pod from the coconut tree and it reminds him of something so he picks it up. He looks for twigs and other bits and soon he has his own canoe complete with oarsmen. Now he too can go to sea. After several attempts he gets his canoe and his men afloat in the sea. He shouts and pats the water excitedly, 'My canoe has gone! My canoe has gone!' (*Tawai Goes to Sea*)

Not long after that, a boy helps his father to make little brass figures for the market. His father gives him one as a reward for his hard work. That evening, he sits by himself in a corner, with the little brass figure in his hand. He raises it to the moonlight. The little figure gets bigger and bigger. Then it opens its mouth and talks to him, 'Come with me my little friend. Close your eyes and come.' He finds himself in the king's courtyard, bustling with people like his new friend and they are very busy, weighing heaps of gold dust. For his new friend is a goldweight! (*The Brassman's Secret*)

Years later in Guguletu, another boy rolls up some clay from the backyard puddle after the rain. He builds a house complete with furniture and separate rooms for himself, his mother and grandmother. Then he builds a car. He is called home to eat. He makes two holes in a slice of bread and places it across his nose. Now he sits in his own car wearing his sunglasses and speeds along the main street of Guguletu. Everybody waves at him in his car, wearing his sunglasses! (*Charlie's House*)

Not far from Guguletu in a place called Stree, an angel lands in a huge storm on top of the school building. He is the new regional angel, appointed in heaven to go and sort out the intractable problems of the place. Precocious Brahms is the first and only human being to see the angel. Later, the angel meets with him and they become friends. Together, they cure the place called Stree of its ills! (*Brahms and the Angel*)

If you are wondering why these are all boys, rest assured. For they have female kin, the most famous is Alice (*Alice in Wonderland*) — alone eclipsing them many fold! These boys are only here to suggest that Africa too has its share of such occurrences even if only small and not as old or as famous as those of Alice and many others around the world.

Fantasy

We refer to the events and experiences of these children as 'fantasy' as distinct from 'reality'. It must be noted, too, that the three stories are not folktales — fairy tales, myths, legends or fables — although they share the common element of magic. This makes it hard sometimes, to distinguish one from the other.

The distinction between 'folktale' and 'fantasy' is a thin line determined by the time in which the magic takes place. In folktales such as myths and legends, things have already happened within a time when magical events were possible — 'A long time ago when nobody was born' — Some call it 'dreamtime' (*The Linguistic Constriction of Reality*). That is 'liminal time'.

But fantasy happens even today. We can think of it as floating 'magical time bubbles' within which incredible things happen. When they happen, they are for the duration of the bubble only. Except that the things that happen in fantasy do not follow the logic which underpins the physical world.

In the world we know, twigs do not become men and a coconut pod is not large enough even for a rat to float on. Neither do little brass figures talk. The laws of the physical world simply do not permit such things to happen. Unlike folktales, fantasy does not offer any clever explanations for life's mysteries or wise instructions on how to cope with them. So what do we gain from fantasy? I would like us to take a closer look at 'fantasy' and 'reality' to see if we can find any answer for the question.

'Real world' and 'fantasy world'

The physical world is apprehended through our senses which affirm its existence. The conditions of fantasy do not submit to the scrutiny of the senses.

So although questions about 'reality' itself are not fully answered, we consign 'fantasy' to the 'sphere of the mind' rather than the physical world.

The conditions of fantasy are experienced only by the activity of the mind — the imagination. Thus, we are looking at two worlds — a 'real world' because our senses say so and an unreal 'fantasy world' located in the mind.

Sense, mind and reality

This raises questions of 'Cartesian' dimensions which we cannot go into. However, the differences between the imagined 'fantasy world' and the sensory 'real world' have significant implications for writers of children's books. This is clearer if we take a closer look at the roles of the senses and the mind.

We know that our senses only function as primary conduits of data — it is not actually my tongue which determines the saltiness of the banana nor my eyes the jet-black colour of cow's milk. These attributes of the world are determined and confirmed by the mind of which the senses are extensions. Ultimately, it is the mind that makes 'reality', if we separate sense from mind.

But the mind does not always require the inflow of sensory data, like signals from the external world, in order to act. It is also capable of autonomous and spontaneous activity. This is why it can generate situations not bound by the practicalities and limitations of the physical world. How about dreaming while fast asleep and remembering vividly the experiences we had in the dream?

Other questions about reality explain that the world is nothing but data. We construct reality from the jumble of data by ourselves. The mind encodes the data so that it can manipulate it. It observes the external world, then organizes 'recurrent elements' into kinds. The sets of recurrent elements form the basis of a concept of 'what is out there' and what is 'to be expected'. This becomes 'knowledge' of what is taken as the 'real' world. But without language, this 'knowledge' does not become 'reality'. It remains essentially private knowledge until effectively communicated from one to another.

Language itself is codes of conventions by which we submit to common meanings and values. It is a body of conventional sound symbols which embody the sets of recurrent elements called 'knowledge of the world' accrued and shared by a group of people who recognize it to be true. The images and concepts that they express and define collectively, constitute their 'real world'.

If we accept this, then we can say that reality is in fact a social construct. It suggests that reality is not necessarily and exclusively determined by finite things of the physical world disclosed by our senses. Society is a non-physical phenomenon after all and so may be the state that we call reality.

From the foregoing, reality depends on our capacity to perceive it, rather than it suffusing us by spontaneous self-disclosure. This is why we have to continually learn and search in order to discover what was already there. It is again why there are variances in our knowledge of the world. So then, what we take to be reality can only be an approximation of it. Even so, there is no certainty that this collective image is formed from uniform perceptions.

This breaches the line between 'fantasy' and 'reality'. We can notice from the incidents of fantasy that, in all cases, there was room for the extraordinary possibilities that occurred. In other words, the fantasy fulfilled some need of the 'real' person rather than the 'real' environment. And here, I become my 'real' African self for by 'real person' I include all the possibilities that are part of the person — the past, present and future.

The children who by their imagination experienced the extraordinary events in their stories, actually created reality for themselves. They transported and situated themselves where they 'really' wanted to be. In other words, they found themselves in what I described above as the 'magical time bubble'. Perhaps it actually begins with those of us who create fantasy.

In spite of the great traditions worldwide across literatures and other media, the perception of fantasy as a genre in literature is feeble. Most common definitions of fantasy deny it any seriousness while some even go further to undermine its place in literature so that it appears that only children or child-like adults, read it.

When it is referred to as 'disordered mental images; weird; illusion, characterized by highly fanciful and supernatural elements', it appears as if fantasy is the product of low activity of the mind. We can only think that way if we overlook the importance of imagination in our so-called 'real' life. We also forget that imagination is itself fashioned from our 'knowledge of the world' mentioned above, which constitutes the real world for us.

On the basis of the brief explanations of how we create both reality and fantasy in the mind, fantasy is the extension of reality, just as the senses are extensions of the mind. Fantasy and reality are not two separate things.

To conclude, going back to imagination and the idea of the 'imagined world', our dreams and our imagination form an important part of our being. We stagnate without fantasy — without imagination. It is therefore important to be able to dream and imagine and fantasize.

Of utmost importance are the elements which are available to us to fashion our fantasies from. We can only have a good, productive, happy, beautiful world if our fantasies are good, constructive, happy and beautiful. This is what we have to bear in mind when we write fantasy stories for children.

36
Reality and Fantasy
in Children's Picture Books

NIKI DALY

According to the *Chambers Twentieth Century Dictionary*, reality is 'that which is real and not imaginary'. Added to this, perhaps unwisely, is the word 'truth'. Reality shaped by Newtonian physics has been replaced by Quantum physics. So what was previously 'determined' is now only 'probable'. 'Reality happens when you look at it', chant the Quantum gurus. What happens when you're not looking at it'? Moreover, how should you look at reality for it to be real?

So I'd like to revise the Chambers definition as follows:

Reality:That which is probably real, but maybe not; forget truth.

Quantum theory is baffling and exciting. It fosters concepts normally associated with science fiction and fantasy writers, such as the 'many worlds theory'. According to this bizarre theory, right now, there is an identical ZIBF conference going on in another dimension. And as I turn my page so will it be turned by my Quantum self. It is reminiscent of Alice's experience as she 'jumped lightly down into the Looking-Glass room' and found a real fire blazing away as brightly as the one she had left behind.

This brings to mind some lines from 'The Man with the Blue Guitar' by Wallace Stevens which provides a bridge from 'the home of reality' to the 'home of fantasy':

They said, 'You have a blue guitar,
You do not play things as they are.'
The man replied, 'Things as they are
Are changed upon the blue guitar.'

The following is the *Chambers* definition of 'Fantasy':

Fantasy, phantasy: 'n. Fancy; imagination; mental image; preoccupation with thoughts associated with unobtainable desires. (I hear a teacher's voice saying, 'Stop dreaming, boy!')

Jane Curry, an American children's book writer, recalled that there were two spellings of 'fantasy' — with an 'f' and with a 'ph'. According to the *Oxford English Dictionary* of 1901, *fantasy* and *phantasy* are apprehended as separate words, the predominant sense of the former being 'caprice; whim;

fanciful invention' while the latter is 'imagination; visionary notion'. Jane Young goes on to explain that these are at either end of a continuum.

In the one our attention is focused primarily on the story or action itself; and in the other it is the feeling, the emotional dimension that holds us.

Fantasy will probably have a linear story line whereas phantasy deals more with being and becoming, with potentiality more than actuality.'

These differences are helpful because 'phantasy' has lost its sway over children's picture book writers. Whereas 'fantasy' abounds. I refer to 'fantasy' picture books in which animals dress up as people or are anthropomorphized in some way.

'Phantasy' has more to offer writers, illustrators, and their readers than 'fantasy'. In addition, 'phantasy' is a deeper and more powerful antidote against the overload of 'reality' that we suffer from.

As a children's picture book writer and illustrator, when I do books on my own they are rooted in my own sense of intrigue, but when I work with other people, our experiences coalesce into a shared vision, or 'negotiated reality'. Although this difference may be invisible to readers.

Illustration is cousin to fine art. Not a poor cousin but a specialized picture making that co-exists with the written word. I have found illustration closer to acting than to painting in that it requires interpretive skills. To draw something convincingly you must become it.

As the actor interprets a story's action and emotion on stage, so the illustrator does on paper. So I think of my work as 'a performance'. This is clear when comparing two interpretations of the same story. The illustrator's interpretation and materials contribute to his 'style'. In addition, a more intangible ingredient is added to the illustrator's style. Walter de la Mare in his tribute to the illustrator, the late Harold Jones, describes it beautifully:

Even his commonest objects tell
His love for what he sees so well,
And such is the delight he shows—
In stool or table, bird or rose —
That, sharing them, one hardly knows
Which for pleasure gives richer cause —
What he draws or how he draws!

The same can be said of Antoine de Saint-Exupéry as an illustrator of his book, *The Little Prince*.

Influences

Realism in children's books is usually good drawing in an academic sense. Those who use realism are influenced by the principles of perspective and chiaroscuro developed through Renaissance painting. Another influence is the invention of photography on late 19th Century Impressionists, namely Degas.

Later still, the Photorealists of the late 1960s provided a not altogether good mould that shapes much of contemporary realistic illustration. 'Not good' because illustrators who use photographs as a resource, especially for figure drawing, can use them badly.

'Drawn-from-photograph-characters' often lack convincing body language appropriate to the written situation; their eyes seldom connect to other characters because the models have been separately photographed and mechanically put together. The result resembles a tableaux of emotionally disconnected people. However, because many lay-people are impressed by skilfully done realistic pictures, photo-based illustration has been more popular than imaginative illustration.

Lisa Klopper in an article 'Will the real drawings please stand up' featured in *Books for Keeps* Magazine No. 110, May 1998, writes:

> To be able to draw freely means to give form not only to what we see around us, but also what we cannot see — the depiction of the imaginary.

Some days I can't draw. While on others, my heart, eyes, hand, and the right hand side of my brain amaze me. Take note of the vital organs associated with drawing — *heart*, *eye*, *hand* and *brain*. The *heart* is the most vital or else your books look 'as though they've been untouched by love'.

Interesting marriages

While realistic images reinforce stories that deal with reality, they can provide a powerful complement to stories that depart from reality. Likewise, non-realistic illustrations (influenced by primitive art, naive art, medieval art, expressionism, surrealism, Dadaist, and modern day art forms like graffiti) can be effectively used to tell stories that are real.

Reality represented in picture book stories

I cannot comprehend 'reality' as an absolute. As an artist, I capture life as I see and feel it; an act of unforgivable subjectivity and indulgence. The most I can offer is a 'Niki Daly World'. It irritates me that reviewers and librarians do not have such a category! Instead, they throw me on to the 'multicultural' pile, where I can be misunderstood.

When reviewing a book about blacks (no matter the race of the author), I ask two questions: Does it accurately present the black perspective? Will it be relevant to black children? The possibility of a book by a white answering these questions affirmatively is almost nil. Lester continued:

> . . . whites can only give a white interpretation of blacks, which tells us about whites, but nothing about blacks — whites will never understand the black view of the world until they get it straight from blacks, respect it and accept it.

This statement was part of a correspondence between Julius Lester, the distinguished African American writer and the *New York Times* children's book editor. This extract was taken from a letter published in 1970.

This issue, expressed so bitterly in Julius Lester's letter, has softened over the years. In South Africa, the cultural edges have softened, melted and begun to merge, as a new generation of artists share our cultural stew — like children around a pot that never grows empty as long as it is shared.

We have a mysterious capacity to empathize with one another. Call it *ubuntu*, humanity or our purpose for being. It's a pity when we doubt one another's capacity to be human, as Lester did back then. It's a tragedy when it's suggested that writers and artists should stay in their own skin. It's precisely their gift to jump out of their skins that reminds us of what we are: first and foremost — humans with tremendous abilities and potential. I first heard Archbishop Desmond Tutu use the term 'jumping right out of our skins'. It is a lovely image of jumping from one life into another; one gender into another; one time and space into another; and from one reality into another.

References

Klopper L. (1998), 'Will the real drawings please stand up'. *Books For Keeps*, No. 110, May, London.

Stevens W. 'The Man with the Blue Guitar', resourced from 'Poetry from the Planet Earth', web site HYPERLINK — <http://redfrog.norconnect.no/~poems/>

The editor, *Books for Keeps* (1997), 'White writer, black characters' No. 105, July.

Young J. (1993), *Towards More Understanding: The Making and Sharing of Children's Literature in Southern Africa*, Juta, Cape Town.

Zohar D. (1990), *The Quantum Self*, Bloomsbury, London.

37
Publishing Comic Books in Africa

WOELI A. DEKUTSEY

A ll over Africa, it is common to see cartoons on political as well as social subjects in newspapers and magazines. But nowhere on the continent has the preoccupation with the cartoon blossomed into a fully-fledged comics industry where a story is developed beyond a three-panel strip, and where the protagonists are realistically drawn. We are yet to witness a burgeoning comics industry on the scale of Asian countries, particularly Japan where the comic has developed into a genre called the *manga*,[1] which delights children and adults alike. In Malaysia,[2] such comics are enjoyed by 63 per cent of children in primary school. One such magazine, *Bib*, has a circulation of 85,000. In West Africa, the closest we have come to the comic is the popular *Ikebe* (Nigeria) and *Funtime* (Ghana). East Africa, particularly Kenya, has its share of comics. In Zimbabwe there used to be a popular comic *Molo Songololo* but this folded up. It would be worth our while to research the rise and fall of comics in Africa. But even in their heydays, no African comic can boast of the dizzying print run figures of south-east Asia. Tejumola Olaniya was right when he observed that 'Comics are not yet a widespread practice in Nigeria outside of low-brow imports and fitful local imitations'.[3] The dearth of comics is not only true of Nigeria, but for the rest of Africa.

Perhaps, a reason for the comic genre's inability to sink its roots deeper in Africa would lie intrinsically in the word itself. The comic has always been associated with the frivolous. No wonder in Kenya[4] and Ghana, the official policy is against the use of comic books as a medium of instruction. In Zimbabwe it is held in low esteem among educationists. And who can blame the policy-makers when in Nigeria and in Ghana, respectively, pages of *Ikebe* and *Funtime*, for example, are full of titillating and salacious celebrations of tabooed subjects? Clearly such comic books are designed to give the readers a good laugh. The argument is always advanced that comics have a tendency to interfere with good reading development. Again, this is for a good reason. The few indigenous comic books published in Africa are often produced by semi-literates, whose language is wobbly, even though they may be gifted artists. The standard of editing is generally low; but one is forced to concede that sometimes the storyline is good; so that with some good editing, the general presentation could be markedly improved.

In the light of the foregoing, serious publishers do not want to be associated with 'low-class' publishing. But one fact that is lost on many publishers is that animated comics or cartoons enjoy a following among children and a good number of adults. In Ghana children are glued to television sets on Saturday mornings when their favourite programme, Cartoon Network, is being beamed. Characters like Scooby Doo, Dexter, and so on, are engaged in all kinds of adventures and kids are simply enthralled. Kabena Ntrakwa,[5] a children's librarian, mentioned that among the most borrowed books in her library are Tintin[6] and Asterix[7] comics. She disclosed that many teachers (and parents) enjoy these books any time their library receives a new consignment. The wonder is that these series seem to be ageless. The Tintin series started as a cartoon strip in a Belgian newspaper, *Le Vingtieme Siecle*, in 1929. The originator, Georges Remi, who wrote under a pseudonym, 'Herge', was both the author and the artist. Tintin is a curious teenage hero who is a young reporter as well as an amateur detective all rolled into one. He works in association with two dumb-witted police twins, Thompson and Thompson. There is also a swearing Captain Haddock whose language is as much fun as it is nonsensical. Completing this motley group of characters is the deaf and absent-minded Professor Calculus who adds spice to the narrative by getting into all kinds of scrapes. The fact that the Tintin series has been around for 50 odd years, has been reprinted several times and translated into many languages including Chinese and German, attests to the fact that it is hugely popular.

The other popular comic which has come much later than *Tintin* is *Asterix*. Although the comic hero, Asterix, lived in the far past, during the Roman era, his adventures are as exciting and entertaining as they are historical. This series, created by Rene Goscinny (text) and Albert Uderzo (illustrations) first appeared in a French comic weekly, *Pilote*, in 1959. Many comics have their beginnings in newspapers and magazines. Some started as cartoon strips and developed into narratives. In the 1980s, the *Guardian* newspaper of Nigeria resorted to using multi-panel cartooning where the story is developed from one segment to the other. Some comics are conceived as stories told in pictures. The *Drum* magazine in the late 1960s started serializing segments of a noted Ghanaian artist's story about an Asante princess who fell in love with an enemy prince. Unfortunately, the magazine fell on evil days in Ghana and the large appetite that this series whetted could not be satisfied. An interesting cartoon series built around the exploits of a folk here, Ananse, was started by a local language newspaper published by the Bureau of Ghana Languages in the early 1960s, but departmental re-organization spelled the doom of this government newspaper which was published in six selected local languages spoken in Ghana. Once again the discontinuation of this series which brought folklore to life, left readers bereft. For Kenya, Henry Chakava reported that sales of a comic series his company, East African Educational Publishers, inherited were in the region of 30,000 per week![8]

The popularity of such serializations shows that the comics genre has a lot of unexplored potential. We need to elevate the comic's low-brow image. One popular Ghanaian cartoonist, Yaw Boakye,[9] affectionately known as 'Ghanatta', recalled two comics he did for the Ghana Water and Sewerage Corporation (which sought to educate Ghanaians on conservation of water) and another he did for the State Insurance Corporation (which sought to explain the various benefits Ghanaians could derive from buying insurance premiums). These comics proved effective learning tools for educating the public on serious issues affecting their lives.

This medium has many advantages — they combine sparse text (through the use of dialogue boxes) with visual images and employ cinematic techniques. The only difference is that the cinema uses sound and images on a celluloid medium while the comic uses dialogue and visuals in panels (which can be likened to the frames of a film strip in the cinema). Such freezing of the action in the story on panels printed on paper loses the immediacy that the cinema enjoys. However, the comic technique benefits from 'stage directions' which the writer/illustrator signposts to signify time lapse. The cinema's stage directions (of the action) are limited to the constraints of the camera lens. Furthermore, the cinema resorts to a range of techniques to indicate passage of time. The cinema can be enjoyed by literate and illiterate but the comic belongs to the literate (and, to some extent, the semi-literate).

The comic is like the cinema in using different perspectives — close-ups, medium distance or long 'shots'. Not many African artists show this versatility and astuteness in telling their story so our artists need some training in this regard.

Publishers need to explore the comic medium for serious themes like re-telling folktales or abridging published serious novels. Students of literature would love to have an encapsulated view of their setbooks published in comic format before plunging into a serious study. I have come across an art student using the comic format to tell the story locked up in a poem!

The fact that an experiment has been successfully carried out using the comic for serious literary works, shows that African publishing is not enterprising enough. Our publishers are too conventional and conservative to break out.

In conclusion, we have established that the comic has a potentially large market (among children and adults alike) which has has not been fully exploited in Africa —perhaps because of the image the genre has, as well as lack of training for artists. More importantly, the reluctance of African publishers to explore this medium could be attributed to the high discipline that this genre requires for it to succeed. As we approach the threshold of the 21st century, African publishers need to break new ground and explore other horizons, for there is a bigger world of the comic waiting to be explored.

Notes and References

1   Asian/Pacific Book Development, a quarterly newsletter of APPREB Vol. 28, no. 3, p. 3.

2   Ibid.

3   Olaniya, Tejumola, 'The tradition of cartooning in Nigeria', Glendora Review 2(2): 102.

4   Information on the situation in Kenya and Zimbabwe was supplied by Henry Chakava and Paul Brickhill, respectively.

5   Conversations the author had with Mrs Abena Ntrakwa, a children's librarian at the Ghana International School, Accra.

6   The Oxford Companion to Children's Literature. Oxford: Oxford University Press, p. 528.

7   Ibid, p. 33.

8   Op. Cit., Henry Chakava.

9   Conversations the author held with Mr Yaw Boakye who is the doyen of Ghanaian illustrators; he achieved some notoriety by his plucky cartoons of Kwame Nkrumah upon the latter's overthrow in a coup d'etat in 1966.

38
Voices from the Past

GCINA MHLOPHE

In the beginning was the word
The word gave birth to language
Language gave birth to the story
Through stories real fun began!

For as long as there have been people in the world there have been stories, long before all the great, respectable sciences were known to us. The Sun and the Moon were important in a way more special than we can imagine. Stories were like firestones, always at hand to start up many other fires in people's minds and hearts. One person could tell a story and another would be reminded of a story too. So the story was at the centre of people's lives. Where do they come from is an old question but one that is still asked by both young and old. Stories were born in people's minds every day, in a way to try to understand the world they lived in. They tried to find answers in the colours of the sunset, they tried to work out where the rainbow ended and other such mysteries. Different peoples all over the world were puzzled by the same issues and they wanted to have something to tell to their children and to one another. Animals of land and sea continued to puzzle them and they made up stories according to the behaviour they observed. Often the people's own ways of thinking and customary behaviour were translated into 'animal language' as they called it. They taught one another important lessons through stories and children learnt to distinguish between right and wrong.

Politics and religion have successfully used storytelling and reached more people than they could have with their often inaccessible language. Many religions have found parallels in stories that are particularly regional to the people they are trying to reach.

In Africa the art of storytelling has survived in spite of the difficulties people have faced. The different cultures developed and survived with the help of storytelling in all its forms. There are many wisdoms hidden inside the stories that have survived, and we continue to learn from them.

Characters like Aknansi the spider in West Africa, Khalulu the hare in East and southern Africa or Nogwaja the wise hare in southern Africa, have emerged as important players in hundreds of stories told again and again in many languages. We often see people we know and interact with in our everyday lives when we listen to these stories. A question about the Lion being King of the beasts — why does story after story portray him as a sitting duck for little creatures like Hare and Tortoise?

Looking at the monsters like Gongqongqo, Golumolumo, Snake with seven heads, and AmaZimu or amaZimZim the feared ogres, have you ever wondered why they have so many faces and characters? Story versions are regional and take the shape and character of the storyteller. The most fearsome monster can be turned hilarious by an unskilled storyteller and so miss the whole point of the story for the listener. There are many examples of how a good story can turn into a confusing jumble of events. And then there are stories that are so powerful that they take hold of their own lives and show the way for us to know the fun and magic of this undying artform.

Someone once said that stories are like breath, they quietly weave their way around and in and out of us, they demand to be shared, not hoarded or owned by one individual. Sometimes we hear a story as children, we grow up and think we have forgotten it as our interests turn in all directions but then comes a day when that old story comes back like a little magician to help us understand or explain to others something that at first appeared so inexplicable!

When a story has a good intricate plot with unpredictable twists or turns of events, then it stands a better chance of staying in our minds all our lives. That story will easily be the one passed on to the next generation and it will have the same effect on them. Also there are many possible interpretations to any one story and that is exactly what excites storytellers and listeners alike.

Like fire and water, rocks and mountains, light and darkness, birth and death, like life itself, Stories are all around us, we only need the eyes to see them, the ears to hear them and the heart to let the magic touch us.

But why storytelling?

Because storytelling is the mother of all other art forms.

Because no song is a good song without a story to tell, something to inspire, to make one think, laugh or just wonder.

Because a dance is only movement unless it embodies a story or simply reminds us of one. A piece of art, a play, a movie and even the style of dress all bear some resemblance to the 'mother', a story of some sort.

Stories are important in the way they manage to strengthen the survival of a people's culture. They raise questions and stimulate creative listening in both the young and the old. In other words, the listeners have to create their own pictures, find their own answers as they listen to stories, and not be passive recipients who accept everything as the gospel truth. Children who learn very early in life to ask questions, will grow to wonder about all they see and learn in life. They might also learn to accept that others will ask questions and sometimes not believe what they say. If stories manage to influence one's outlook on life, then they have played a role in letting their magic show.

Why stories? Because stories can give voice to one who thinks they have nothing to say. They open the channels of communication between all kinds of people, parents and children, men and women, people from different cultures or different political persuasions. In countries like South Africa, where we have suffered so much pain, again stories can be used as medicine. They can help heal festering wounds if we use them well, respectfully.

What makes a good story?

I am tempted to say; a good story must have a good beginning full of promise, a strong storyline to sink one's teeth into as it were, and then an end that hits us like a bolt of lightning! But must every story be like that? I am not so sure.

One thing is certain, though — a strong storyline is like a backbone that survives and is remembered when all else threatens to disappear into forgetfulness. Tellers must surely know why they are telling a certain story and where it is taking the listeners — they must never tell a story they do not like. No one else will like it, because there will be no joy in the characters portrayed, no warmth in the voice that tells it, and no life in the thread that tries to reach the ears of the listeners.

A good story must have a purpose. It must be imaginative and take the mind to countless mysterious places. Also you can trust your heart, the heart knows a good story, it will gently reach out to the mind and say, 'Go on, fly, there is much adventure and treasure to be had, you'll be back soon enough for all your realism and seriousness!!'

Then imagination will gleefully take over. Imagination opens up the wings of the mind and they fly to Storyland where everything and anything is possible.

A good storyteller knows this and looks for good stories everywhere. Even when the mind comes back from Storyland, a good story lingers on in the subconscious and waits to be called up, to play a role in the real world.

Sometimes a good story is a simple story that everyone can understand.

Storylovers all over the world know one truth:

Without stories we die inside;

Without us, stories die.

In the company of words

It is truly marvellous, wonderful and comforting
To know that I have eyes to read
Hands that can write
And an enormous love for words
I am lucky to be speaking a few extremely beautiful languages
For I love words — language's ancestor
When I'm happy, words define my happiness
When I'm sad and confused
Words turn into clay and allow me
To mould and remould my muddled up thoughts
Till I find inner peace in my soul

Had I to choose, between weeping and reading
I'd most definitely choose reading,
A good book
For I have proof, for aches and tensions
It works!
Countless times I've turned my back on pain
And found friends in characters from far off lands
Countless times I've defied anger
And caressed my nerves with an old comic book
Countless nights I've triumphed over insomnia
And had a heart to heart talk with my pen and paper

I come to my desk in the dead of the night
I sit, without a clue as to how I wish to start
But then, before I know it, words of all types and sizes
Come rushing unto my finger tips
As I feel my whole body smile
I welcome them, every single one of them
Like the good old friends that they are
When they start dancing in large circles around me
I am convinced that I was not born to be bored
For how indeed can boredom even begin to penetrate
My timeless word circle
Now you see, why I'm so content
In the company of words   *Gcina Mhlophe*, 1995

39
Storytelling

LYDIA MHANGO

People of all ages need stimulation for their imaginations, dreams and inner development, so we all seek artistic experiences in different forms — theatre, dance, poetry, painting. Storytelling is a way of making literature alive in various ways.

Story-telling as a bridge builder
— Children and adults
Perhaps the best meeting ground is between children and adults because children listen to adults, and in turn love to be listened to themselves — a two-way process. Story-telling involves emotions, therefore it highlights important issues in both children and adults.
— Old and new traditions
It's important to know one's roots and feel proud of them; adults telling stories to children is known as oral tradition. Comparisons can be made between the old and the new to determine what remains relevant and applicable.
   Racial groups
As long as they listen to each others' stories, they can communicate.

   Literature requires access to books, newspapers and magazines but an alternative is oral story-telling. In Africa, this has gone on from generation to generation as a way of preserving culture, entertaining, teaching morals and passing on knowledge, especially in the form of parables. In the evening, children sit around a fire and listen to folklore, music, proverbs and learn to dance, providing an opportunity to interact with adults in a relaxed atmosphere.

   For this reason, people with the knowledge and who have special abilities to do this, must tell stories in order to entertain, educate and spread knowledge to the less knowledgeable.

Story-telling for enjoyment/entertainment
— Enjoyment is the most important reason people listen to stories, and why it should be lively and worthwhile. Very few children forget an enjoyable story.
— Children love to listen to stories. Younger ones ask for the same bedtime story again and again, and ask a variety of questions — 'Then what happened?'

'Why?' 'Say that part again!' They are not happy with 'to be continued'. Answers are not always available but curiosity is good for learning.

— What sounds boring to an adult may interest children; if we are going to tell them stories, we have to be patient with them and not frustrate their interest.

— Story-telling has to be lively. A droning voice will send children to sleep, adults will simply walk out. The audience must hear and see emotions and possibly feel them along with the storyteller, that way their attention is held.

— By the end of the story, the audience should have got the message and the objectives been achieved. (Questions are a healthy sign but too many questions could indicate failure to reach the children).

— Story-telling can be in the form of music — there are no barriers to the enjoyment of good music. Most African songs, drumming and dancing tell a story. A lack of eloquence does not necessarily mean one cannot tell a story in the form of song and dance and entertain others.

Story-telling for stimulation

— Story-telling is particularly stimulating because everything has to be imagined. Any child listening to a story will form certain images in his mind to make the story vivid, and reality is different to each child. Stories make children think, this could lead to research. Thinking in turn helps them develop concentration as well as listening skills. Sometimes visual aids help to achieve a more lasting impact, for clarification and also to avoid vague imaginations.

— In teaching literature, I have been amazed at the variety of pupil's answers given to the same question. I learned the hard way to pay attention to accuracy because I could not rule out my own mistakes. Children believe in us.

— Story-telling sharpens the imagination especially in children: ('Did the monster have big horns?' 'Why did the little boy die?' 'What happened in the end?') Again, curiosity and building up images of characters, fires the imagination, particularly in those that cannot read.

— Children come up with questions, facts and ideas that the story teller might miss; this has to be encouraged as it is a learning process. We may even learn something from them in the process.

— As the child's imagination is stimulated, a message from one story can inspire work on other areas of the curriculum or day-to-day life.

Story-telling for communication

— Story-telling is increasingly becoming a method of sending out messages about the AIDS epidemic, education, gender and environmental issues (particularly over the radio). This is a form of literature. These messages have to be exciting and interesting enough to hold attention — how else apart from the story form?

— Mere hard facts may not be appealing; tell a story, hold a discussion afterwards so that it is not just a story but a lesson from which something can be gained. Story-telling is a source of information or a method of discovery.

— Most people that are illiterate and do not have access to books or magazines spend a lot of time listening to radio stories. Children sit down to enjoy listening to children's radio programmes. It is a method of acquiring information on social issues, politics, wildlife, right and wrong and so on.

— A lot of radio programmes are in story form in Zambia, evidence that story-telling has been recognized as an effective way of reaching and communicating with masses of people. It must be made alive for them.

Story-telling for character building/confidence

— Openness is very important for confidence or character building. When children feel they have taught other children and even adults something, they gain confidence. Also, this strengthens the child-adult relationship and develops trust. The child becomes more fluent with this confidence. Confidence develops character and should be encouraged.

— An appropriate story will dispel children's wrong beliefs but we have to respect them and give them the freedom to express themselves. If we are flexible and friendly, we promote their awareness of their ability to influence things for the better. They open up and we can tell each other stories more effectively.

— Story-telling should not be by adults only, children enjoy being entertained by fellow children. Where talent in story-telling is identified it should be encouraged. Stories can be dramatized to strengthen self-expression.

— Children themselves recognize the need to improve their speech, sentence construction, pronunciation, grammar, adjectives, inflection and so on because they want to reach others and entertain them.

Story-telling for education/knowledge

— My experience in teaching literature revealed that novels and plays came alive during class discussions. When I or the pupils re-told the stories, the level of understanding improved, resulting in better essays, too.

— Even just the teacher reading aloud as the children follow in their books is a form of story-telling and livens up literature. Through sentence stress, emotions like sarcasm, joy, misery, and so on, become alive and the correct meaning is communicated.

— Listening to stories leads to awareness of the written word (related to spelling, vocabulary, grammar). Children learn to write through reading, and good readers are usually good writers. This is essential for their continuing education as it promotes literacy.

— Story-telling by reading aloud presents an opportunity to stop and define unknown words, make reference to other parts of the story, give examples or alternatives of what might not be apparent, as well as allow for questions.

— The question and answer sessions help identify talent. It is interesting to hear them say, 'If I were so and so, I would have done . . . ', or 'Why didn't he. . . ?'. The children are able to relate to characters in the stories and offer solutions and/or alternatives — a sign of mental stimulation and development.

— My best history teacher's lessons were all in story form. Without textbooks he told stories about European history and made it alive. The whole class was attentive. Being old, the effect was almost as though he had been there himself! We read the textbooks to verify his facts and dates. I had not liked European history until then but he effectively used story-telling to teach us.

— Stories that are fiction based on fact will impart knowledge to the children, especially if they are simplified to suit the appropriate age groups.

— Use of story-telling in teaching English Language, for example, essay writing, summary and comprehension.

Story-telling for reconciliation and healing

— Some of the best known examples of this come from South Africa, Zimbabwe, Angola, Burundi and Rwanda, where children have gone through much pain, suffering and death as a result of conflicts.

Children's stories have emerged from real experiences and, apart from entertainment, have also brought about reconciliation and healing between groups — age, racial and tribal as well as political groups. Their innocence in these conflicts touches adults who might not have similar success in bringing about healing and reconciliation.

Conclusion

Story-telling is day-to-day life itself. It is communication, enjoyment, entertainment, stimulation, development and education at various levels and in various forms. Almost every child can tell stories as well as listen to them. As children respond very well to story-telling, much could be achieved through this medium.

Discussion Points
Group Two: Children's Literature

1   Teaching deaf children: Gcina Mhlope asked how Maria Chiswanda had become interested in teaching deaf children to read and Dr Chiswanda replied that it was curiosity — a friend of hers had come to work at the Emerald Hill School for the Deaf and in discussion with her, she felt that she, too, would like to learn more about the problems deaf children have in reading. As a child she had a deaf neighbour of whom she had been frightened and yet she had wondered if she was able to read and write.

2   Donor-funded children's book projects: A participant suggested that it was a case of 'let there be a donor and there shall be a book project' and he wondered if anything would continue when the donors finally left. Godfrey Moyo said that obviously the vision is to be self-sustaining in the long run but they had to start somewhere. Their plan is to sell their books and so continue to fund the project. Eli Moshi said that their project relied solely on donors with very little local contribution. The National Insurance Company and the National Bank of Commerce had made some contribution but they do have a problem of sustainability especially since the project now plays a fundamental role in the education sector. They do collect some money by charging members a fee for learning to use the computer and a fee for the seminars and workshops.

3   Self-sustaining Philippines project: Annari van der Merwe asked Virgilio Almario how he had managed to create a self-sustaining project in the Philippines. He replied that when Marcos was still in power, she had been interested in the project and had offered money and encouragement. Although he did not actually receive much funding, he was stimulated by her interest and he had got a good head start. After the fall of Marcos he already had a lot of titles. By selling the titles and developing more he eventually made the project self sustaining. Initially, it was very difficult to sell 1,000 copies of a title but now he can produce 10,000 copies and sell them in a month. The books are mainly sold directly to the children. However, it had taken a great deal of planning and marketing. He had to organize storytelling groups and form a support group of representatives from different sectors of the book industry. It was hard work but after 20 years it became self-sustaining as the desire for books had been created.

4   Indigenous language publishing: A Zambian participant asked Godfrey Moyo how his project decided what language to publish in. He pointed

out that there are about 73 languages in Zambia (although only 7 official languages). There is a lot of conflict over which languages should be used. Godfrey Moyo explained that the children's book project is a pilot project so they started with Ndebele since the project was based in Bulawayo where this is the dominant language. He thought that they would be able to translate the books into other languages once the project is established and it was important to make a start somewhere.

5   Distribution: A Ugandan participant asked how the two children's book projects distribute their books. Eli Moshi explained that in Tanzania in the first phase the publishers were obliged to submit their books to the project and they handled distribution in the three southern regions which were the most disadvantaged. However, in the second phase each district would receive enough books for six selected schools each year. The publishers post these books to the District Education Officer in each area who has to get the books to schools. The schools fill in a form to confirm they have received the books and this form is returned to the project. This has been successful so far. The publisher gets 80 per cent of the value of the books and the outstanding 20 per cent is paid once the forms have been received. Godfrey Moyo explained that his project acts as the publishers and so they have to go door-to-door to bookshops to sell their books. Also, he mentioned the Book Fund Project Catalogue produced by the Zimbabwe Book Development Council which he feels will help market the books in rural areas. Chirikure Chirikure raised the issue of the difference between a commercial venture and a community project but regrettably time did not allow for further discussion.

6   Storytelling: Miriam Bamhare asked the storytellers what parents could do if they don't know any stories. Gcina Mhlope replied that there are lots of theories about where stories come from but, to quote Lydia Mhango, stories are 'the very essence of everyday life' and explained that ordinary happenings can be embellished and worked upon. She suggested you could even start with a simple chant about members of the family. Godfrey Moyo asked whether we were still justified in saying that we in Africa sit around the fire and listen to stories. The panel replied that this certainly still happens in rural areas although in towns the television may have replaced these traditions. However, as Gcina Mhlope pointed out, we can tell our stories using the electronic media too.

7   In summary, Woeli Dekutsey used two quotations from the papers presented— 'the story is the mother of all art forms'(Gcina Mhlope) and 'stories are the very essence of everyday life' (Lydia Mhango).

Group Three
Scholarship
& Research

40
Children's Literature and the Development of Identity
A Personal Reflection

ELINOR SISULU

O nce upon a time, on a bright, sparkling morning, a group of children set out to school. They hopped and skipped along, looking out for the wild fruits which they knew they would find on the way. First they came to the short, stout *ntuntuluka* tree. They swarmed around the tree like buzzing bees, picking the oval red berries, each one trying to pick more than the other. They ate as they walked, their faces puckering when they tasted the sourness of the big pip of the *ntuntuluka* berries.

The children made another stop on the way to school at their favourite place, where the trees grew thick as a forest, a shady place, cool and quiet like a church. They came to four huge *tshwankela* trees which stood tall and proud, like kings and queens looking down at everyone. They seemed to say, 'You down there, we are special. Our fruit is precious. It is not like the lowly *ntakubomvu* which you have to grovel on the ground to find or the common *ntuntuluka* for which you barely need to stretch out your hand. Ours is special, the fruit of kings and queens, black and smooth like the darkness of the night. You have to work hard to get hold of our treasure!' And indeed, the children did work hard. The brave ones climbed up to the lower branches and carefully reached out for the berries. The others scrambled around in a clump of nearby bushes until they found the long pieces of wire which were twisted with a hook at the end. They used the wires to hook down the *tshwankela* berries. When they thought they had picked enough, they sat down for a while for a small feast. All the hard work was worth it. The *tshwankela* was oh, so sweet, the kind of sweetness which stayed in the mouth for hours afterwards.

As they sat quietly, in that shady place, their mouths full of sweet fruit, they heard voices behind them. 'You eat alone, you children. What about us, your ancestors? You do not offer us any fruit. We are not strong and nimble like you. You should pick some fruit for us!' Startled, they turned around and saw two ancient-looking people sitting on a rock shaped like an upside down basin. They were a strange pair, a ragged old man and a ragged old woman, dressed in what looked like bits of sack and skin. The woman wore a patched apron with huge pockets.

'Well! What has happened to your respect! Do you not answer when you are spoken to?' The children jumped up as if waking from sleep.

'Yes, of course we will give you some fruit' they cried. The oldest girl had tied her pile of *tshwankela* in a cloth bundle. She untied the bundle and poured the plump berries into the outstretched hands of the old man and woman. The woman put the *tshwankela* into her pockets.

After a few moments of nodding their heads at each other, then at the children, the two elders spoke, 'Since you have been so kind and generous, we will reward you.' The woman reached into her pockets and took out some stones. 'What do these look like?' she asked.

'They look like the round pebbles which are found next to the river,' replied the children.

'Ah, but these are no ordinary stones. These are feeling stones, more precious than gold. When you hold this stone tight in your hand, close your eyes and think hard for a while, what you feel and know at this moment, on this day, all that feeling and knowledge will go into this stone. In the time ahead of you, when you want to remember how you felt on this day, you can hold the stone.' She gave a stone to each child and holding the stone tightly in their clenched fists, they closed their eyes and thought as hard as they could. When they finally opened their eyes and looked around, the old man and old woman were gone. The children wondered what had happened. Perhaps they had been dreaming. But when they stretched out their hands, there were the stones, lying warm and heavy in their palms.

Suddenly the children realized they were late for school. Their loud, noisy selves again, they rushed off, clutching their magic stones. They were out of breath by the time they arrived at their school on the hill. Their teacher was waiting for them. Tall and stern he was and he stood no nonsense. He asked them sharply why they were so late. 'Nonsense!' he said when they tried to explain what had happened. 'I have never heard such rubbish. You are lying! You were sitting around eating that disgusting wild fruit. I can see that you mouths are blue black as if you were drinking a bottle of ink!'

'No, we are not lying, teacher! Look! Here are the stones!' The teacher looked at the stones in disgust.

'What worthless things! They are of no value at all! If these old people do exist then they are just filling your head with foolishness.' He took the stones from the children and flung them into the sand. Shoulders drooping, the children filed sadly into the classroom, all except one little girl. She was not sad because when she realized that the teacher would take their stones, she had hidden her stone in her pocket. That day and in the days afterwards she kept her stone in a hiding-place, away from the sharp eyes of prying teachers and gossipy schoolmates.

***

A few years ago, I had the good fortune to come across an article entitled 'The Earth Turns on a Foreign Axis' by Zimbabwean writer, Chenjerai Hove. In this article Hove argues that education in Africa has been an alienating experience because from the time an African child enters a classroom, he finds that his world is not worth learning about:

> Nothing about my own parent's farming routines, the birds of my own sky, the smell of my own land, the cries of the children as mothers sang African lullabies to them and the folk tales which sent ghosts reeling in our imagination. Nothing about the stories of witches and medicine-men and women as they fought to control both the gods and the human beings. All became 'superstition' as we succumbed to the new religion, never to return again, or maybe to remain in some grey area of confusion. A new world, remote and seemingly relevant, grips the world of the little ones. The earth turns round still, but on a different axis.

Hove's observations affected me profoundly because they brought back memories of my own education, memories which I would have preferred to forget. I went to a primary school in Harare in the 1960s. The education system in what was then Rhodesia, was modelled along British lines. Like Hove, my education was an alienating experience, doubly so because I went to a school for children of mixed race. The content of education for 'coloured' children was the same as that of white children and it was designed to root out the African in us. In the year my brother started school, my father's sister came to live with us. Like any good aunt, she told us stories about Chihota where she and my father grew up, as well as tales about witches, magicians and talking animals. Budding storyteller that he was, my brother passed on these tales to his teacher. Her response was chilly. She contacted my mother to tell her this child was disgracing the family by telling stories about witchcraft at school. Thoroughly embarrassed, my mother put a stop to the storytelling sessions, much to our detriment. The irony was that the school library was bursting with stories about witches, goblins and pixies, stories like *Hansel and Gretel* and *Sleeping Beauty*. It was fine to read about witches and other strange creatures, as long as they were white but witches from Chihota were a no-no.

The books I read in school filled my head with visions of the English countryside, white Christmases, goblins and pixies. My favourite writer was Enid Blyton whose British upper class characters were far removed from the reality of most children in Britain, let alone that of an African child. If I came across Africa at all in the course of my reading, it was through the works of Kipling and Rider Haggard, stories and poems such as 'The Great, Grey Greasy Green Limpopo'. I remember the first time I saw the Limpopo river, it was during a particularly bad year and I wondered why it was not grey green and greasy. The consequences of damaging stereotypes, the exoticization of Africa, and the absence of good African literature in my early education resulted in an inferiority complex which was only corrected when I went to university where for the first time I encountered African literature.

Thirty years later I discovered that the folklore stories which were forbidden in our home and school have been published and have received critical acclaim abroad. I was amazed to discover the book *The Lion on the Path and other African Stories* told by Hugh Tracey and published in 1967, a time when I had my nose buried in Enid Blyton. Another book inspired by Zimbabwean folklore was *Mufaro's Beautiful Daughters* by John Steptoe. There are many other African stories which are finding a ready market in Britain and North America.

Does this mean that things have changed in Africa? I look at the books which my children are reading and things have not changed that much. Although my children have more access to stories from Africa, as well as from other cultures, there is still a dearth of stories set in their own environment. While there has been an explosion of multicultural children's literature in the US and UK, these developments have not made a dramatic impact on education in Africa.

***

Now, to get back to my story:

Nothing more was heard of the magic stones, until one day when a group of white missionaries from a foreign country visited the school. As the teacher proudly showed them around, one of them picked up a stone in the playground. 'What have we here?' he asked. 'Oh, that's just a worthless stone,' said the teacher impatiently. 'Interesting,' said the visitor, as he took a round glass out of his pocket, put it against his eye and examined the stone more closely. After that he hardly looked at anything during the tour of the school. His eyes were on his feet as he shuffled through the sand, every now and then bending to pick up something. The children thought he was strange, the teacher thought he was mad, but then missionaries were often that way.

When the missionary went back to his far away overseas country, he showed the stones he had picked up to the other white people. They were fascinated and many people flocked to see the stones. Some stones were put into museums, others were sold for a lot of money. Some of the white people wrote books about the wonderful stones.

The owners of the stones, the children at the school, grew up and some of them became just like the teacher and believed that the stones were worthless. Others felt sad about how they had lost the stones. When they had their own children they tried to tell them about that wonderful day. 'Take us there,' said the children. 'We too want to eat those fruits, we too want to feel those stones.' But when they went back they were terribly disappointed. The *ntuntuluka* trees had disappeared, the *tshwankela* trees had been cut down by people who wanted to build a road where the trees had stood. The quiet, shady place had been replaced by a gaping wound in the earth. And try as they might they could not find any stones. They would have to take their children to foreign lands to find the gifts of two ancient people.

As for the little girl who had kept her stone, she found out that whenever she held her stone and felt the joy of that day in her childhood, she could paint the most wonderful pictures. She grew up to be a famous artist who travelled around the world, but wherever she went she always carried her stone.

References

Hove C. (1993), 'The earth turns on a foreign axis' in *Common Cause*, July-September.

Tracey H. (1967), *The Lion on the Path and other African Stories*, Routledge and Kegan Paul, California.

41
Current Reforms in Education in Zimbabwe

GABRIEL M. MACHINGA

No reform in the education sector being initiated in most countries of southern Africa can avoid taking due cognizance of the comprehensive socio-economic reforms such as the economic structural adjustment programmes aimed at achieving macro-economic stability. In Zimbabwe, economic reforms which have been characterized by public expenditure restraint, stringent budget deficit reduction measures; comprehensive cost-recovery and cost-sharing measures; commercialization and privatization of state enterprises, have already impacted on the education sector just as dramatically as the civil service reforms have done on the human resources sector. It is evident that no education reform process in this region can ignore the new demands by the general public led by civic organizations for openness and transparency as prerequisites for accountability and good governance. These demands have promoted active stakeholder involvement and wide consultations in all socio-economic and public sector reforms being undertaken.

Commission of Inquiry into Education and Training

At the beginning of this year, the President of Zimbabwe, Robert Mugabe, appointed a 12 member Commission of Inquiry into Education and Training Systems to advise on the changes necessary to meet the challenges of the 21st Century. The Commission of Inquiry is expected to take cognizance of the fundamental need to develop an education system that responds to the aspirations of the people, to the changing socio-economic environment, to technological changes and to the imperatives of global trends. The composition of the Commission and the nature of its work plan also take into account public demands for openness, transparency and comprehensive consultation and involvement of stake-holders and key players in the education sector.

It is our expectation that the Commission of Inquiry into Education and Training will effectively address the critical issues of access, equity, relevance, efficiency, and quality in our education system. It is also expected to deal with issues on the financing of programmes and infrastructure; monitoring and evaluation of education; information technology and its application in Zimbabwean schools; the establishment of an appropriate framework for effective organization and management of the education system; comprehensive curriculum reforms and the retention of quality human resources in the education and training sector.

On-going Reforms

The quality of written and oral submissions already made to the Commission of Inquiry at public hearings held so far in different regions of the country demonstrates the enormous interest by the people of Zimbabwe in the work of the Commission. The Commission is expected to submit an interim report shortly which will highlight some of the most dominant reform proposals and the nature of submissions so far made.

It is important to stress that although the final recommendations of the Commission will constitute the most far reaching education reform proposals, there are many other on-going education reforms which are being undertaken and which we expect will have equally serious implications on our education system. This is as it should be for education reforms should be regarded as a process and not an event.

It is my intention, therefore, to highlight some of the on-going education reforms in Zimbabwe to illustrate this and especially those reforms that touch on some of the issues of this year's Indaba.

Reform of the Curriculum Development Unit

As the main function of textbook writing has been decentralized to commercial publishers it has become necessary to reform the structure of the unit responsible for curriculum development and review. Through an effective system of strengthening the knowledge-base of classroom teachers in subject areas, and of equipping these teachers with the necessary textbook writing skills, many classroom teachers could become competent textbook writers whom commercial publishers can commission to write the required textbooks. This move has, therefore, made it unnecessary for government to maintain a team specifically for writing education materials.

Equally important has been our decision to reform the human resource management and structure of the unit that reviews national curriculum and is responsible for syllabus production. Here again our decision has been to develop a strategy that uses classroom-based teachers working in panels and co-ordinated by full-time subject specialists to review national curricula. This arrangement makes it unnecessary to finance an independent and fully fledged curriculum development unit while encouraging all teachers to see themselves as contributors to curriculum development and review. In many respects this approach helps to bridge the gap between the classroom and the curriculum developer. The classroom, therefore, becomes a firm testing ground for national curricula.

Reforms in textbook supply
Currently being implemented are reforms in the distribution of educational materials. Arising from various studies conducted in Zimbabwe on both the pupil–textbook ratio and the supply of textbooks to schools, new strategies have been adopted to effectively decentralize the supply of relevant and affordable educational materials to schools. A forum for regular consultation between the ministry and representatives of book publishers and booksellers was set up. This greatly enhanced the capacity for the commercial publishing sector to access financial resources provided by co-operating partners as part of comprehensive budget support aimed at enhancing efficiency in the supply of textbooks — especially to disadvantaged children. This partnership has brought about effective planning for reprinting textbooks and also ensures that publishers do not face unnecessary financial constraints by warehousing materials no longer needed by schools. Through this regular forum, publishers and booksellers have begun to contribute to the improvement of mechanisms in schools for identifying the required education materials and for ensuring that the book procurement procedures are transparent, consistent and efficient.

Reforming the education administrative structure
Currently, the government is rationalizing the structure of the Ministry of Education, Sport and Culture as part of reforming its administration. Some objectives of these reforms are the creation of distinct career pathing structures and the removal of structures which have led to under-use of human capacities and the rapid turnover of specialists in such areas as policy analysis, research, monitoring, evaluation and information-technology management. They will enhance the proper deployment of adequately trained and motivated education personnel. They are also expected to create an effective institutional framework for sustained participation in decision-making at various levels of the education system thereby guaranteeing professional commitment and ownership of both the education system and the education policy by all education personnel.

Another critical reform in this regard is in the management of information in the education sector especially in such areas as planning, evaluation and monitoring. The establishment of the education management information system will not only improve access to relevant and critical information but will also enhance the diagnostic capacity of the planning and evaluation units of the Ministry of Education, Sport and Culture.

In the context of improving the internal efficiency of the education system, and as a means of contributing to the improvement of the quality of teachers, we have adopted a concept of a Better Schools programme that is establishing teachers' resources centres throughout the country. All schools in Zimbabwe have been grouped into clusters. Each cluster of schools will be serviced by a well-established teachers' resources centre where teachers will access a wide diversity of education materials and benefit from in-service training and specialized school management programmes. Equipped with both information technology and a wide variety of reference materials, these resource centres should greatly enhance the quality of education. Through these centres publishers will be able to inform teachers on their recent publications, their future textbook plans and any publishing projects which may be of interest to them. Many teachers in our schools are enrolled with different local and international universities for different degree programmes. Publishers of tertiary educational materials will be expected to exploit these teachers' resource centres to promote their publications and appropriate educational computer programmes.

A major component of the Better Schools programme is the broadening of the teachers' horizons and awareness in order to handle many new subjects such as HIV/AIDS education, human rights education, civic education, population education, and so on. These are subjects which many of our teachers did not come across during their teacher training and yet are a prominent feature of the school timetable. The Better Schools programme will be used to discuss new ideas and all reforms being introduced in our education system.

42
Writing for Children in Indigenous Languages
A South African Perspective

TSLETSI W.D. MOHAPI

Writing in all societies has been preceded by an oral tradition, which developed into oral literature as classified by academics in literature studies. The stories have been related through the ages for entertainment and in an attempt to provide answers to questions on nature and its genesis, to understand human behaviour and thoughts, and to address the aspirations and fears of humankind.

In African cultures, storytelling has been a common feature handed down from generation to generation. However, the narration of these stories assumed different forms in terms of presentation, content and effect. They are known in Sesotho as *ditshomo*, in IsiXhosa as *lintsomi*, and in IsiNdebele as *linolweani*. These are what are referred to in English as folktales. According to Alan Dundes, folklore, which comprises folksongs, folktales, riddles, proverbs and other materials preserved in words, has diverse functions. The most common of these are aiding the education of the young, promoting a group's feeling of solidarity, providing socially sanctioned ways for individuals to demonstrate their superiority, serving as a vehicle for social protest, offering an enjoyable escape from reality, and converting dull work into play.

Folktales have a purpose in the rearing of children because they instruct as well as entertain. Dundes declares:

> Even African folktales, which are regarded as fictitious, are
> considered to be important in children's education since many
> of them are fables or other story forms that teach morals.

Folktales have been identified as an essential element in the rearing of children in the African culture.

What is children's literature?
Children's literature can be defined in various ways depending on the context, for example: literature about children, by children, for children and a combination of all of these.

This critical analysis is about literature written by adults for children and will confine itself to primary school children whose mother tongue is one of the indigenous languages of South Africa.

Writing in the early years

When the missionaries came to South Africa, their mission was to convert Africans to Christianity. The first hurdle they faced in achieving this was illiteracy; they had to make Africans literate if Africans were to read the Bible. This entailed teaching them the alphabet and then to read books. Most of the publishing in African languages was done under the direction of the churches. Presses such as the Morija Press, Mazenod Press in Lesotho, Marianhill Missionary Press, Loveday and the Missionary Press were controlled entirely by missionaries. They also published books for primary and secondary schools. Books in African languages for primary schools were known as 'readers'. Some of these readers were written as early as the 1930s and 1940s. In Sesotho, *Paliso tsa Sesotho* (South Sotho reader) was published in 1940 with an issue of 5,000.

The books included cultural, religious, social and geographical materials as well as animal stories and poetry. This represented a radical move away from the folktale format. For the first time, parts of the human body were seen to be conducting a conversation, for example in a story entitled *Puisano ya Bahlanka ba bahlano* (a conversation among five gentlemen). In this, the eye, the ear and the mouth discuss their indispensable roles in the human body. This was a new turn in the content of such stories.

Some of these readers were a combination of grammar and short stories, as is the case with the Xitsonga grammar books, *Xitsonga xerhu*, produced for Standards 1 and 2. In Sepedi a series on wild animals and children was prescribed for schools. These works had titles such as *Ditaba tsa serapa sa diphoofolo* (The news of the animal park) and *Ditapa tsa bana ba mabu* (The news of the children of the soil).

Immediately after the introduction of Bantu Education in 1953, a number of publishers became interested in publishing for and in African languages. These publishers generally confined themselves to educational material. These children's stories were therefore written either by teachers or school inspectors, and by non-first language speakers of African languages.

In Sepedi, a reader entitled *Balang ka Lethabo* (Read with pleasure) was written by Phatudi, Mojapelo and Goslin. The book comprised modernized folktales, Biblical stories and some accounts of social events. At the end of each story there is an explanation of terms in English and Afrikaans. But one ends up not knowing whether the reader is for Sepedi, English or Afrikaans.

Also in Sepedi, there was a series of *A re baleng* (Let us read) for Substandard A to Standard 4, written by Hoffman and van Heerden. These were elementary readers with the letters of the alphabet introduced in isolation and in short simple sentences of one or two words. In Standard 4, the reader assumes another form by graduating to stories of three pages long.

In IsiXhosa the *Stuward Xhosa* readers were first published in the 1920s and were revised in the 1960s. According to Shepard (1945) they were prepared under the editorship of W.G. Bennie and were well graded according to level of difficulty and designed to sustain the children's interest from the beginning. They were for novice readers and ran through to Standard 6. The content was folktales, riddles and interesting stories.

To engender a love of reading for its own sake, the then Department of Bantu Education encouraged the publication of a children's magazine, called *Wamba*. It contained stories written by teachers and inspectors of schools and letters from pupils. It also had a cartoon strip from T.O. Honiball about a naughty jackal.

In Sesotho a series of readers were written for Substandard A to Standard 5, entitled *Ntataise* (Guide me) and *Matshohlo a Puo ya Sesotho* (Thoughts of the Sesotho language). They were both written by Thejane and Englebrecht. They were later revised to bring them in line with the new Sesotho orthography.

The pattern that has been illustrated in the examples cited was maintained in all nine indigenous languages in the writing of children's literature.

Observation

1 The readers were written by inspectors of schools and non-speakers of African languages. It may have seemed a good idea to allow inspectors of schools to write children's literature but they were not in a position to keep abreast of the tastes and interests of pupils. Sufficient proof of the folly of allowing non-speakers of the languages to write readers for children is to be found in stories which are not culturally compatible with the pupils they were written for. An example is the book *Balang ka Lethabo* (Read with pleasure) which cannot be declared a Sepedi, English or Afrikaans reader. Furthermore, the authorship was confined to those who sought to 'civilize' the African people through western standards rather than liberate them.

2 The readers were not written for pleasure but as learning aids. In a book

like *A re baleng* (Let us read), for example, there are short uninteresting sentences which do not make for enjoyable reading.

3   The illustrations are only in black and white and they do not encourage children to use their senses to enjoy and comprehend the story. M.M. Nhlanhla is of the opinion that the amount of reading a child can do depends on internal and external influences.

4   The level of the stories is beyond the children's comprehension as the stories do not reflect the children's day-to-day reality.

5   Although the writers tried to bring folktales into the readers, they failed to exploit the plot structure of the folktales and in some instances the illustrations are modernized while the content is not.

6   The illustrations show white people in civilized situations such as the example from a passage on 'Let's go to town'. Only whites are depicted walking in town.

Writing of children's literature in the 1970s

In the 1970s the Department of Education and Training introduced a new syllabus which encouraged the study of oral literature from Standard 6 to Standard 10. A number of books were written on oral literature in all nine African languages. The books were written in African languages by African folktale experts and education subject advisers. These were taken from research at universities and written mostly by non-speakers of African languages.

There was an upsurge in the publication of children's literature in indigenous languages from the 1980s to the 1990s. There was a need for original works for primary schools. The increase came from translated works from English with stories that come from Europe and some from central Africa. A number of publishers took the opportunity to publish the stories.

Recommendations on the writing of children literature

1   African literature, particularly children's stories, will be of value to the international community if they are written according to the structure of the folktale, highlighting cultural values and norms through artistic creation in order to link with what has been lost in culture.

2   The stories should uphold the African renaissance philosophy by emphasizing the importance of African cultural values that will build the personality of the child to be a better citizen of Africa.

3   The publisher should commission writers who are conversant with African

culture, African values and aspirations. Sekou Toure (*The Wretched of the Earth*, p. 206) says:

> In order to achieve real action, you must yourself be a living part of Africa and of her thought; you must be an element of that popular energy which is entirely called forth for the freeing, the progress, and the happiness of Africa. There is no place outside that fight for the artist or the intellectual who is not himself concerned with and completely at one with the people in the great battle of Africa and of suffering humanity.

The publishers need to consult African languages writers' associations to find out what they would like to achieve in African languages for the African child.

4 The stories should address the question of multicultural schools in South Africa which is in its infancy. Do children from other cultures know and accept the African experience or is it as a foreign concept although they live on the continent? Multilingualism should be reflected in the choice of literature in all institutions where children's literature may be accessible.

5 The media should also be encouraged to promote the African children's literature through television, radio and cinema. It is possible to do so — consider *The Lion King* where the setting, naming and moral lesson were maintained in the film.

6 The stories should incorporate the dynamism inherent in current African communities — not only have rural settings, but say something about the urban African child who has the same social problems as any other urban child. Problems of drugs and child abuse should be tackled as they were addressed in folktales — for example, the story of Tselane who was warned not to open the door for Dimo.

7 Theatrical performances of indigenous children's stories would also promote better understanding of culture and encourage reading.

Conclusion

In a nutshell, there should be a deliberate glorification of writing in indigenous languages for children but not its exploitation. Let us be proud of our heritage that has brought us as Africa to where we are today, emerging amongst nations, soaring high as an eagle to the future unknown.

43
Co-publishing for Children
And the Economics of Indigenous Language Publishing

DON LONG

It's just not economic to publish in your language.

How often has something like this been said to you? It's the excuse for not publishing in indigenous languages given the world over. yet half of the world's 6,000 languages are in danger of disappearing, according to Stephen Wurm, the editor of the Atlas of Languages. The disappearance of any language represents the loss of an incalculably precious portion of the human heritage.

The Pacific Islands comprise over 20 countries and territories, spread across 30 million square kilometres of ocean — about a third of the surface of our planet. In the Pacific we speak around 1,200 indigenous languages — almost a quarter of the world total. Yet there are only about 10 million of us. And some of us live in very poor countries. Tuvalu, for example, may be the world's third poorest country. And we are young. Half of the people in Tuvalu are 19 or younger. Even in more developed countries, like New Zealand, half of the Pacific Islands population is under 20. Our languages survive or disappear with our children.

Children's book publishing in small indigenous languages in the Pacific faces the same problems found in other developing economies. Overwhelming problems force us to find innovative solutions. We don't want to lose our indigenous languages. As we migrate between our different Pacific societies and into our cities, the last thing we want to do is lose our languages of identity and heritage.

Indigenous languages

The indigenous languages are spoken in both the island states of the Pacific and by Pacific Island communities within the so-called Pacific-rim countries (though in reality this means in about a dozen major cities, like Los Angeles and Auckland). In New Zealand, for example, about a third of the children are Polynesian. Of this third, about two thirds are Maori. Maori may be one of only five or six of the world's smaller, indigenous languages which are in a state of recovery, according to UNESCO. The balance of New Zealand's Polynesian population is made up of people from other Pacific Island countries: principally Samoa, the Cook Islands, Tonga, and Niue. Tokelau has been part of New Zealand since 1948. The Cook Islands and Niue are internally self-governing in free association with New Zealand (which means that Cook Islanders and Niueans are also New Zealand citizens). Two indigenous languages are spoken in the Cook Islands and by the Cook Islands community in New Zealand: Cook Islands Maori and Pukapukan. (More speakers of Cook Islands Maori and Pukapukan live in New Zealand than in the Cook Islands.)

The Ministry of Education publishes resources for New Zealand schools in English and six Polynesian languages. By world standards the total number of speakers of these languages is small. There are only about 12,000 Niueans in the whole world, for example, with about 10,000 living in New Zealand. Of the 6,000 or so Tokelauans in the world about 4,000 live in cities like Wellington and Auckland. So imagine the demographic challenge that has to be overcome to publish in these languages: few of them represent substantial markets to publishers.

The economics of publishing

The economics of publishing children's books essentially comes down to this: the larger the print run the lower the unit cost.

The Ministry of Education in New Zealand publishes a new resource in Maori on average about once a week. It publishes a new resource in Samoan, Cook Islands Maori, Tongan, Niuean, or Tokelauan on average about every twelve days. These Polynesian-language resources include children's books, audio cassettes, issues of journals for children, and a newspaper (in Maori) for teenagers. Even the newspaper is published in full colour. And all these resources are available on free issue to schools.

This publishing programme is contracted to a government-owned publishing company, Learning Media, which also publishes for the Ministries of Education in Samoa, Niue, Tuvalu, and Tokelau and to privately owned publishing companies, such as Huia.

Because of the approach to teaching reading in New Zealand schools there is little to distinguish readers published by the Ministry of Education from trade children's books for sale in bookshops. Trade children's books sometimes use larger formats and occasionally come out in hardback but otherwise they look much the same as the reading resources published for the Ministry and they draw upon the same pool of authors and illustrators.

When the Ministry publishes a children's book in English it usually does so in a print run of about 40,000. This drops to about 20,000 for a book in Maori. Books in Samoan, Cook Islands Maori, Tongan, Niuean, and Tokelauan are combined into print runs approaching 20,000.

In contrast, first editions of trade children's books are generally published in English in editions of 3,000 to 5,000 — sometimes with 1,000 to 2,000 copies each in Maori and Samoan (the Maori and Samoan editions are usually supported by a grant from New Zealand's arts council).

Co-publishing — publishing the same book in a number of different language editions (sometimes for several clients) — has a dramatic consequence. Combined with grants from an arts council, it allows trade publishers to publish children's books in the most widely spoken Polynesian languages, like Maori and Samoan. It allows Learning Media to economically publish full-colour children's books in Polynesian languages for Ministries of Education — even in languages with relatively few speakers, like Niuean and Tokelauan.

When you publish a children's book many of the costs are the same, whether you print a few hundred or thousands. Illustrators tend to work by commission for agreed fees, with the publisher retaining copyright. (In contrast, freelance writers prefer to license their work to publishers for royalty payments, retaining the copyright in their words.)

If you contract an illustrator to illustrate a book for US$1,000, printing 100 copies that would cost US$10 per book — just for the artwork. Already, the book's uneconomic if it's a children's book — with that single cost alone.

But spread that cost over 10,000 copies, and the cost of those illustrations drops to only ten cents a book. Precisely the same equation applies to many of the other costs involved in publishing a children's book — from the salary you pay the editor through to the cost of the colour plates.

Big print runs are the key and co-publication is an excellent way to achieve them. By printing different language editions of the same book in one print run you can dramatically increase the size of the total print run.

There are some constraints and a few concessions — you must keep all the words on the black plate. The colour plates are shared across all the different versions and should remain unchanged. So you sacrifice colour in the titles. All the text is in black. This forces the designer to find other ways of creating interesting covers — using interesting fonts, for example in place of colour in the lettering. And the illustrator and designer need to work to the language that will take up the most room on each page. And you can only combine languages that read in the same direction.

We combine print runs in several ways. Sometimes we publish in several languages for one client (as we do for the New Zealand and Samoan Ministries of Education). Another way is to publish simultaneously for several clients (as we have done for the Tuvuan and Tokelauan Departments of Education and the Institute of Education in Fiji).

This is how it works taking, for example, a 12 to 16 page full colour children's book in 210mm by 147mm format. Publish 1,000 copies in one language and the unit cost is around US$3,50. Publish 2,000 copies (spread across two languages) and the unit cost drops to around US2,30. By the time you reach 20,000 copies, spread across five languages, the unit cost has fallen below US$1. It is a numbers game in which small languages can help each other by joining forces.

Adding another language at a later date is almost as cost effective. Black plates run out at about US$50 each and the cost of putting a job back on the press tends to add about another 50 cents per book. This is the way the Asia/ Pacific Cultural Centre for UNESCO's co-publication programme works. They publish a master version in English, designed in such a way as to leave lots of room for Asian and Pacific language versions. The most recent title in this programme has so far been published in about 24 languages, for a total print run of 200,000.

Once unit costs reach these levels, full colour children's books can come out at about the same unit cost as small editions of poorly illustrated, photocopied books — of which we have seen far too many in our languages.

Consequences and benefits

These poorly illustrated, black and white books carry an insidious message. In bilingual educational settings — quite common in the Pacific — children can't help but compare such books in indigenous languages to full colour books published in English or French. What does this convey to children? Doesn't it start to say something about the relative importance of their languages?

Co-publication is typically a book published in the language in which it was written, together with translations into other languages, the same book published in the same language but slightly different editions or a combination of these.

This has important social and regional consequences.

Looking back at the reading resources published for the Pacific Islands schools in the 1940s and 1950s, there are a lot of European folktales translated into Pacific Islands languages. Children of the Pacific used to be more familiar with Little Red Riding Hood than they were with traditional stories from a neighbouring island.

Publishing books in different Pacific languages means that children not only have access to the work of authors writing within their own cultures and languages but also to the work of other Pacific Islands writers, too. In the Tupu series published by my company, we publish a children's book each year by a Samoan writer, a Tongan writer, a Cook Islands writer, a Niuean writer and a Tokelauan writer — but each of these books is published in five separate language editions — so the series actually creates 25 separate children's books each year. We've calculated that for the same budget, we could publish only about seven children's books if we were not translating and co-publishing.

In multicultural societies it's important to grow up reading each other's stories. This raises all kinds of issues: of identity — what exactly is the culture of a multicultural society — of tolerance and mutual understanding.

Countries that share small languages (in the sense of total number of speakers) can co-operate within combined print runs to publish full colour children's books. Even if each country has different spelling or orthography, you can just change the black plate between each version. Regional co-publishing of different editions (if only with different imprints or title pages) is definitely a way to achieve economic print runs and the quality that children deserve in their own languages.

44
Translation and Communities
Working across Cultures: The Role of the Translator
A Summary of Wangui wa Goro's Presentation

CHARLES R. LARSON

In her provocative paper, Wangui wa Goro, a Kenyan, identifies her role as a translator of African literature as 'subversive'. In the first 20 years of her life, she attended schools that denigrated African languages. She remembers a teacher who forced a piece of paper down a pupil's throat if the child spoke in a tribal tongue. This literal gagging serves as a metaphor of the colonial attitude toward African languages which persisted in Kenya after independence. Thus Wangui asks — if this is the attitude toward African languages in general, what would be the attitude toward literary works in African languages?

A true African literary work is one written in an African language. The African literature tradition ought to be founded on such works. Wangui, like her mentor Ngugi wa Thiong'o, is well aware that years of debate have persisted about this issue. Ngugi stopped writing in English and switched to Kikuyu mid-stream in his literary career. Wangui acknowledges that the Nigerian writer, Chinua Achebe, says that African writers ought to be able to write in any language they want. If that happens to be a European one, it doesn't make them any less African.

As a translator of Ngugi's own works (from Kikuyu into English), Wangui admits that major complications exist. These difficulties may be of culture or of gender — let alone of the languages themselves and inadequate words in the European language to express African expressions. As a woman translator, for example, Wangui asks, how is one supposed to translate something by a male writer that she is conflicted about? What about race, class, or even technical issues/inadequacies of translating from one language to another?

Thus, as a translator, she feels she has to intervene in order to challenge world perspective about the culture the literary text describes. The academic community is not sufficient preparation for training a 'subversive scribe'. A translator, thus, uses her imaginative self to create a partially new text, especially when the translator (like Wangui) sees herself as 'a translator for social change'. Only then does authentic African literature pass from one language to another.

45
The Academic Seminar
A summary of Terence Ranger's Reportback

CHARLES LARSON

Professor Ranger's report began by praising the steps that have been taken by this year's ZIDF to add a strong academic component. At the two day University of Zimbabwe seminar that preceded the Book Fair, an extensive variety of regions and disciplines were represented by a variety of scholars. In future years, he noted, this conference might not be a prelude to the Fair but run concurrently with it, immediately after the Indaba.

Surprisingly, in spite of the focus on children at this year's Book Fair, there has not been that much actual research done on African children. Yet in the next century, children (those 18 or younger) will constitute a majority of the population of the African continent. He cited, for example, the thousands of children who live on the streets of Harare. And he asked how many people have studied them seriously.

More importantly, the conference asked a crucial question. How do we get to hear children's voices? A great amount of research, for example, has been devoted to the study of African women, but how do we get to understand children themselves learn of their choices (as children) outside of the domain of the adult world? How can children tell us about themselves from their own point of view?

African children often want to define their own roles in life especially in the absence of adults around them. Street children often set up their own night classes for reading, teaching one another. They know they need to be literate, but once literature, what kind of literature exists that is relevant to their lives? Publishers don't like to publish books about children. Academics, publishers, and especially adults need to learn to listen to children's voices on their own terms and not exclusively to the adults who traditionally have dominated and controlled their lives.

46
Children in Context
The National Inquiry Services Centre

MARGARET CRAMPTON

C hildren are growing up in a world different from the childhood of their parents and even more different from that of their grandparents. Never before has there been such confusion between generations and a need for understanding, counselling and information. The nuclear family is disappearing, serial marriage is common, many are dealing with the problem of step-parenting and there is a reversal of the traditional male and female roles. Many families are headed by a single parent and mothers are employed in the business of making a living. Society needs information tools to tackle the social, educational and health aspects of these changes and problems.

To quote a WHO News release (WHO, 1994):

> Studies have demonstrated that the family is changing throughout the world. Among the factors affecting the change are: the reduction in family size due to the control of fertility and the decline in the extended family; migration and urbanization; increasing numbers of women entering the work force; divorce and family breakdown; increasing numbers of people 'living together' without formal status; and the growth of single parent families, 90 per cent of which are headed by women. Single parent families now account for nearly 20 to 30 per cent of all families in Africa, Latin America and the Caribbean, 15 to over 35 per cent in Europe, and about 15 per cent in Asia and the Pacific. (p.1)

In Africa children now comprise the greatest population group by age (Goliber, 1997).

> For sub-Saharan Africa as a whole, 45 per cent of the population was under age 15 in 1997. The population under age 15 exceeds 40 per cent in every country except Gabon and South Africa, which have relatively low fertility. In contrast, 34 per cent of the population in Latin America was under age 15, as were 32 per cent in Asia and 22 per cent in the US. (p.10)

There are an estimated ten million children on the streets of Africa, driven from their homes by poverty, abuse, abandonment or orphaned by AIDS. Most are boys (McCauley, 1995). According to Grier (1993) with AIDS in Africa, 16 million new orphans could end up on the streets in our continent by 2015.

These are a few of the many challenges facing Africa. We need to plan for Africa's youth and comprehend and chart the impact of the changing world.

Information tools

Information resources have been developed for professionals working with children to build on the experience of others. The National Inquiry Services Centre (NISC) offers access to a vast amount of useful and specific information.

The publication of bibliographic databases

NISC is a database publishing company with the parent company in Baltimore, US, and branches worldwide, many in developing countries. We offer a platform for the publication of databases, alone or in combinations. These serve needs in a multitude of disciplines. Our mission in South Africa is to provide information databases for Africa, about Africa and by Africans. The NSICs worldwide contribute databases from their regions and by combining resources, we provide sophisticated and relevant information in many subjects.

CD-ROM and Internet

NISC offers access to most titles with the option of CD-ROM or Internet, in both cases with powerful and user friendly software and at similar prices. Online access to the Internet tends to be slow, bandwidth too narrow and response time frustrating and variable with the time of day. Tele-communications are unreliable and not always available so the best technology is CD-ROM. The discs are robust, portable and can be sent by mail. CD-ROMs hold increasingly large quantities of information. The plastic discs are relatively cheap and can be updated and re-issued. The software is powerful, intelligent and user friendly with context sensitive help at all times. Response time is instant. CD-ROM drives are standard on all new computers.

Free titles

We promote free access to information essential to the wellbeing of Africa's children helping them grow up with the support of informed professional care givers. Access to information is a cornerstone of a free, peaceful society.

NISC supports the free distribution of POPLINE in Africa. This is the world's largest population database from the Population Information Program of Johns Hopkins University, School of Public Health and the National Library of Medicine, in Baltimore. It contains over 251,000 citations and abstracts from published and unpublished sources. Topics include population, family planning, AIDS, fertility, population laws and policies, health care instruction and maternal and child health. Subscriptions are free to developing countries.

'Child Abuse and Neglect' CD-ROM is available free to libraries and organizations. This has over 23,000 references and access to the world's largest collection of bibliographic information on the subject. Featured are documents, legal statutes, public awareness materials, audiovisual materials and more.

NISC gives a free 'ERIC' CD-ROM to subscribers in Africa if they maintain their subscriptions. This is the world's largest database on education with 954,000 records. Each year about 33,000 new abstracts are added.

NISC discs giving child information

Many of our CD-ROM and Internet titles are relevant to those working with children. To identify them a general information search was conducted:

Child or infan* or teen* or adolesc* or boy or girl or pubert* or pubesc*

This search was not exhaustive and the number of records retrieved understate the total available. The software has built-in intelligence and automatically searches singulars and plurals. Where a word is truncated with an asterisk it will locate references which begin with the truncated word. The software detects spelling variations and versions of compound words.

This search identified thirteen discs with a concentration of child-related information. These are listed alphabetically in Table 1 where it is indicated which of the three main disciplines is served by these discs. The broad categories identified are Psychology and Sociology, Education and Health.

The table shows an approximate analysis of NSIC discs. The figures have been plotted on a Log Scale. In this figure the top bar for each title tells the percentage of the total records on the discs which have child information. The second bar is the total number of relevant records for child information and the third bar represents the total number of references on the disc as a whole.

PsycLIT, from the American Psychological Association and ERIC, the education database, have the largest number of references with approximately 200,000. Nevertheless as a percentage of the total information on the disc, children account for 20 per cent for ERIC and 25 per cent for PsycLIT. These titles offer excellent resources for general psychology and education.

For information on aspects of child related health, POPLINE and the new NISC disc African Health Anthology have 78,000 and 61,000 references respectively. POPLINE is also relevant for sociological and demographic information. Both these titles have excellent references from and about Africa. Family Studies is another relevant disc with more than 60,000 references.

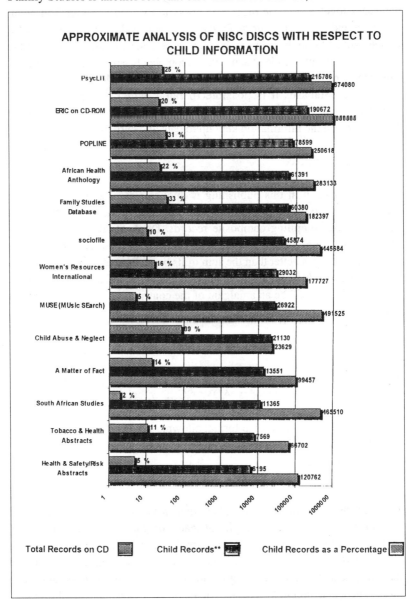

APPROXIMATE ANALYSIS OF NISC DISCS WITH RESPECT TO CHILD INFORMATION

Anthology publishing

NISC has perfected a method of integrating anthologies or suites of related databases together on one disc. It is possible to integrate large and small databases and provide a platform for databases which alone might be too small or specialized to publish. In combination each adds a unique flavour to the whole and the result is a blend to produce a completely new information source. This can be by discipline and/or by region as in African Health Anthology. In combining databases it is possible to range widely over time and be comprehensive. These resources are updated quarterly intervals. The medium is dynamic and the information kept up to date and current.

Composite records

A potential hazard in this publishing is duplicate records where the same reference appears in more than one database. NISC has turned this to an advantage, by compiling composite records. Duplicate detection software identifies the duplicates and retains that which is unique. The resulting composite record is better than the sum of its parts. Different facets of a topic are exposed and different abstracts given equal weight. The keywords in the composite record will be an amalgam of the contributions from the different databases.

Searching features

Three levels of search are provided to cater for each user's personal style: NOVICE provides a basic index. ADVANCED offers distinct field searching and EXPERT, for the information professional, is innovative and a full-powered update of the traditional online format allowing set searching and the repeat of previous searches. It is dynamic, interactive and flexible.

Online help

An online help system is available, featuring an overview of NISC DISCover. It includes such things as: examples of search operators and concepts related to database searching; highlights and sample searches from the three search modes; and techniques for manipulating records and using different record displays; instructions on printing or downloading search results and much more. There is a thorough field specific help system available at all times.

Discussion Points

Group Three: Scholarship and Research

1 Eleanor Sisulu asked Gabriel Machinga what was being done to capture the children's imaginations and make them independent readers and what was being done with regard to African folklore. Gabriel Machinga replied that independent reading was a crucial issue and he had been encouraged by being involved recently in the launches of many supplementary or non-curriculum books. So much was already being done that he felt we were heading in the right direction. He also felt that a start had been made on preserving, renewing, translating and transmitting our folklore.

2 Alois Mlambo asked what the realities of the new curriculum were in the context of economic structural reform and the imperatives to maintain quality with equity? He commented that one impact of the economic adjustment programme was to undermine Zimbabwean education. He also suggested that we need to focus on the entire book supply system, rather than just textbook supply, especially since we have been focused on exams. Gabriel Machinga agreed that the current reforms had resulted in limited finances, especially since 94 per cent of the vote went on salaries leaving little for books. However, education gets 26 per cent of the total budget. Despite these constraints, a lot was being done with the support of the Netherlands and many schools now had enough core texts and were even buying supplementary texts. Regarding the redefinition of education, the commission of inquiry would have a fresh look at the entire system and its structure. Regarding the school and its interaction with the surrounding community, in terms of cultural anchorage, much needed to be done.

3 A Zimbabwean participant commented that education occurs in a specific cultural context and more thought needs to be given to our world view and identity so the community can contribute to the educational system and so that an *ambuya* can feed her fund of indigenous knowledge into schools.

4 The discussion topic, Role Models for the Future — African Women Writers and History, included the description of a project to document voices of African women in Zimbabwe as an example of recovering lost voices. These are being translated into English for the database.

5 Wanguru Wa Goro from Kenya bemoaned the lack of awareness of African women in the diaspora who have a story to tell and are telling it excitingly.

6 A participant pointed out that there is a tendency to not document details of original sources. However, a panel member felt that womens' voices

were being effectively recorded. Further discussion raised the issue of recovering material from the Ndebele women praise poets of the 1960s. In response, the panel agreed there were problems of missing records and archives but much was being done. A Namibian participant suggested that, depending on the language group, some voices were completely shut out and neglected. Also, at times, academics were out of their depth and needed to call on the help of non-governmental organizations and other activists.

7   A participant involved in an organization of indigenous knowledge, commented that most individuals involved in these development projects are university based and élitist with little in common with peasants — making for insurmountable class contradictions. However, in response, the panel acknowledged that university personnel involved are trained to a high level but awareness exists of the ambivalences and contradictions of intellectuals speaking on behalf of peasants, as given in the example and writings of Gramsci and his dilemmas as an Italian intellectual communist in the 1930s. A participant from Botswana noted that their group had Ph.Ds but they got on with their jobs, although this experience was not common in other parts of southern Africa where grassroots people were also involved. A university lecturer from Rome commented that there was no reason to apologize for being an academic. She also enquired about the indexing of various works in the different languages or cultures. She was assured that some sort of bibliography would be published.

9   After Wangui Wa Goro's paper about gender and translating of *Matigari*, a participant asked whether the main character could have been altered to a woman in view of the gender imbalance. In reply it was agreed there was an opportunity to have a female protagonist but Ngugi had not agreed. Further discussion about translation suggested it was creative literature, citing examples of Shakespeare being translated into Kiswahili. African narratives are now part of the global narrative and issues of tribe and village fall away. They are universal stories and translation removes issues of nationalism because you are already dealing with two cultures.

10 Alois Mlambo raised the issue of 'built-in racism' in languages and wondered whether the 'dynamics' of translating from African languages were the same and this became a discussion of the pros and cons of colonial languages, racism and so on. However, the point was made in defence of English that some of the most liberal and liberating works have, after all, been in English! Also, languages do get cleaned up — words like 'nigger' have almost disappeared from English, and languages are also getting more sensitized to gender.

Group Four
Access & Technology

47
Performing Children

ELDORADO DABULA

The first time in our life we face theatre is when we are children. We face it in two ways: as actors or as spectators. As we play we make believe and into that make believe we add a piece of cloth to simulate father's stomach or we use our mother's dress so our first props are used. In Africa theatre has been present in all great events such as great hunting trips, initiation rites or before important battles.

Children, having been the most active spectators, begin to perform by imitating what they have seen. They try to imitate reality. It's good for children to play sport but it's even better for them to perform as theatre increases their physical and mental development. In theatre performance they create and enrich their capacity to work in groups and develop their talents which in turn removes any social barriers they face in school. When taught theatre they learn the importance of their ability and other people's appreciation. They learn to analyze situations and they begin to question. Why this, not that? They begin to use the magic *if* which transforms situations; . . . suppose things did not happen like this, . . . suppose the end can be different . . . suppose there was another solution. This magic *if* gives them the capacity to create different points of view, imagine different developments of the same problem. This is good because it opens their minds and makes them begin to search for other answers.

Some children are part of organised theatre groups, some times professional or semi-professional working days and nights and receiving a monthly income. In southern Africa we have lived through wars and we know that one of the consequences of war is the separation of family, children being the main victims. We know about the so-called street children, washing and guarding cars to make money to take home to their families. However, children take part in theatre to develop their ability and for fun and if they earn income, that helps, too. It's important to generate a healthy spirit among the members of the group so they feel integrated and develop good relationships which make them feel useful. Even the decisions must be consensual so they feel that everyone is important. During orientation, it is important not to say this is good or bad but to encourage children to experiment.

Choosing scripts

Once I had the opportunity to direct a school theatre group and I suggested that since there was no script, we could create one. After a few rehearsals I was living in a new world and finding out how the children judge their elders (with justice, purity and simplicity). I could feel their philosophy of life which was written into the script. They criticised the severe way adults judge young people. Their main messages were something along these lines:

Please father, look back, you have been young like me and try
to understand me. I'm doing my best but I'm still young and so
I make mistakes. I'll get to your stage that is why I am studying.
Please try to be patient with me.

This play was presented at school for parents and teachers and I could see some parents saying timidly, 'Yes, I get the message'. Of course there were others who said'Come on, if you have my experience you will know life is difficult, there is no time to make mistakes'. These children were performing children expressing their point of view of the problems they face.

Once I was invited to attend an amateur festival of theatre and a group of children were chosen as the best. They were acting a common story of a miner who went to South Africa leaving his young wife needy and hungry in the village. After a few years she decides to prostitute herself. She was also supporting her father-in-law. When the husband came back his parents kept quiet but one of his friends told him what was going on in his family. The family forced him to forgive his wife and to forget everything. After the performance one of the children asked me why the father did not tell the son the truth. It is not normal that he should lie, is it? This play disturbed these young children, it was a bad beginning. They should begin with simple stories and only after they mature can they be expected to perform such deep plays.

Summarizing, in this kind of work it is important to know who is going to do which job, what information they have or need, which message they want to put over to whom, whether he or she is the right person to convey that message to these people? Is he or she happy about delivering this message? Did they understand the whole message completely? Children are the men and women of tomorrow and they are in the growing process so they have their own messages in their own lives. They have time to understand the world and they will take care of the future so it is important to develop their ability to analyse problems at their own level and not to take them early to the world of the adults with all the traumas that that can cause.

48
Zimachitika

SIMON SIKWESE

Zimachitika is a family health radio soap opera, broadcast nationally in Malawi, created by The Story Workshop Educational Trust, an 'educating through entertainment' media non governmental organization.

Once upon a time, an elephant, so loved by people because of its friendliness, grew tired with the heat of the sun and decided to take a rest below a fruit tree. Up the tree, a monkey was busy eating fruits. When monkey plucked one of the fruits, he discovered it wasn't ripe enough to eat. So the monkey threw the fruit away without seeing that it would fall on the resting elephant's tusk which it did. The beloved elephant's tusk was broken and rumours circulated around the village that the elephant's tusk had been broken by a falling fruit. Some old men hearing this were puzzled. 'A fruit can't just fall on its own to break an elephant's tusk. Something or someone caused the fruit to fall.' When the village gossips came to tell them the news the old men said, 'Don't just say a fruit has broken the elephant's tusk. Instead, you should find out exactly why the tree fruit fell and broke our elephant's tusk.' And so the people went back to the tree only to find a monkey eating fruits of the tree while throwing unripe ones to the ground.

This is one of the many traditional Malawian proverb tales which story characters in our radio soap opera called ZIMACHITIKA often use to illustrate the advice they give to other characters on the show. We use these well-known proverbs repeatedly in our dramas as a means of preserving our Malawian cultural heritage while at the same time we attempt to educate families on how to improve maternal and child health in the country. The radio soap opera is broadcast weekly on MBC, our national radio, as part of a campaign aimed at exposing local conflicts which act as barriers to health messages and to find realistic resolutions within the people's social context.

ZIMATICHITIKA is sponsored by the Ministry of Health and Education and is a UNICEF-funded project which came about because Malawi is one of the countries whose maternal and child death rates are high. Coupled with poverty and illiteracy rates (as most of its population is predominantly rural and unemployed) behavioural issues emerge over and over again as significant cultural and social barriers to better family health. These barriers have been identified through our research to be:

1   Women's lack of power within their families and communities which means they are not in charge of their own health practices even though they bear the major responsibility for their family's health and well-being.

2   Traditional beliefs and community practices which reject the scientific view of 'cause and effect' in preventing, diagnosing and treating illnesses.

3   The attitude of health service providers, their failure to be supportive of villagers who seek medical treatment and their failure to use educational opportunities to inform people about the treatments, the options they might have and the preventative practices they can employ in the future.

4   Village peer pressure (including the threat of witchcraft) for social conformity which rejects individual behavioural change, especially by women, who want to adopt new ideas.

These are the four underlying barriers to health behaviour change which our weekly radio stories on ZIMACHITIKA are designed to both expose and explore so that Malawian family health improves and children have a more positive environment in which to grow.

What is ZIMACHITIKA?

ZIMACHITIKA means 'it happens'. It's a favourite Chichewa expression for coping with life's unexpected problems. (The play is serialized in 52 25-minute episodes.) The play format integrates elements of both a radio soap opera and serial drama for maximum entertainment.

A serial drama is an indefinite number of episodes using continuing characters who are in new conflict situations in each broadcast. The African-American television programme, The Cosby Show, is a good example of this.

A soap opera has a continuing story with many interrelated sub-plots about a place or group of people whose stories are intricately related. It has no real beginning or ending only an expandable middle. It can stay for decades.

We have mixed these formats so listeners can enjoy each episode separately but we use the extended village family and sub-plots for sustained interest. Each story introduces a new conflict so health issues are mixed with tense social entanglements that entertain while examining underlying values and beliefs that motivate behaviour.

Why has the play grown so popular?

1   The characters are based on real people. They were chosen from people our writers and researchers met and interviewed. They are not educated

but they are intelligent and capable of combining traditional cultural wisdom with the emerging values that can lead to health seeking behaviour.

2   The storylines mix traditional Malawian parables, songs and proverbs with the 30 local heroes, heroines and villains. Because these go with stories told by one of the leading characters, Gogo Nasibeko and the singing blind musician, Tadeyo, the play attracts the attention of children.

Dramatizing family health issues

Each ZIMACHITIKA episode has a proverb title to which the storyline is tied. Most Malawian proverbs are also stories. The following is an example of how it works. The show is called Konza *Kapansi Kuti Ka Mmwamba Katsika* (Prepare the one below for the one above to come down).

In this episode, two young girls are being coaxed by a sugar daddy. He buys them Fanta (cold drinks) and biscuits and offers them a ride in his car and money to start small businesses. Fortunately one of the girls' mother finds them and she takes them to granny who tells them a tale: A man for the sake of his pregnant wife, went hunting. At one fruit tree, he found a bush baby down the tree eating fallen ripe fruits. He caught the bush baby. As he was about to leave, he discovered there was another one up the tree. Carefully he thought of how he could catch it. He gathered a lot of ripe fruits and started to feed the bush baby he had caught. Seeing this the bush baby in the tree trusted the man's generosity and came down to join the friend and the man. Without problems, the man caught it and went home with two animals for his wife.

In the end Gogo tells the girls that the sugar daddy was buying the drinks, offering a ride and money so that they would be be easily trapped.

What proverbs do different cultures have that can teach the consequences of behaviour through an entertaining story?

ZIMACHITIKA stories focus on the meaning of the proverb '*Umanena Chatsitsa Dzaye Kuti Njovu Ithyoke Mnyanga*' (You must know what caused the fruit to fall and break the elephant's trunk). The story attached to this proverb is about cause and effect. Things don't happen without a reason and the cause must be identified if the situation is to be corrected. All the episodes in ZIMACHITIKA try to lead the audience to social change through dramatizing and realistically resolving local cultural and social barriers that generate conflicts in local understanding and acceptance of health messages.

A forced bone breaks the clay cooking pot

In ZIMACHITIKA, one character, a young woman named Zione, is being forced to stay in marriage by her marriage counsellor (*nkohswe*) in spite of the husband's promiscuity. When she runs away, her uncle and grandfather force her back saying marriage survives with persistence (*Banja ndi kupirira*). Zione is infected with STDs and diagnosed HIV positive while she is pregnant. Upon hearing this, her grandfather (a chief) realizes his mistakes and remembers, 'A forced bone breaks a clay cooking pot'. They forced Zione into a marriage she did not want. The bone is the message for social change while the pot is the social wellbeing of the people. Most donor-funded projects have brought messages to or forced them on people and met resistance.

When messages are forced on people without first identifying any barriers they are rejected (the pot breaks). Many educational dramas have artificial resolutions that depend on the ignorant learning from the educated. In these dramas, the educated person informs the illiterate one and with this 'new' knowledge the illiterate person immediately changes his or her ways.

In real life, social change doesn't happen that way. What we know is often not what we do. An example of this is that most of us know about HIV-AIDS and yet we continue the behaviour that has led to Africa's epidemic. In our field research supporting our dramas we found that most people are acting on traditional beliefs and peer pressure when they reject development messages. The concepts of good versus bad and educated versus ignorant need to be eliminated. We need to focus on family and community realities so that the real barriers to social change are exposed and discussed. In this way, realistic solutions can come from within the family or the community as we ourselves identify the improvements we want and how we can achieve them.

Why do we use traditional stories in ZIMACHITIKA?

Storytelling is an ancient art form and a vital part of nearly all cultures. All of us, especially children, enjoy identifying with and imagining ourselves as story characters. At one time in Africa, traditional stories were a part of everyday life. Proverbs and parables were shared in social groups as people debated this and that with their friends. And around fires at night our grannies would tell us folk stories which carried moral values, stories of life events symbolized in metaphors and parables. These traditional stories have always helped us to make better sense of our life experiences, especially if we enjoy the story enough to identify with the characters.

As Africa urbanizes, we are losing some of these traditions, but through the *Gogo* stories and the traditional music featured on ZIMACHITIKA we are trying to preserve the cultural meaning and fun of the story at the same time we apply it to new circumstances. Thus we educate and entertain.

Why radio drama?

People outside Malawi often ask us, why radio? We answer that we believe radio is the most visual medium of all. Can you say why?

Pamela Brooke in her book on radio drama, *Communicating Through Story Characters*, wrote, 'Radio draws on the imagination of its audience for the drama's pictures'.

If you asked children listening to a *Gogo* story to draw images of the characters and scenes, you would get pictures that fulfil the fantasy of the individual listeners. Every child would imagine the story characters and scenes in his or her own way. With radio, instead of the one image television provides, you have all the mental pictures from the entire audience's participation in the drama. As radio script writers, therefore, we try to set imagination in motion, trying to create the entire universe out of nothing but atmospheric sound effects, music and human voices.

Malawi has no television and radio is the only medium through which messages can reach a wider population. Radio drama is especially popular in Malawi and since we have one tribal language, Chichewa, that is understood by most of the country's different ethnic groups, we are able to reach and involve a national audience through a single drama.

Although there are many such groups in South Africa, Kenya and Zimbabwe, The Story Workshop Educational trust is Malawi's first educational entertainment media non-governmental organization. We are just finishing our first year of field work, scriptwriting and production and hope in the coming years to extend the radio story characters into printed comic books for children, teens and adults to meet a variety of different educational objectives in health, agriculture, social welfare and social change.

In Malawi, there is a saying which goes *Mmera mpoyamba*. In English this saying would be 'The strength of a crop (seedling) is detected at the nursery' which means charity begins at home. If we are to talk of safe motherhood, maternal or child health, environment, gender issues, and so on, the wellbeing of the family supporting the child should be our prime target so that our children develop in an environment that is responsive to the changes needed to educate and protect each child.

49
Children's Science Books
The Kawi Project

EMMIE WADE

The scarcity of science reading materials on the African continent has already been confirmed. The few that are available draw on irrelevant experiences making it difficult for children to enjoy learning. Science education in Africa has remained a school activity leading towards examinations, with the teaching methods being rote learning and drilling. Science teachers are inadequately trained and insecure so they discourage exploratory questions from students. The poor infrastructure and use of alien learning materials prevents real scientific experiences among children.

This backdrop prompted UNESCO to set up a project to increase the availability of science materials in Africa. The books will enable students to interpret real life experiences in scientific terms. The rationale is that Africa must use local resources to communicate science. This project will primarily address the energy crisis being experienced the world over; in Africa it is the over dependence on wood-fuel. Environmentalists have provided sufficient data warning about the dangers of continued unchecked use of wood-fuel. In addition the absence of modern technology to be able to tap other forms of energy has exacerbated the problem.

The project is called Kawi, kiswahili for energy, to capture the African spirit. Traditional practices of energy use and conservation will be incorporated into the project. This is consistent with APNET's goal, which is to ensure that Africa has in its possession and within reach high quality, appropriate materials.

UNESCO has made progress in getting African governments to use alternative energy, particularly solar energy. It convened the first conference in Rio de Janeiro in 1992 where Agenda 21 was adopted. The World Solar summit was held in Harare in 1996. UNESCO concluded that a cheap and reliable supply of energy facilitates rapid industrial growth and assures human comfort. Wherever there is a crisis in energy supply, industrial production goes down and people's comfort is compromised.

The private sector already offers alternative sources of energy on the market. Farming communities and industrial centres in remote areas use alternative energy sources since it is too costly to link up with the main electricity grid.

In Zimbabwe, the Energy Forum is co-ordinating everyone concerned with energy supplies. Non-governmental organizations' programmes in Africa are focusing on adequate energy sources and increased access to energy for marginalized communities. With increased awareness societies can reduce energy costs, save foreign exchange and establish an energy supply base without heavy investment. This provided the basis of APNET's decisionto invest in reading materials on the subject.

Aims and objectives

The project will produce six culturally relevant popular reading books on renewable energy in Africa for the 12 to 17 years age group. The books must be fun and reader friendly to interest children. The project will:

- Enhance science writing capacity placing emphasis on Africa's contribution to the development of science and technology. There is an assumption that there is no science and technology in Africa. The process of colonialism encouraged the denial of African science and technology. Through this project children will begin to understand their own environment in scientific terms.
- Involve APNET membership in the publication of popular science materials. Publishing in Africa has been dominated by school texts where the market is understood and guaranteed. The aim is to introduce innovative ways of publishing materials. The project seeks to influence curriculum designers and science teachers so they become more creative in the teaching of science.
- Focus on issues related to renewable energy and the crisis in Africa as far as energy sources are concerned. Knowledge and information on renewable energy is not easily available. The project will package this information for the consumption of children.
- Contribute to a literate environment through access to culturally relevant popular science books. If books are to be useful, they must respond to local needs and aspirations. It is a local book industry that can be in complete harmony with local interests and requirements. Books can also be used to narrow the gap between the intellectual and the common man

Implementation

Several steps have been identified in order to achieve the stated objectives. The first step was to request APNET membership and affiliates to nominate professionals and experts who would ably contribute to the entire process of developing reading materials on renewable energy. This exercise allowed project staff to compile a list of experts with various backgrounds who represent the diversity of the African continent.

Once these experts were categorized, a selected team was invited to participate at a meeting held in Nairobi in February this year. The participants' backgrounds ranged from science teachers, curriculum developers, non-governmental orgaizations working on energy, publishers, researchers, media personnel, and UNESCO and APNET staff. These experts were able to:

- Refine the project concept and suggested improvements to its design.
- Discuss the situation regarding the teaching of science in Africa.
- Agree that materials will be generated in English, French and Portuguese in order to reflect the spectrum of APNET's membership.
- Visit projects to bring themselves up to date with actual projects serving communities with renewable energy.
- Develop a manuscript outline.
- Adopt a writing format and assign each country a book to develop.

The books will have the following titles:

Sources of renewable energy	Guinea
Uses of Energy	Mozambique and Malawi
Conservation of Renewable energy	Kenya
Energy Changes	Lesotho
Storage of Renewable energy	Tanzania
Socio-economic and Political Issues	Ghana

It was agreed that each chapter should:
- include an introduction to a particular energy form — solar, wind, biogas, hydropower and wood fuel;
- discuss its scientific principles;
- highlight traditional and/or local examples;
- include new information and a developmental lesson;
- show concern for the environment;
- develop an activity /assignment/exercise which interests the readers and invites them to participate.

In order to ensure that the scientific information becomes popular, we have insisted that:
- Examples of traditional African scientific knowledge be incorporated.
- The language must be accessible to rural communities.

- Illustrations and symbols must be relevant and interpret the daily experiences of readers.
- Books should be non-racist and non-sexist.
- The diversity of African ecosystems, housing and dress must be included.

The writers are in the process of writing and we are discussing each chapter of each book by e-mail — making suggestions and corrections where necessary. Generally, the books are interesting and include typical local examples and stories to support the scientific theories. For example: the use of charcoal irons; various drying methods for food processing; the use of a mbaula or 'coalpot'; the long distances women walk to fetch water; water shortages and drought and so on.

In Malawi when a child is born the remains of his umbilical cord are buried in a hole and a tree is planted. The tree becomes an indicator of his birth-place. The child nurtures this tree and ensures its conservation. This contributes to afforestation programmes and ensures continued supply of wood-fuel.

In Kenya the word El-nino has become a household name signifying hardship. The East African country suffered from floods this year attributed to the El-nino phenomenon.

Lesotho has developed an activity for children which demonstrates the principle of wind energy when blowing a whistle made from a bamboo stalk.

Ghana's manuscript is targeting older children and presents information that encourages greater understanding of the economics of energy and political considerations. The writers have presented figures showing the disparity of supply and usage of energy between northern countries and poor southern states, bringing in numeracy.

The books will have 60 per cent text and 40 per cent illustrations using common and daily examples. They will be brightly packaged to draw children's attention. It must be emphasized that these books are not textbooks although they will supplement various curricula.

The final drafts will be submitted in November 1998. The next step will be to edit the books. From the already developed database we have identified a team of scientists, environmentalists, educationists and publishers to become an editorial team. This exercise will be co-ordinated from the APNET secretariat.

How do we ensure accessibility? Accessibility begins with the conceptualization of the project. Experience has shown that some writers write for themselves and not for the target group. We have made provision for children to be involved so that the books are relevant. APNET has developed mechanisms to increase accessibility in other projects. Some are to do with selling copyright, facilitating and co-ordinating co-publication, resource mobilization to publish commissioned work, fostering north - south linkages and developing and administering buy-back schemes.

The buy-back scheme

The buy-back scheme has been incorporated into the project. It refers to the purchase of up to a third of the print run which the publisher receives in advance to cover production costs. The scheme will be developed and implemented in such a way as to encourage fair participation on the market. To ensure this the publisher will only receive 60 per cent of the market value of the books up front, 30 per cent on delivery of the books and the remaining 10 per cent once the project team are satisfied that they have secured orders for the remaining copies. It is not the intention of the project to create unfair competition on the market. The books are being developed as a set and will be marketed likewise.

To sensitize the market the project has developed promotional materials and is working on book jackets — a weak area in African publishing, since production costs are high and inhibit rigorous advertising. The stimulation of a sustainable readership is being carried out by service institutions such as book councils. The books will also be marketed outside Africa.

Following book launches, the books will be distributed to identified schools, educational institutions and communities. Already some non-governmental organizations have indicated that the books will be useful in supporting their energy supply programmes. For example the book on *Conservation of Energy* is likely to be popular and serve the needs of out-of-school readers as well.

Concurrently a manual on 'How To Produce Science Books' is being developed. This has only just begun. In addition, the project team is collecting science materials developed and produced in Africa. The collection will become part of a permanent collection of the African Publisher's Network.

Conclusion

The success of this project lies in consultation, review of materials and observation of cultural life. Most publishers have little time to fully concentrate on this aspect of book production. Therefore they are often pressed to bring out new untested materials to meet curriculum needs. We already know that these books will be useful as supplementary material to natural science subjects, physical science, environmental science and social studies.

50
Enticing Kids to Read
Summer Reading Programmes at San Francisco Public Library

YOHANNES GEBREGEORGIS

There are 26 branches and one main library in the San Francisco Public Library system. The branch libraries serve unique neighbourhoods throughout the city. Even though there is a mixture of all races in the city, there are pockets where certain groups are dominant. For example, the Chinatown branch is located in a predominantly Chinese area. It holds the largest Chinese language collection in northern California. The Mission branch serves a largely Hispanic population, and contains a large Spanish interest collection while the Walden-Bayview branch serves a mostly African-American populace, and houses the largest African-American collection of all branches.

The New Main Library

The New Main Library is a very modern, state of the art library. It is a seven-storey building with a five-storey skylight atrium and seating capacity for more than 2,000 patrons. It holds over 1, 272,000 books, 750 magazines, 340,000 bound periodicals and 2,221,600 government documents. It is wired with new information technology-on-line and multimedia and Internet access.

It was built with $104 million bond money and $30 million from private donations, which was used for furnishing, carpeting, computers, and so on.

The Children's Centre of the New Main Library
The Children's Centre has the largest collection of children's materials — board books, picture books, readers, fiction (including mystery, adventure, science fiction and fantasy) non-fiction (including biographies), folklore, international languages (more than 55 languages represented), audio cassettes (children's songs, stories, folklore, and language learning), videos, early childhood collections (materials for parents, teachers, and day care providers). It has a children's reference collection as well as extensive materials on all aspects of children's literature. There is also the Effie Lee Morris Historical and Research Collection of Children's Literature, which includes such rare works as the original *Alice in Wonderland* and the Beatrix Potter collection.

A variety of children's programmes are provided at the children's centre: storytelling, puppet shows, films, art and crafts, individual and group performances and authors and illustrators' presentations. Using its abundant display space, the children's centre hosts various types of public displays of photography, art, poetry and crafts, made by children throughout the city of San Francisco and beyond. 'The Giant who Swallowed the Moon: Indonesian Children's Art from Java and Bali' was displayed in February and March 1998).

The Electronic Discovery centre is a network of 12 computers connected to a CD-ROM server for children to develop reading and art skills, play interactive games, explore encyclopedias and connect to the World Wide Web.

What is Summer Reading Club?

Summer Reading Club is a programme to encourage reading and library use during the summer months when children are out of school. Libraries organize stimulating programmes to get children to visit the library. These include music performances, storytelling, craft making, authors' and illustrators' presentations, multicultural performances, magic and puppet shows, clowns, and so on. It is full of fun, activities, reading, stickers, bookmarks and prizes. All children up to the age of 13 can join by signing on at one of the 26 branches. The club runs from 6 June–8 August. (There is a teen reading programme for those over 13.)

Planning for summer reading

Planning for the summer reading programme is an ongoing process done by a Summer Reading Committee. The committee is made up of children's librarians from the branches and the co-ordinator of programming. Librarians choose what committee they want to participate in depending their own interest.

The Summer Reading Committee's work includes:
— Creating a theme for the reading programme.
  For example, Reach out for the world — Read 1996; Read Around the City 1997; Reading — What a Trip 1998.
— Creating and designing reading records, posters, cards, and so on.
— Producing flyers and other promotional materials.
— Choosing prizes to be awarded.
— Soliciting donations for prizes.
— Providing information to librarians throughout the system.
— Publicizing the summer reading programme.

School visits for Summer Reading Club
Just before the summer break, librarians arrange school visits to reach children in each of their designated schools. They do book talks, distribute flyers, explain the Summer Reading Club and encourage children to visit their libraries.

Read and Win: Rules of the game
Different libraries use different approaches to how children account for the reading before they get their prizes. There is controversy and heated discussion as to the merit of counting the number of minutes or hours read versus how many books read. After counting the number of books read, San Francisco Public Library system has adopted counting the number of hours read.

The rules
On the first day of the Summer Reading Programme, which is determined by the date schools close, children register at their local library. They either take books home to read or read in the library. They have a time log sheet where they register time started and time finished reading. After reading in increments of 15 minutes, they come back to register the number of hours read on their reading record which is kept at the library.

After two hours of reading, she or he gets the first prize, the second prize after four hours, the third prize after six hours and a final prize after eight hours. The child has completed participation in the club after eight hours and receives a certificate and other prizes. However, children can continue reading as many hours as they can and enter for extra prizes.

Community involvement
Gifts and donations — One of the tasks of the Committee is to solicit gifts and donations for prizes for those who participate in Summer Reading Programmes. For many consecutive summers certain institutions and organizations have supported the club by donating passes, tickets, T-shirts, books, and so on. The San Francisco Zoo, the Planetarium, the Discovery Museum and the SF Giants, have been donating prizes for several years.

Kid Power volunteers — Kid Power volunteers are between the ages of 10 and 16 and they register children, record times read, explain the rules to participants and give out prizes. They file records and keep the summer reading table clean. Kid Power volunteers have to participate in Summer Reading Club and they are expected to be exemplary.

At the end of Summer Reading Programme, they receive a certificate of appreciation, a T-shirt, books, a special drawing and a thank-you party.

51
Enticing Children to Read

MYRNA MACHET AND SANDRA OLEN

Research has established that many of the skills which are used in reading are learnt before the child goes to school (Heath,1983). In Africa many parents are illiterate and cannot afford books. They opt out of the child's education not because of disinterest, but because they think that they have nothing to give the child that will be of any value. Many children are no longer experiencing the rich oral culture of storytelling — an important preliteracy experience. Even in a developed country like the US, only half the infants and toddlers are read to by their parents (Trelease 1995:48). In developing countries the number of children whose parents read to them is far less.

Emergent literacy

Many of the skills for successful reading are taught through reading aloud to a child. In shared reading between an adult and a child, labelling, scaffolding and repetition play an important role in the child's early language development. Labelling (Ninio and Bruner, 1978), where parents name vocabulary items and begin a give-and-take dialogue, is one of the first language games. The lexical and syntactical features of a child's language is expanded through scaffolding (Wood, Bruner and Ross, 1976). For example the child may say: 'Look, a bus' and the parent replies, 'Yes, it's a big red bus'. Children frequently ask for a repeat reading of a favourite story and this serves as a basis for language acquisition as well.

Parents' style of storybook reading and the use of interactive methods affect literacy development (Stoll, 1998:24). The language development features — labelling, scaffolding and repetition — play a key role in early language acquisition and also promote the child's enjoyment of books. Being read to in the home is regarded as the best single predictor of future academic success.

Children look forward to the shared intimacy of 'lapreading' and this helps them develop a positive attitude to reading (affective development). Reading offers exposure to the decontextualised language of books and a world of knowledge that is often beyond the experiences of the child (cognitive development). The differences between the context-embedded talk of everyday life and the more decontextualised form of written language becomes familiar (Heath,1983).

There is also linguistic development as reading increases vocabulary acquisition and syntactic structures are strengthened (Elley, 1989; Feitelson *et al.,* 1993). Also, children learn how to hold a book properly, to turn the pages, and to interpret the pictures and gradually learn that the text is written from the top to the bottom of the page and from left to right. They learn to sit still and concentrate on a story for short periods of time. They become familiar with story schemata. This extends their ability to produce or retell a story verbally.

All these aspects contribute to the child's readiness for school. Wells (1986:193) and others found that children who have been read to have a head start.

During a research project we carried out, interviews were held with a sample of primary school pupils who came from fairly affluent homes in an established urban township (Machet and Olen, 1997). The pupils' parents were white collar workers. The average number of books in their homes was five and these were usually textbooks. Some of the children could not differentiate between a book, comic or magazine so there may have been even fewer books. This also indicates a lack of emergent literacy skills.

Although the parents read newspapers and magazines at home, the children did not observe them reading books so they did not appear to endorse reading and as Wells (1986:193) has indicated, parents are important role models.

In many deprived communities, libraries are regarded as places of study and are seldom used for borrowing leisure reading books. Few parents belong to libraries and both parents and children seem to spend most of their leisure time watching television. Preschools are few and far between and often overcrowded and staffed by unqualified caregivers. Children in the rural areas or informal settlements are probably much worse off than children in urban townships. So most children will enter school without emergent literacy skills.

The role of the school and teachers

Teachers in deprived schools can still use various strategies to assist in reading and writing development. For example, they can fold a sheet of paper to create small books and then children compile booklets, like one on 'Colours' where they use crayons to put a different colour on each page. They copy the word for each colour onto the page. By providing each child with their own book to read the teacher is making reading material accessible to the children. The children can swop books with each other and this helps to extend limited classroom collections.

Another idea is to use a series of pictures so that children learn to create stories with sequencing. A story structure also helps pupils develop visual literacy. Children can relate a brief item of news which the teacher writes on a strip of paper and pins on the board. Children then 'read' the different news items. Many other strategies which have been devised by creative, caring teachers are discussed in the professional literature.

The role of libraries

Libraries play a vital role in introducing books to young children. A regular story hour for young children in the library or in an alternative venue, like a clinic, should be investigated. Many parents are unaware of libraries and story hours are non-threatening. Children can then be invited to become members of the library. Many parents who are not readers are nervous about joining a library so an informal meeting about the library would help. Picture books with no writing ensure that illiterate parents can 'read' these books to their children. They can play an important role in helping children develop emergent literacy skills.

The role of publishers

Publishers have an important role to play. Many of the books available have been published overseas and do not reflect indigenous culture. Publishers need to develop indigenous writers so books reflect the local culture. Publishers are faced with the problem of multilingualism, poor distribution channels, limited disposable income and a lack of reading culture (Machet, 1993). However, it is difficult to develop a reading culture if there are few relevant books available. Publishers need to use ingenuity to develop interesting books that can be sold cheaply.

Selection of books

Books selected for children need to be as accessible and appealing as possible because children need every possible motivation to read. Research indicates that children have a more positive attitude towards reading if characters reflect their ethnicity, lifestyle and values (Saracho and Dayton, 1991:43, Shelley-Robinson, 1996:16). An important factor is accessibility of text and illustrations. Text in books for second language readers has to be simple but rewarding (Heeks and Kinnell, 1997:80). The text should be examined not only for vocabulary but also for hidden assumptions that the child may not understand. Librarians and teachers selecting books need to look for books that help concept formation.

Second language learning

In second language learning there are four areas of development. For affective development, an informal environment is preferred. Cognitive development is more complex. As Ô'Malley (1988) points out, most second language programmes fail to meet the needs of pupils who are moving from a context-embedded language environment of written language, especially as pupils advance in school. The pupils require additional support to gain the necessary skills for school success (Stoll, 1998).

Free voluntary reading and interactive reading

In 1995 we carried out a pilot project on grades three to seven pupils to determine the effect of free voluntary reading on their English second language comprehension (Machet and Olen, 1997). It was found that free voluntary reading significantly improved comprehension, and even more so in the grades three to six age group.

Interactive reading uses 'why?' and 'what if?' questions. Wells (1985:253) has described how reading programmes where the teacher uses an interactive style are more effective. He noted:

> If stories are simply read as part of a daily routine, without being further discussed, they are likely to remain inert and without much impact on the rest of the child's experience . . . However, where, through discussion, stories are related to children's own experiences and they are encouraged to reflect upon and ask questions about the events that occur, their causes, consequences, and significance, not only are their inner representations of the world enriched, but also their awareness of the ways in which language can be used in operating on these representations is enhanced.

Thus linguistic and literacy development for second language pupils requires interactive participation and support. Reading competitions and Readathons are more effective with older pupils as they encourage reading a new book each time — younger readers benefit from re-visiting stories already read.

Conclusion

It is not enough to teach children to decode. We need to teach them a love of reading and provide them with books that will encourage and support the reading habit. We have to make reading a priority and ensure that suitable books are available and accessible to encourage this. Many government officials believe that story books and school libraries are a luxury that can easily be dispensed with and do not take cognisance of the fact that effective learning cannot take place without effective reading. It is false economy to do away with libraries because more money will ultimately need to be spent on children repeating classes or dropping out of school, If we are to develop a love of reading in children we have to start as early as possible to introduce children to books. This is the responsibility of the community as a whole — we have to work together to ensure that the next generation does not reflect the high illiteracy rates of present generations. The only sure way to do this is to inculcate a love of reading in children. Literacy is essential for development. Without a literate population the gap between the developed and developing world will grow larger and the possibility of closing it will diminish. In conclusion, it is hoped that teachers, librarians, parents and publishers will be aware of the importance of reading and work together to entice children to read.

References
Elley W.B. (1989), 'Vocabulary Acquisition from Listening to Stories, *Reading Research Quarterly*, 24(2):174-187.
Feitelson D., Z. Goldstein, J. Iraqui and D. Share (1986), 'Effects of Listening to Story Reading on Aspects of Literacy Acquisition in a Diglossic Situation', *Reading Research Quarterly*, 28:71-79.
Heath S.B. (1983), *Ways with Words: Language, Life and Work in Communities and Classrooms*, Cambridge University Press, New York.
Heeks P. and M. Kinnell (1997), *Learning Support for Special Educational Needs: Potential for Progress*, Taylor Graham, London.
Machet M.P. (1993), 'Publishing and Bookselling in South Africa with Particular Reference to the Black Market', *South African Journal of Library and Information Science*, 61(4):166-176.
Machet M.P. and S. Olen (1997), 'Literacy Environment of Pupils in Urban

Primary Schools', *South African Journal of Library and Information Science*, 65(2):77-84.

Ninio A. and J. Bruner (1978), 'The Achievement and Antecedents of Labelling', *Journal of Child Language*, 5:1-15.

O'Malley J. (1988), 'The Cognitive Academic Language Learning Approach', *Journal of Multilingual and Multicultural Development*, 9:43-60.

Saracho O.N. and C.M. Dayton (1991), 'Age-related Changes in Reading Attitudes of Young Children: a Cross-cultural Study', *Journal of Research in Reading*, 14(1):33-45.

Shelley-Robinson C. (1996), 'The Voluntary Reading Interests and Habits of Jamaican Sixth Graders', a paper presented at the International Association of School Librarianship, 25th Annual Conference, Jamaica, 30 July 1996 (Unpublished).

Stoll B.B. (1998), 'The Effects of Differential Exposure to Stories on Second Language Discourse Skills of Pre-primary Children', MA thesis, University South Africa, Pretoria.

Trelease J. (1995), 'Reading Aloud for Reading Readiness', *Youth Services in Libraries*, 9(1):43-53.

Wells G. (1985), Preschool Literacy-related Activities and Success in School' in *Literacy, Language and Learning*, Olsen, Torrance and Hildyard (eds), Cambridge University Press, Cambridge.

Wells G. (1986), *The Meaning Makers: Children Learning Language and Using Language to Learn*, Hodder and Stoughton, London.

Wood D., J. Bruner and G. Ross (1976), The Role of Tutoring in Problem Solving', *Journal of Child Psychology and Psychiatry*, 17:89-100.

52
The Role of IBBY

The International Board on Books for Young People

F.M. GENGA-IDOWU

In discussing the role of IBBY, we address questions like: How well are the publishers in the North and South doing? Are the publishers in the North doing better? What are some of the most recent experiences in the publishing field? And, consequently, do children and young people read or not read, North and South? Why? How best can readership be achieved?

The focus is on access to, variety and quality of books for children and young people in the North and in the South. Within this framework, IBBY's role is better explained through its aims and activities since its birth in 1953.

High literacy and artistic standards in the market for children's and young people's books is the concern of IBBY. With its international network of people committed to bringing books and children together, IBBY's place in the book market is outstanding because it represents countries with well developed publishing and literary programmes and other countries with only a few dedicated professionals doing pioneer work in children's book publishing and promotion. The link is a common platform with these basic aims:

- To promote international understanding through children's books.
- To give children everywhere access to books with high literary and artistic standards.
- To encourage the publication and distribution of quality children's books with high literary and artistic standards.
- To stimulate research and scholarly works in the field of children's literature.

The basis of IBBY's work

In addressing the aims, the national sections play a prominent role. The national sections ideally should represent all fields of children's literature, joining publishers, authors, illustrators, translators, librarians, booksellers, educators, researchers and government officials involved in book promotion. The ideal goal would be to establish the national section as independently as possible, at the same time involving governmental and private organizations in a way that would allow for maximum efficiency and some autonomy.

Activities of the national sections

- Publication of information and publicity materials such as book reviews and recommendations as well as newsletters or journals for professionals.
- Organizing conferences and exhibitions, children's events, award programmes and competitions.
- Co-ordinating research and collecting documentation on children's literature.
- Forming the international network by participating in IBBY's activities.

IBBY's international activities

- The Hans Christian Andersen Awards, given biennially to an author and an illustrator of children's books whose complete works have made an important contribution to children's literature. These 'little Nobel prizes' are the highest international recognition in the field of children's literature.
- The IBBY Honour List, a biennial selection of some 100 titles of outstanding, recently published books, honouring writers, illustrators and translators from member countries. The latest IBBY Honour List 1998 has just been published and will be distributed throughout the world in 3,000 copies. South Africa was the only participating African country and IBBY encourages more African member countries to take part in 2000.
- IBBY congresses, which have been held every other year since 1953 in different countries. Members come together to share a mixed programme of lectures, working groups, poster sessions, exhibitions and social events that strive to satisfy the expectations of the participants from some 60 countries to communicate, to exchange information, ideas and experience.
- Regional seminars and conferences co-organized by national sections for it is not possible for all members to attend the biennial congresses.
- IBBY workshops and seminars for developing and newly emerging countries on writing and illustrating, production, publishing, promotion, and distribution of children's books which have been held since 1988 in co-operation with UNESCO and other organizations.
- The IBBY-Asahi Reading Promotion Award of 1 million yen (about US$10,000) sponsored by the Japanese newspaper company, Asahi Shimbun, which is presented by IBBY every year to a group or an institution which is making a significant contribution to book promotion programmes for children and young adults.
- The IBBY documentation Centre of Books for Disabled Young People, established at the Norwegian Institute of Special Education in Oslo (1985), as a follow-up to several IBBY projects in co-operation with UNESCO

after the International Year of Disabled People 1981, has published catalogues and organized exhibitions of internationally recommended books for and about disabled young people.

- *Bookbird*, A Journal of International Children's Literature, which is the quarterly of IBBY, is published in the US. Each issue has a special theme, the latest one being African children's literature. IBBY encourages active involvement of literature departments in universities and other institutions in this international publication and profit from the possibilities provided by *Bookbird* with its wide range of information on children's literature from all over the world.

- The International Children's Book Day is celebrated on 2 April (Hans Christian Andersen's birthday) to inspire a love of reading and to call attention to children's books. Each year a different national section of IBBY sponsors the day. A well-known writer of the country is asked to write a message to the children of the world and an illustrator is requested to design a poster to go with it. These materials are shared with the other national sections and distributed widely. So far only one African country has sponsored International Children's Book Day, namely Ghana in 1989, under the motto: 'Share the Reading Experience — Read!' The poster showed the well-known Anansi spider holding a book!

- Close co-operation with other organizations and children's book institutes around the world. IBBY is prominently present at the children's book fair in Bologna and participates in several other fairs around the world. It has operational relations with UNESCO and UNICEF, and is a member of the International Book Committee.

How IBBY manages its affairs

Policies and programmes are determined by the Executive Committee, elected biennially by the national sections. The daily management of the Secretariat in Basel is the responsibility of the Executive Director, Leena Maissen.

IBBY is a non-profit organization, financially dependent on the dues of the national sections. Additional funding, sponsorships and in-kind contributions (such as free printing) are necessary to meet expenses. Despite this and despite the fact that new criteria have been developed for assessing the dues, the financial situation remains difficult and burdens the agenda of the Executive Committee and the Secretariat to an ever increasing degree.

The challenge remains, how to strengthen IBBY's role in the North and in the South, develop new guidelines and find solutions to renew our structures while keeping up our ideals of building bridges for international understanding.

53
Hans Christian Andersen Awards
The Possibilities for African Regional Co-operation

JAY HEALE

Being a member country of IBBY seems awfully expensive.
What do we get for our money? Is it worth it?

Yes, with the small amount of money we have available for children's literature in Africa, it is expensive. And, Yes, it is worth it.

The main point about being a member of IBBY is sheer pride. If you take children's literature and reading seriously then how can you not be a member of the world body on children's books? Sportsmen consider it essential to be a member country of the International Olympic Committee and other sports bodies. Being a member gives you opportunities. Your soccer team doesn't expect its membership of FIFA (the world body on football) to result in your country immediately winning the World Cup! In the same way, your membership of IBBY will not result in immediate cash rewards for your authors, illustrators and publishers, but it does open the door to opportunity.

It isn't just a question of what you can get out of IBBY — it is also a question of what you can put in. Most of the so-called First World is far too ignorant of what is happening inside Africa in the field of children's literature. They need our input for them to know how best to help us.

The first key word is contacts. Through the IBBY network, their magazine *Bookbird*, their genuine friendliness, you will find yourselves in contact with more people who know more. In South Africa, we have been visited by children's book delegations from the US and Sweden, by individual visitors from the sections and even by the President of IBBY (Dr Ronald Jobe 1993).

Through the Zimbabwe International Book Fair, we shall build up a stronger network of children's book contacts within Africa. We need to correspond, to send each other our newsletters, to exchange copies of our best books. Our librarians need to exchange ideas on how to get children to fall in love with books. Our publishers need to talk through the possibilities of co-productions which will bring more books to more African children. My own personal dream is for a Southern African regional IBBY conference.

If a country takes children's literature seriously, then there will be an organization dedicated to it. It may be called the IBBY section (Japanese IBBY is called JBBY; the US IBBY is called USBBY) or it may have its own name (in South Africa, there is the South African Children's Book Forum which is the South African national section of IBBY). If there is a children's book organization, it should contact IBBY to join. If there is no such organization, then think hard about starting one. Even if such a national section seems an impossibility at present, you may be able to join IBBY as an individual member.

Every IBBY Congress (every second year) there is a display of the Honour List. Every member country has the right to choose and submit examples of its best children's books which then go on display around the world. Member countries select IBBY Honour Books, not some committee far away in Europe! they say: 'This is the author, the illustrator, the translator we are most proud of,' and the representative books are given international recognition by IBBY.

The Hans Christian Andersen Awards may seem more remote. They are more expensive to take part in but they are the highest international honours in the field of children's literature. First awarded in 1956, the winners include names like Eleanor Farjeon, Astrid Lindgren and Maurice Sendak. This year there were 50 entries altogether for the two awards.

To be chosen as your country's candidate for the Hans Christian Andersen Award is, in itself, the highest honour – as memorable as competing in the Olympic Games. It's not always the rich publishing countries whose candidates succeed, although the 1998 winners are from the US (Katherine Paterson) and France (Tommie Angrier). Andersen medals have been awarded to authors and artists from Finland, Iran, Israel, Denmark and the Czech Republic. What is vital is that the author or illustrator you submit has made considerable impact within the children's literature of your country. And that raises the original question: Do you take children's literature and children's reading seriously?

You owe it to your book creators to give them the international exposure and prestige of IBBY. It is not a rich organization itself. Its worldwide network is run from a three-roomed office in Switzerland with a full-time staff of Leena Maissen, the Executive Director, and a part-time secretary. Many national sections have no office at all, and nearly all are staffed by unpaid enthusiasts.

In South Africa, our publishing industry is in crisis, our education system in chaos, our parents are apathetic — but we still have children who want to read. And we have volunteer enthusiasts who think they deserve the best books possible, and that the authors and illustrators and publishers who create those books deserve our support, better publicity and more of a feeling of pride.

54
Children and Culture
The Outside Threat of the Modern World

ASENATH BOLE ODAGA

What does culture mean? It is the collective values, ways of life, aspirations, beliefs, patterns of behaviour and inter-personal relations which are predominant within a given community. It is intellectual development and artistic aspects of a society and its way of life which forms part of its heritage and traditions that have been handed down from one generation to another. Children and culture therefore mean the culture in which they are born and are brought up. I was asked, 'Do children have a culture?' To which I answer, 'Yes. They are part of the culture of their birthplace. Everyone has a culture; it is a way of life. And each of us has a way of life.'

The outside threat of the modern world refers to foreign concepts and ways they destabilize cultural ways. The ensuing development often causes confusion and changes which affect children directly or indirectly. Children are important — they are the inheritors of any culture as successors to adults. In normal circumstances, they are demographically more than adults. For instance, in Kenya 65 per cent of our population is below 20 years of age. In Zimbabwe, I read that 50 per cent of the population is about 15 years old!

Children imitate what they see around them. They learn by example. First, of their immediate environment: parents, family, peers, siblings and the village. From these backgrounds, they learn the language, mother tongue (which is the basic carrier of cultural values), play, behaviour, songs, art, kinds of animals and birds. They also learn their gender roles as constructed by their society. This means that outside threats of the modern world are real for children in view of their malleable character. They are thus susceptible to influence and easily become victims of seemingly attractive and more appealing practices.

Any society is dynamic and subject to continuous changes from internal as well as external factors. So is culture. Consequently, the changing circumstances have an effect on children's values, behaviours and attitudes.

Much of the threat comes to children through books, literature, television, radio and mass media. This is in contrast to the traditional African set-up where children were told stories and encouraged to take part in games, songs, riddles, story-telling, puns and tongue-twisters. The cultures tended to be homogenous although not totally free of outside influence. A community may have been in contact with the outside world which gave them a different version so the stories were told and retold, from one generation to another. Today the threat of the outside world to the traditional set-ups is much more critical than previously due to difference in strength and means of presentation.

Stories from oral literature of illiterate people fulfilled the functions of written literature and embodied cultural values. This is still the case. Among the cultures which children learn from literature and other media are Christian, Muslim and Western. Underlying these are universal cultural values. Some of these put a high price on human life — they support human rights, for example. They teach children to honour parents, respect other people's possessions as well as their collective responsibilities, especially at funerals, weddings and other important ceremonies. Children in Africa through most of their stories learnt that in times of difficulties one was expected to take action.

In a Kenyan oral narrative, Obon'go told his sister not to go on a journey because the route passed through a forest full of ogres who liked beautiful girls. Obon'go's sister was a beauty. She defied his warning and went. After a night away the girls left to return home. On the way they found a stool on the path, blocking their way. It was a trap. The ogre, Apul Apul, had hidden himself in a nearby bush. All the girls sat on the stool and passed over it, except Ndai, Ogon'go's sister. When she sat on it, she got stuck there! She regretted disobeying her brother's warning. She began to cry and sing. The other girls ran to get home quickly and reported the incident. When Ogon'go heard this terrible news, he took his spear and rushed to the forest to rescue his sister.

So, Obon'go acted responsibly; a reflection of the culture of his community.

The African child was exposed to cultural activities which they could create or expand but certain aspects were fixed — these were the conventions. People were often rated according to how well they had acquired the behaviour and beliefs expected of them as part of that culture or community. Outside influence was minimal. However, threats of modern cultures have gradually intervened through mass media and education with adverse effects on the children.

At the advent of colonialism, much of the threat came with formal education — with authority and force unmatched by the local culture. It appeared stronger and superior as it was well defined and accompanied by glossy and appealing books. Today there are video, televison, radio, magazines and newspapers and African narratives produced by outsiders are also glossy and appealing.

A further threat is the fact that cultural activities have been commercialized and are being marketed as commodities of trade, refined to attract consumers in a highly competitive market. Advertisements make people believe, for example, that children who drink Ribena are healthier, cleverer and stronger than those who drink fresh orange juice or who eat wild raspberries which are natural, free of chemicals and have the same content of vitamin C. These adverts and other literature have a bad effect on children.

At another level the threat of the outside world presents a challenge to African culture. We should evolve our own cultural literature and programmes, equally well packaged, and supported by the unique African soul that should emphasise values that nurture and safeguard the sanctity of the human race.

The outside threat is part of globalization which in one sense is wonderful since it means growing closer like members of one village. But it has come too soon after the end of colonization; at a time when Africans are beginning to appreciate their roots and to adjust to new thinking. The outside threat is causing cultural confusion and our youth need a clear cultural perception.

Development is fast replacing colonization and neo-colonialism. Development packages are mechanisms that transfer, impose and import cultures and practices. Some, if not most of these, pose threats to our children.

Most people cannot adapt to lifestyles and cultures from outside. Indeed, only a small percentage of the élite can cope with current rates of change. This has an adverse effect on our children as people cannot cope economically. The grandmother nursery school is a dying institution. Formal education has to be paid for — children learn from teachers, books, television, videos. Grand-mothers' unrecorded stories are lost and certain cultural values, phrases, idioms, names of animals, plants, various skills and knowledge, with them.

Most of African cultures required children to be obedient and to respect each other and elders religiously; and they did. Today, defiance of norms and rules at home, school and in general by children, is widespread.

Culture did not allow children to drink alcohol or to take drugs. Now they do so openly and in disregard of customs. In the past street children did not exist. And child abuse in all its various forms would be unthinkable. Increase in population, unemployment coupled with the breakdown of tradition, have forced many parents to abdicate their responsibilities.

These examples show that children and their parents are at cross-roads — nobody is quite clear of what path to take: the threat from outside is real.

Children need access to suitable literature and values to discourage them from imitating foreign cultures. We must accept, though, that certain information will reach us as a threat. But if we lay a strong foundation for our children, then the threat will no longer be harmful but could be seen as enrichment and challenge — even opportunities — to be harnessed or harmonized for the development of children.

55
The Rushinga Twin Schools Project

DAVID MUNGOSHI*

There were four phases in the Rushinga Twin Schools project: The *preparation phase* which was taken up with discussion, planning, consultations with interested parties and rigorous negotiations preceding the signing of the agrements between the Zimbabwe Writers' Union and Norwegian People's Aid; the *writing skills workshop* targeted at teachers and schools on 28 and 29 August 1997 respectively; the *post-workshop phase* which included two progress-monitoring visits to Rushinga in October and November 1997 which included the final evaluation of the materials submitted; and finally the *production phase* which is still to be entered subsequent to the acquisition of the necessary funding.

It became clear early on that there would have to be a workshop to start off the project and also propel it forward. This would have to be properly planned, efficiently organized and effectively conducted.

As agreed, the general objective of the workshop was to provide technical competence to pupils and teachers of Gwangwava, Gwashure and Mukonde schools in the Rushinga district for the writing and promotion of teaching and reading materials. To provide this, Zimbabwe Writers' Union drew up objectives of what would have happened by the end of the workshop.

* The Zimbabwe Writers' Union acknowledges their indebtedness to the Norwegian People's Aid for co-ordinating the efforts that led to the twinning of three Norwegian schools with the three Rushinga schools which are the subject of this report and the main beneficiaries of the Twin Schools' Writing Project. And in particular, to Vitalis Chipunza, the acting country representative of the Norwegian People's Aid in Zimbabwe, for his continued interest and assistance, to N.G. Chikwema, Education Officer, Rushinga District who contributed in no small measure to the outcomes, to Mrs Chitiyo, the Assistant District Administrator for her various facilitative roles throughout the first phase and finally to the parents, children, headmasters, teachers and chairpersons of the School Development Committees of Gwangwava, Gwashure and Mukonde Schools for their effervescent enthusiasm and exertion.

The children were to have:
- begun to acquire the skills necessary for writing manuscripts in their chosen area.
- begun to work on their ideas for the manuscript.
- submitted pieces of writing emanating from the workshop for use by Zimbabwe Writers' Union in selecting project participants.

The teachers were to have
- acquired insights into manuscript supervision, origination and compilation.
- begun to work on their ideas for teaching materials.
- submitted pieces of writing emanating from the workshop for use by Zimbabwe Writers' Union in determining the project participants.

And finally:
- Representatives of each schools development committee were to have acquired insights into the project.

To measure achievement it was necessary to think in terms of its specific outcomes which were outlined as follows:
- Technical competence where the pupils were concerned meant that the pupils would be able to:
  — write different types of texts.
  — create reading materials for their peers.
  — illustrate their writings.
  — collect information.
  — use the information they collected in their writing.
- Technical competence where the teachers were concerned meant that the teachers would be able to:
  — design questionnaires.
  — conduct both structured and unstructured interviews.
  — synthesize information from different written sources.
  — interpret the information that they collected.
  — produce teaching materials which are relevant to their situations.
  — do preliminary editing of the children's work.
  — design effective art briefs.
  — compile first draft manuscripts from the work of the children.

Owing to the fact that Zimbabwe Writers' Union had no previous background information relating to the creative or academic propensities of the participants in terms of writing, we opted for a basic skills package, hence the nature and content of the programme. The general pattern was lectures with corresponding activities. This is how the manuscripts were written.

There were question and answer sessions, as well as readings, recitations and drama. The participants also tried illustrating their manuscripts. In addition, teachers and pupils filled in fact files so that the Zimbabwe Writers' Union could develop profiles.

Table1 Teacher fact file

ACADEMIC WRITING

Sometimes	Never	Regularly	Interest	
			Average	High
7	4	2	5	8

Most teachers needed some orientation in academic writing. They needed training in writing skills but at least they all indicated they were regular readers.

Table 2 Children fact file

READING BACKGROUND

Reading in English

Textbook only	1 Fiction/other	2 Fiction/other
53	12	10

Reading in Shona

Textbook only	1 Fiction/other	2 Fiction/other
6	39	30

In the context of the organic link between reading and writing, the fact files were predicators of the work that might materialize. They also indicated the things needing attention. A salient fact was that the participants needed more training which was confirmed in their evaluation of the workshop.

Table 3   Evaluation by teachers

Happy with the workshop	Wanting more workshops	Attrition
12	10	1

One teacher had to leave prematurely owing to a bereavement.

Table 4   Children's evaluation

Spoilt papers	Happy with workshop	Wanting more workshops	Attrition
8	46	46	21

Some children had to leave before the end to catch their buses.

Zimbabwe Writers' Union recommends, on the strength of its observations, the adoption of the following measures:

- As a matter of urgency, structures are needed to establish viable libraries to ensure children can and do read. The importance of a reading culture for academic and development purposes cannot be overemphasized. It is recommended that school development committees look into the funding of libraries at each school.
- Further, when such libraries are set up, they should contain sufficient reading matter for the teachers, including educational journals and reference materials so teachers can attempt to write academic texts. Unless this is done, the teachers are likely to engage only in creative writing and this would negate the Twin School Programme vision.
- School development committees should secure funding for this very important aspect of the project.
- Much of the children's writing is likely to be in Shona, so translation will be necessary but it can only be done in the later stages of the project, and then only after careful grounding and training. School development committees need to fund an ancillary translation project.
- Success of the project will depend on the adoption and implementation of a development-oriented paradigm.

Table 5 Analysis of pupil submissions

School	Total No. of pupils	Possibilities	Definite	Falling Short
Gwangwava	27	8	18	1
Gwashure	25	15	5	5
Mukonde	82	32	13	37
Total	134	55	36	43

1 The total number of items supervised is 134, as a number of children were quite prolific and each submitted several items.

2 There are 36 items that we found definitely usable, 55 others can make the grade with further work along the lines of the supervision comments supplied to the writers on their manuscripts. This brings the total of items that could be published to 91.

3 43 items were found to be unsuitable for various reasons including lack of originality, unwholesome details, adult themes and poor creativity.

Of the eight teachers who submitted materials only two submitted academic writing. One teacher submitted an essay on the post-funeral rites of Rushinga while the other submitted an item for use in religious education. The remaining six tried creative writing and wrote poetry, short stories and longer pieces.

Two of the parents who participated in the workshops submitted interesting articles. One specialized in the history and culture of Rushinga while the other used his knowledge and experience of hunting to produce something engaging.

While there could have been a wider spread in terms of the variety of texts attempted, there was a sufficiently varied number of texts to warrant classification as follows: poetry, short stories, essays, instructions, folk stories and games. Attempts to produce humorous articles were largely unsuccessful as the jokes tended to be private ones.

In order for the teachers in the long run to be involved in the production of school materials it will be necessary to do the following things:
- run workshop/s on school materials for teachers;
- provide resources for further reading and research;
- compile pupil materials, after further development, into an anthology.

The question of translation from Shona to English for the benefit of the Twin Schools in Norway needs be addressed, since the overwhelming majority of items were in Shona, with only two promising articles in English.

The Norwegian People's Aid, on receipt of the final report, were satisfied with the way the project has been run so far. Zimbabwe Writers' Union on its part has found the project instructive in terms of opportunities for developing and sharpening negotiating skills. Further, the enthusiasm shown by all concerned has been most gratifying. It is reassuring to observe that during the post-workshop consultations all three schools expressed the following wishes:
- to have more writing workshops focusing on specific areas of writing so as to enable them to expand their repertoires *vis a vis* knowledge and skills;
- to be assisted in obtaining books to establish school libraries that would serve the community and assist in the development of a reading culture;
- to see the project continued until after publication.

Zimbabwe Writers' Union has managed to secure membership for the three schools of the Children's Book Fund, a project being run by the Zimbabwe Book Development Council (ZBDC) to assist member institutions to acquire books over a three year period. Given sufficient goodwill, consistency and determination, the Rushinga schools should soon have the beginnings of what should, in future, become viable libraries.

In the immediate future Zimbabwe Writers' Union hopes to enter into final negotiations with the Norwegian People's Aid in order to obtain funding for the production phase of the project. Efforts will also be exerted to enter into partnerships with a willing and competitive publisher.

56
School Textbook Supply

RICHARD CRABBE

A ny discussion of textbooks must take into account the local context. The size of the school-going population, the government's educational policy, income levels, availability of textbooks and the general attitude towards books and their use are critical factors that any analyst must consider. Further, one should take into account whether textbook supply remains the preserve of government or whether the sector is open to private participation.

Educational policy framework

This is what sets out the goals of the country's education system and the means to achieve them. It includes elements such as who should receive education, the types and quantities of textbooks required, how they will be procured, funded and distributed. Generally, it is accepted that textbooks should enhance the learning process. Thus provision of textbooks is expected to improve the quality of education. Implementation of any educational policy must be backed by the political will to see it through and the allocation of adequate resources for the various aspects of the policy, including textbook supply.

Finance

Many countries claim to have education as a national priority. Putting up funds to support the assertion often assumes challenging dimensions. Education budgets are not immune from cuts in times of austerity budgets. Further complicating the situation is the perceived reduction in purchasing power of parents and guardians of school children.

Increasingly many African countries require external funding to meet shortfalls in providing their textbook needs. In our recent experience this support has come in as donor funding or through World Bank loans and multi-lateral (inter-governmental grants). Today the World Bank's financing for education accounts for more than US$2 billion per annum. The bank is the single largest source of finance for textbook procurement for most African countries. Whatever the source of funding, it is important to ensure that the country as a whole is adequately catered for.

Distribution

Quite often, higher income urbanized areas tend to receive better supplies of textbooks than the poorer rural areas. Urban areas usually have centres of supervision. Also, the infrastructure needed to stimulate book distribution such as bookshops and trained personnel is more likely to be found in urban areas. The state of the roads in rural areas poses a formidable challenge to the regular distribution system. Less privileged areas in our countries need more attention in order to improve textbook supply. In many African countries, there is currently a gradual shift from state-controlled textbook provision (from conception to distribution and use) to partially or fully privatised systems. Where the state has been in charge, the basic infrastructure for distribution is inadequate to support private participation in textbook supply. In some places publishers are not used sending their books to schools or marketing them to bookshops.

Access to books

This is discussed separately from distribution, because much more is involved. Much has been said and written about the textbook/pupil ratios in our schools. I know schools where textbooks are locked up after use in cupboards in the head teacher's office or where there is one book per subject for a class of more than 40 children. These are in government-run schools. Private schools generally achieve better book-to-pupil ratios. For the quality of education to improve and for our children to learn better, we should improve their access to textbooks and other reading material.

Sustainability

A more serious issue relating to financing textbook supply is sustainability. Yet textbook supply schemes overlook it. We only mortgage the future of our people if we fail to adequately address this issue. The high rate of population growth, averaging 3 per cent across the continent, means the number of children entering schools will continue to increase. We need to consider how we will cater for their textbook requirements.

Recommendations

The following may provide discussion points towards developing effective strategies for textbook supply.

The right to education — This should include equal opportunity or access to educational materials.

National planning and co-ordination — It is the responsibility of government to provide quality education for the people. But the enormity of the challenge and the complexity created by the factors involved, demand a pooling of efforts from various sectors. Textbook supply can no longer be left to governments alone. As many stakeholders as possible should be included in the planning and delivery process. We must ensure that books get to our schoolchildren when they need them. It is important to address issues relating to book use. This should include a teacher-training component. We cannot ignore the fact that the attitude of teachers to books and book use can strongly influence their pupils and students.

Partnership between government and the non-governmental organization/private sector would have to increase. Non-governmental organizations dealing directly with government in textbook provision should begin to involve the local publishing industry: writers, publishers, printers, distributors and booksellers.

Community level libraries should be established and equipped to provide supplementary access to textbooks and general readers.

Building capacity in the local publishing industry is integral to securing textbook supply. With increasing dependence on external sources of funding, I would advocate a two-pronged approach: First, ensure that a significant local component is built into any book supply scheme. This is to develop the local publishing industry. Second, increase local participation through improved access to finance for local publishers.

Conclusion

The questions to consider are: for how long will African countries continue to receive external funds for textbook schemes? And how will we continue to provide textbooks, should those inflows dry up? We must satisfactorily answer these questions to brighten the future of educating our children. Their future is the future of our countries — it is the future of Africa.

Discussion Points
Group Four: Access & Technology

1 A librarian originally from Ethiopia gave an example of science in operation from childhood — a 12 year old watching men loading a barrel onto a truck who finally had to use poles to roll the barrel up. This is the kind of material that would be useful for the children's science books project.

2 David Mungoshi said that a previous example of the localization of science was the ZimSci project which was for under-priviledged rural schools. Emmie Wade assured him that although the books would be extracted ɪrom the children's life and locality, there will be no hiding from current realities — merely broadening children's experience. ZimSci certainly offers a good alternative where laboratories are unavailable.

3 A participant from the Rural Library Association of Zimbabwe raised the issue of indigenous languages and the status of books. Emmie Wade replied that whether in local or an international language, the 'Africanness' would be communicated. Also, it was a matter of available resources and terms of reference. If local languages were used, it would be a different project with a different agenda. Regarding status perceptions, she said there was a genuine interest in discovering what African science is, which would elevate the status of local scientific wisdom. A Nigerian participant suggested we might be 'over flogging this Africanness'. The world is getting smaller and he pointed out that there were over 200 languages in Nigeria. Emmie Wade replied that it was merely making education more relevant, basing it on realities from the children's lives.

4 In the discussion on enticing children to read, Yohannes Gebregeorgis said it was important for African societies to make use of traditional storytelling resources — better still, in conjunction with books. In the US where books abound, the importance of storytelling has been rediscovered.

5 A participant commented that in urban environments, sometimes it was also a matter of children teaching their parents and reading for them as a means of coping with the demands of new, urban environments. Susan Scull-Carvalho agreed that community involvement was important. Even though teachers are overburdened and underpaid, there were plenty of creative things they could still do. In Nairobi, the newspaper, *The Nation*, was persuaded in 1994 to publish a reading resource supplement, pre ɔared by teachers and subsidized by local companies which has lasted and g·own

from four to eight pages in four years. This has encouraged children and parents to write stories.

6   David Mungoshi raised the issue of reluctant readers and the panel suggested that children are only reluctant because they lack preliteracy skills. If this is neglected until they are over 11, then you may lose them as readers.

7   After the presentations about IBBY, David Mungoshi asked whether an organization needed to be exclusively involved in children's books to join and the answer was that the only requirement was a serious committment to children's books. For example, the Indian section is the Association of Writers and Illustrators. It was also pointed out that individual membership is possible where no organization exists. A Kenyan participant asked if IBBY in South Africa had problems getting members pay subscriptions and Jay Heale said they had used different means to raise funds for the country subscription. They published an expensive newsletter and even offered services like copying and postage, thus raising the money to cover the country membership.

8   Dr B. Townsend from the International Reading Association explained that it is an organization focusing on teachers, whose goal is to improve literacy throughout the world. They have affiliates throughout the world although membership is for individuals and the affiliates would need ten individual members. They produce several publications for teachers including four journals and a bi-monthly newspaper. In answer to questions about the organization, she explained that it was started by a group of professors in Canada and America with the aim of ending the isolation of teachers. They have individual members in 90 countries and 40 affiliate members. The association offers book awards which publishers from all over the world can enter. The national affiliates are independent and carry out their activities fairly autonomously, although there are international organizations committees which liase and identify issues and policies for interested governments and parties worldwide.

9   In response to Asenath Odaga's presentation on children and culture, a participant from South Africa commented that authors should create mechanisms to promote and sell their books, taking a more active role instead of moaning. A Ungandan participant argued for looking at the positive side of technology and making use of it to promote our cultures, for example, the Internet could be very effective for this. He urged people to not always blame outside influences but look deeper to see what may be wrong with our attitudes and practices. For example, he thought we

might inadvertently encourage drinking of local brews which can lead to other kinds of substance abuse. A participant from Ghana commented that some of us should accept we are city people with no villages to turn back to and some of our children are born of at least two cultures. So we should not bemoan what we cannot go back to. At best we can expose our children to both rural and urban life. Culture is dynamic and we must move on with it and celebrate our diversity. Another contributor agreed that we should not see the world as hostile but move forward with it. While accepting new things, Asenath Odega commented that we should still retain our values and identity and Shimmer Chinodya ended with the plea, 'Let us be proud of our culture and its rich complexity.'

10 In response to Richard Crabbe's presentation on textbooks, a Nigerian participant added that in a World Bank University refurbishment of 20 federal institutions, the programme insisted on at least 20 per cent being used on libraries and this has left lasting benefit in that some money has had to be spent on books and journals, which benefits present and future generations of students. Engelbert Luphahla said that in Zimbabwe any aid to do with books includes a requirement that all books up to 'O' level must be sourced locally, which makes local publishers more viable, resulting in self sufficiency in the supply of books up to 'O' level. A South African participant commented that while we have competent people, governments are not playing their part and not giving education the priority and resources required.